Highlights of the reports

Health (reports: *Doctors and nurses*, *In sickness and in health*)

A total of 4.5 million people in the UK reported that they had both poor health and a limiting long-term illness in 2001; 5.9 million people said that they provide care to family and friends on an informal basis. The amount of this informal care is provided in direct proportion to the rate of poor health in areas across the UK. However, higher numbers of practising, qualified medical practitioners tend to live and work in areas where the rates of illness are lower. This is an example of what has been called the 'inverse care law'.

Education (reports: *Teachers*, *Sons and daughters*)

An 'inverse education law' also appears to exist. Areas which have the highest proportions of young people with no qualifications tend to have the lowest availability of teachers. The proportion of 16-17 year olds with GCSE-level qualifications also varies widely across England, Wales and Northern Ireland, and areas with a high proportion tend also to have many adults (around the age of these young people's parents) with degree-level qualifications. The situation in Scotland is different, with little variation in the rate of young people with qualifications, and no relationship with the education of the older generation.

Housing (reports: *Changing rooms*, *A place in the sun*)

Overcrowding and underoccupancy vary widely across the UK. Areas with high levels of overcrowding tend not to have many underoccupied homes. The Census also recorded 185,000 unoccupied second homes and holiday residences. In areas where these are prevalent – particularly remote rural areas – there are more people who may be having difficulty entering the housing market.

Employment (reports: *The office*, *Open all hours*)

Well-paid, high-status jobs are most likely to be found in London and the South East. In areas without many high-status jobs available, people with very good qualifications are more likely to be working in lower-status jobs. This suggests that someone's location is sometimes more important than their qualifications in determining what kind of job they do. Areas with low levels of unemployment tend also to have many people working long hours; conversely, areas with high unemployment tend to have few people working long hours. The country appears to be divided between 'work-rich' and 'work-poor' areas.

Poverty (reports: *Top gear*, *Home front*)

There are about the same number of households in the UK which might be said to need a car but which do not have one as there are households which might be said to have more cars than they really need. The areas in which many households may need a car but do not have one are geographically distinct from those in which many households have more cars than they might really need. Child poverty remains widespread in the UK. Areas where many families have no parents in paid employment tend also to have many young people providing care on an informal basis.

Read the full reports to find out more about how and why some areas and some people have the resources and amenities they need, while others do not.

The research was funded by the Joseph Rowntree Foundation and further details can be found at www.jrf.org.uk or www.sheffield.ac.uk/sasi

JOSEPH ROWNTREE FOUNDATION
The POLICY PRESS

SUMMARY

The latest Census reveals that people who live within the UK can still live in very different 'worlds'. For some, resources and amenities abound, for others life is characterised by deprivation and difficulties, especially when their need for support is great.

Since 1801 successive governments have asked the population to assist in the taking of a Census. The 2001 Census marked the bi-centenary of Census taking in the UK. It is the most comprehensive social record of life in this country now available.

This project has produced a series of 10 short reports showing key patterns and inequalities in life in the UK as revealed by the 2001 Census. The project focuses on differences between areas within the UK, highlighting those where services and opportunities appear not to be available or accessible and often finding that they are lacking or missing in the places that need them most.

How to use this pack

- Each of the **10 reports** stands alone as a description and analysis of what the 2001 Census can tell us about a particular issue in contemporary Britain. The series taken together gives an overall view of poverty, inequality and place.
- The **technical report** can be consulted for project background, details of data and methods, further analyses, and overarching observations and conclusions.
- Finally, each of the **five posters** gives a striking insight into one of five themes, raising issues and illustrating them with maps and photographs.

The reports are:

1. ***Doctors and nurses,*** on illness and the provision of formal care
2. ***In sickness and in health,*** on illness and the provision of informal care
3. ***Teachers,*** on qualifications and the provision of teachers
4. ***Sons and daughters,*** on children's and adults' educational qualifications
5. ***Changing rooms,*** on overcrowded and underoccupied homes
6. ***A place in the sun,*** on holiday/second homes and private renting
7. ***The office,*** on employment and the distribution of skills
8. ***Open all hours,*** on people working long hours and no hours
9. ***Top gear,*** on households with many cars and no cars
10. ***Home front,*** on children caring for others and those living in poverty

HOME FRONT

175,000 young carers

The 2001 Census revealed that 175,000 (about 2%) of young people aged 5-17 in the UK provided care on an informal basis for relatives, friends or neighbours. Of these, 30,000 were providing care for 20+ hours per week, a substantial undertaking given that almost all of these children were also in full-time education. Additionally, there were around 1.3 million families with dependent children where no parent was in employment. This report shows that areas with the highest percentages of young people providing care also tend to have high proportions of families where no parent is in paid work.

Child poverty and young carers

Child poverty has a host of detrimental effects, harming both current and future health, impacting on educational outcomes, and restricting future opportunities, achievements and living standards. It is also an experience that is unpleasant, restrictive and stigmatising[1].

In 1999 the government set an unprecedented and impassioned policy goal: to eradicate child poverty within a generation. A number of policy initiatives have been devised to achieve progress toward this target, with some success. In 2001-02 there were 3.8 million children living in poverty (children living in households with incomes below 60% of the median after housing costs), a fall from 4.4 million in 1996-97[2]. Many of these 'poor' children will be living in households where there is no adult in paid work and the family is totally reliant on benefits. In other households, low pay is the main cause of family poverty. Many children who have been lifted out of poverty (in technical terms) by benefits and tax credits will still be in families who are only just above the poverty threshold.

Life in Britain

The latest Census reveals that within the UK people live in very different worlds. For some, resources and amenities abound; for others life is characterised by deprivation and difficulties, especially when their need for support is great.

The 2001 Census marked the bi-centenary of Census taking in the UK. It is the most comprehensive social record of life in this country now available. Since 1801 successive governments have asked the population to assist in the taking of a Census.

This report is one of a series of 10 showing key patterns and inequalities in life in the UK revealed by the 2001 Census. These reports focus on geographical inequalities, highlighting where services and opportunities appear not to be available or accessible to those people and places that need them most.

The public manifestations of social exclusion (truancy, area de/regeneration, homelessness) have received a great deal of attention in recent policy debates but the experience of poverty in the privacy of the home has gained less attention[3]. Young people who provide care, usually for other family members, are a group who are often socially isolated and socially excluded in a way that is not easily visible from outside the home. A 2003 survey of over 6,000 young carers in the UK found that 56% lived in lone-parent families, and 22% were missing school or having educational difficulties. Although figures on employment were available for only 1,000 of the adults being cared for by these young carers, 43 (4%) of the adults were in employment[4].

The Census provides simple measures of both children in poverty (as estimated by those living in households with no parents in employment) and of children who provide care, so here – in this series of reports on geographical inequalities – we consider whether these two groups tend to be geographically coincident.

This analysis uses data from the 2001 Census to construct two measures that tell us about the lives of some of the most disadvantaged young people. Firstly, the Census data describe household structures, and also include information on the employment circumstances of all adults. Therefore, it is possible to calculate the number of parents with dependent children living in circumstances where no parent in the household works. While it would be simpler to have a count of the number of children (rather than parents), or families where no parent works, the slightly cumbersome count of parents is what is possible with standard data tables released from the Census. However, the figures available do reflect children living in relatively impoverished circumstances, with families totally reliant on state benefits.

Secondly, the 2001 Census asked, for the first time, a question on the provision of informal care. The question asked:

Do you look after, or give any help or support to family members, friends, neighbours or others because of:

- **long-term physical or mental ill-health or disability, or**
- **problems related to old age?**

Possible responses were: No; 1-19 hours a week; 20-49 hours a week; 50+ hours a week; and the data released from the Census breaks these responses down by age group. It is therefore possible to calculate the number of young people (aged 5-17) providing informal care in this way.

This report describes analysis of these two measures – parents in households with dependent children where no parent works, and young carers – across the UK. As for other reports in this series, the UK is divided into 142 areas consisting of counties, unitary authorities and former metropolitan authorities. The two measures can be calculated for each area, and the report addresses the question:

Do areas that have lots of families with no working parents tend to also have lots of young carers?

Findings

The 2001 Census revealed that there were 1.7 million *parents* living with dependent children[5] in households where no parent worked, around 3% of all people. The Census does not include relevant information on the numbers of families, but it does indicate that 935,000 of these parents are *lone parents* and 815,000 are in *couple* families. These figures can be used to estimate that around 1.3 million *families* were living with dependent children and no working parents in 2001. The Census gives numbers in the relevant data tables for parents with one dependent child or 'two or more' dependent children. This means it is also possible to state that these families with no working parents include *at least* 2 million dependent children.

Responses to the informal care question reveal that 30,000 children aged 5-17 were providing 20+ hours of informal care a week at the time of the 2001 Census. That is three in every 1,000 children in this age group in the UK. A further 145,000 children in this age group (15 in every 1,000) were providing care for 1-19 hours a week. This means a total of around 18 per 1,000, just under 2% of young people providing informal care. Most of these children are likely to be providing care for their parents, grandparents or for siblings. The low percentage shows that it is fairly unusual for children to be put in these extreme positions. However, the events that result in children being carers do not occur at random, neither socially, nor across space, and never have.

Comparing areas

Figure 1 illustrates how the two measures are associated with each other across the 142 areas of the UK. This clearly shows a strong positive association – areas with a high proportion of households with parents not in work tend also to have higher percentages of children providing informal care.

Table 1 lists the five areas used in this analysis that have the highest percentages of young people providing informal care for more than 20 hours a week. In these areas at least 1 in 200 young people are providing this amount of care. These areas are similar to those with the highest rates of informal care provision overall, which are discussed in another report in this series, *In sickness and in health*.

Figures 2 and 3 illustrate how the two measures vary across the UK. The highest rates of non-working parents are found in South Wales, cities of the North and Midlands of England, and Glasgow. The highest rates of young carers are found in Wales, cities in northern England, southern Scotland and Northern Ireland.

100 years ago

In 1886 Charles Booth started a 17-year street-by-street survey of the extent of poverty in London. He set out to disprove an earlier report that claimed that a quarter of workers in London were in receipt of wages not sufficient to maintain life. In fact, Booth found that 30% of London's population lived below the poverty line that he had devised.

One of Booth's conclusions was that the circumstances of irregular and poor employment, rather than 'habits' or 'character' (what we would call 'lifestyle') were the major causes of poverty. For those who could not find regular work, the workhouse was the last resort. Booth's notebooks described the micro-geography of Victorian London.

For more information see Charles Booth online archive (http://booth.lse.ac.uk/); Davey Smith, G., Dorling, D., and Shaw, M. (2001) *Poverty, inequality and health in Britain: 1800-2000 – A reader*, Bristol: The Policy Press.

Table 1: The five areas of the UK with the highest proportion of young people aged 5-17 providing care for 20+ hours a week

Area	% of 5-17 year olds providing 20+ hours care a week	% of people who are parents in households where no parent works
Glasgow City	0.7	5.9
Blaenau Gwent	0.6	5.3
Denbeighshire	0.5	3.2
Neath Port Talbot	0.5	4.5
Caerphilly	0.5	4.6
UK	**0.3**	**3.0**

Figure 1: The association between the two measures across the 142 areas of the UK

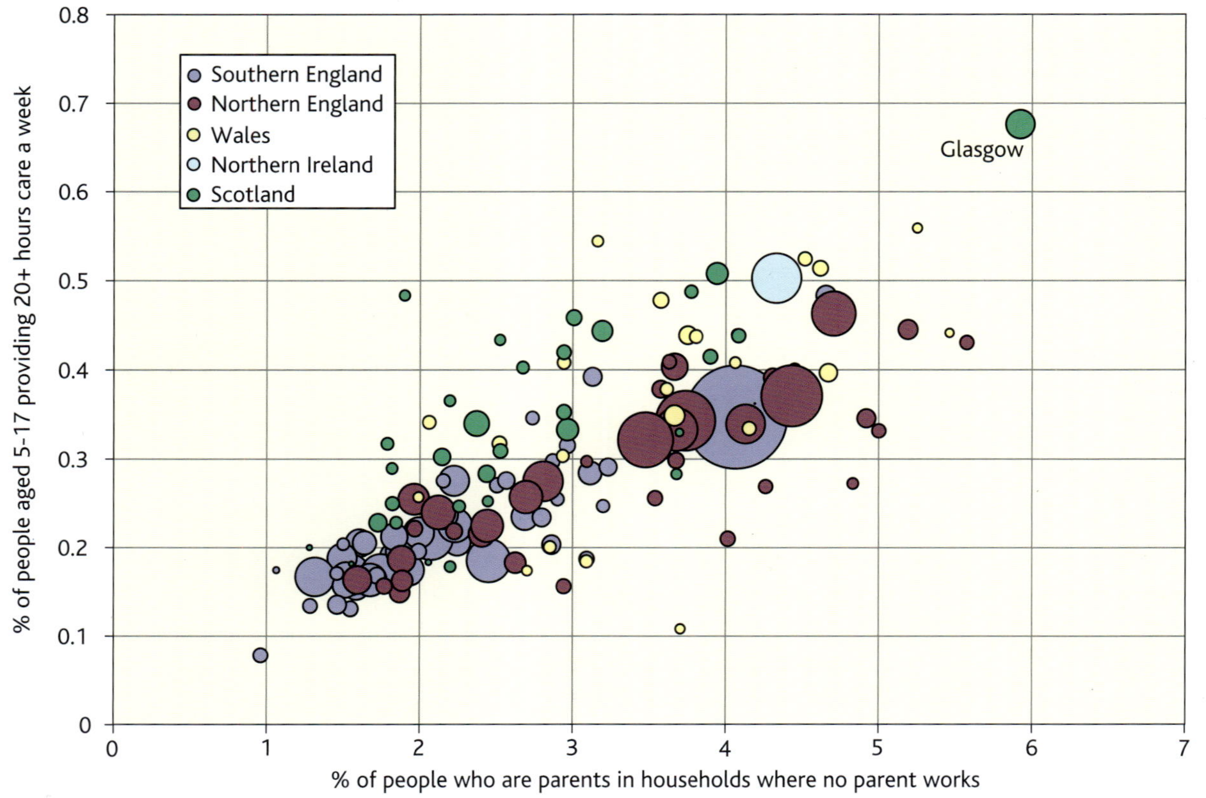

Note: Each circle is a county, unitary or former metropolitan authority, drawn with the area in proportion to the total population in 2001 (the largest circle represents London, with a population of just over 7 million). Areas in northern England are those that lie west or north of the counties of Gloucestershire, Warwickshire, Leicestershire and Lincolnshire (the Severn-Humber divide).

Since 2001

In 2002/03 3.6 million children in the UK were living in poverty[6]. It has been claimed that unless a further £1 billion is spent on tax credits the government is unlikely to meet its interim target of reducing this to 3.1 million children living in poverty by 2004/05[2]. Although the number of children living with parents not in work will have fallen, it is unlikely that there has been any great rise in the proportion of those children living with parents who have got well-paid jobs.

Informal care by young people has only been formally recognised in the past decade[7]. The government established a Young Carers Forum in July 2001, and has implemented a Young Carers Strategy. In addition, the Department for Education and Skills has taken on responsibility for policies to ensure that young carers gain an education[8].

Discussion

Child poverty reflects family poverty. Children may live in impoverished situations because their parents are unable to work, sometimes through poor health, in which case these children may also be providing care for their parents. Children may also provide care for others, such as siblings and older relatives.

These Census data do not allow analysis of individual families, so it is impossible to be sure whether or not the children providing care are living in families with no parents in paid work. However, this is a reasonable explanation for the close relationship between the two measures. Certainly, both of these indicators can be read as measures of the social exclusion experienced by young people and their families in these areas. The government's definition of social exclusion describes it as what "... happens when people or places suffer from a series of problems such as unemployment, discrimination, poor

Figure 2: Maps illustrating variation across the UK of households where no parent works

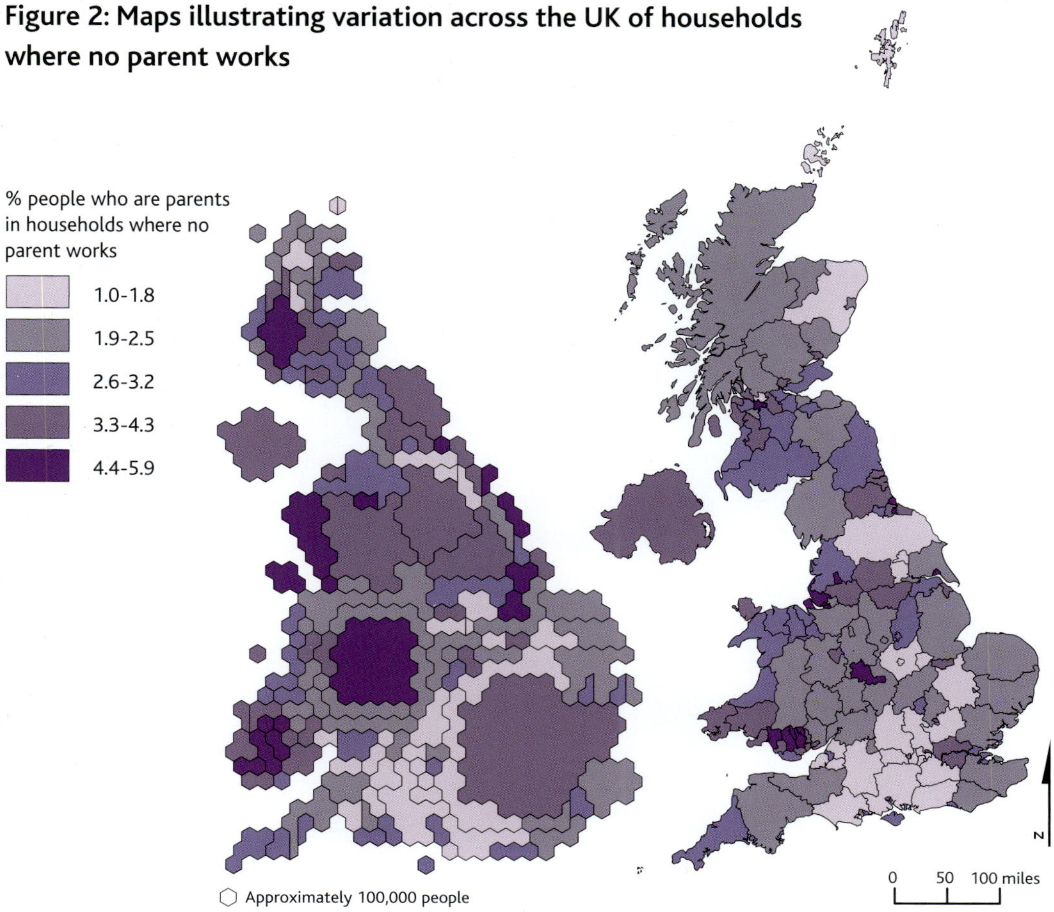

Figure 3: Maps showing the percentage of young people caring for 20+ hours a week

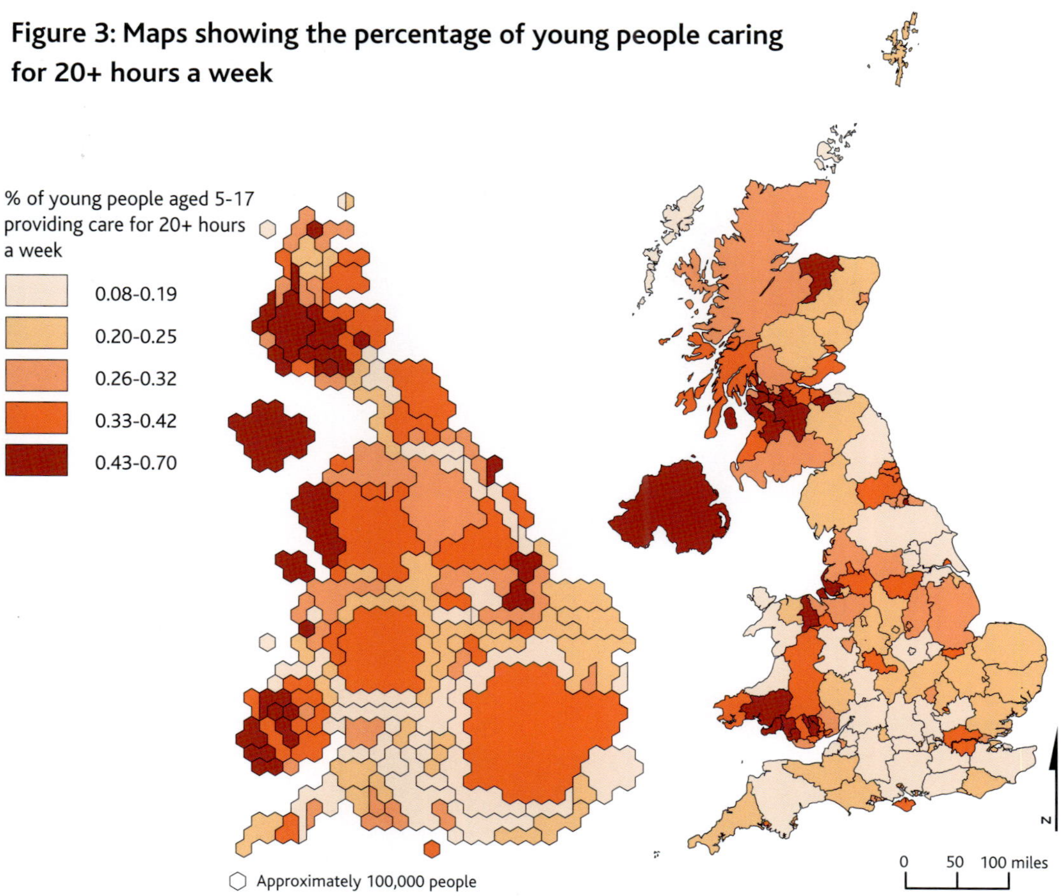

Note: Both maps in each figure represent the same places, shaded identically. The map on the left is a cartogram – each area is shown in proportion to the size of its population in 2001. The largest area is London, since it has the highest population of any of the places[TR]. The map on the right shows the actual boundaries of the areas.

skills, low incomes, poor housing, high crime, ill health and family breakdown. When such problems combine they can create a vicious cycle"[9]. Social exclusion is therefore about areas as well as people.

Providing informal care will impact on children's experience within the home as well as beyond it. Caring can contribute to personal development, a sense of reward by fulfilling social expectations, the pleasure of social interaction and the mutual exchange of laughter, affection and love[10]. However, home can also become the limits of the young carer's social world. The burden of caring – in terms of time and energy (both physical and emotional) – can mean that young carers find it difficult to form and sustain long-term friendships. Their education may also suffer – they may have to miss school, or feel tired at school, which means they may not reach their educational potential[3]. Their labour within the home thus has an impact on their life outside the home as well as inside it.

Similarly, growing up in conditions of poverty can affect the experience of home life as well as the world beyond, as Ridge says: "... the effects of poverty and disadvantage can permeate every aspect of their lives; from the material and more quantifiable aspects of their needs, to the social and emotional requirements so important for children, both in childhood and beyond" (p 131)[1]. Both child poverty and young caring are thus experienced in the home, but have ramifications for the lives of young people far beyond that sphere.

Most importantly the geographical distribution of where children find they need to care does not arrive by chance – it reflects the general distribution of childhood poverty. Although a minority of child carers may not be poor, for as long as child poverty remains we can expect some children to have to care for their parents or other members of their families who are ill and in need of many hours of help a week. Poverty reduces the options open to families in need to care. A very simple interpretation of Figure 1 could be that if child poverty were reduced to the levels of the best-off places, fewer than 1 in 1,000 children would be found caring for more than 20 hours a week in the country. Ninety-nine point nine per cent would have the time to study and play that most children enjoy. Of course, the future does not tend to play out as such statistical relationships suggest, but the fact that where children are most likely to be found to be carers is also where they are most likely to be poor provides yet more evidence of the need to abolish poverty.

Notes

1 Ridge, T. (2002) *Child poverty and social exclusion: From a child's perspective*, Bristol: The Policy Press.

2 Brewer, M. (2003) *What do the child poverty targets mean for the child tax credit? An update*, Briefing Note 41, London: Institute for Fiscal Studies.

3 Roche, J. and Tucker, S. (2003) 'Extending the social exclusion debate: an exploration of the family lives of young carers and young people with ME', *Childhood*, vol 10, no 4, pp 439-56.

4 Dearden, C. and Becker, S. (2004) *Young carers in the UK: The 2004 report*, London: Carers UK (available from www.carersonline.org.uk).

5 The Census defines a dependent child as "... a person in a household aged 0 to 15 (whether or not in a family) or a person aged 16 to 18 who is a full time student in a family with parent(s)".

6 CPAG (Child Poverty Action Group) (2004) *Poverty: The facts (summary)*, London: CPAG.

7 Aldridge, J. and Becker, S. (2003) *Children caring for parents with mental illness: Perspectives of young carers, parents and professionals*, Bristol: The Policy Press.

8 www.dfes.gov.uk

9 www.socialexclusionunit.gov.uk

10 Benn, M. (1998) *Madonna and child: Towards the new politics of motherhood*, London: Jonathan Cape.

TR Further information on this point is available in the accompanying technical report.

What do we know?

- Child poverty is a significant problem in the UK, and the subject of major government targets.
- Many children living in poverty are in families where no parent is in paid employment.
- Young people who provide care on an informal basis may be socially isolated and socially excluded.

What have we found?

- 175,000 children and young people (aged 5-17) in the UK provide informal care.
- Areas with lots of young carers tend also to have lots of families where no parent works.
- In the best-off areas as few as only 1 in 1,000 children need to provide care for more than 20 hours a week, while in other areas this figure reaches 7 per 1,000.

Other reports in the series

The companion report to this, *Top gear*, looks at whether areas with many households that might need a car tend also to have many households that have more cars than they might really need.

1. *Doctors and nurses*
2. *In sickness and in health*
3. *Teachers*
4. *Sons and daughters*
5. *Changing rooms*
6. *A place in the sun*
7. *The office*
8. *Open all hours*
9. *Top gear*
10. *Home front*

Contact details

The reports were prepared by Ben Wheeler, Mary Shaw, Richard Mitchell and Danny Dorling. The authors can be contacted via:

Professor Danny Dorling • Department of Geography • University of Sheffield • Winter Street • Sheffield S10 2TN

e-mail: danny.dorling@sheffield.ac.uk • www.sheffield.ac.uk/sasi

Project funder: Joseph Rowntree Foundation

JOSEPH ROWNTREE FOUNDATION

The POLICY PRESS

DOCTORS and NURSES

Inequalities in paid healthcare persist

In this report the 2001 Census is used to demonstrate that an 'inverse care law' is still in operation in the provision of paid healthcare, despite more than 50 years of NHS provision free at the point of delivery. In 2001, nearly 4 million people in England and Wales reported poor health and a limiting long-term illness. Overall, there were 23 qualified, practising medical doctors for every 10,000 people, but this figure varies widely by area, from 4 to 56 per 10,000. In a continuing demonstration of an inverse care law, the areas with the greatest needs for health services tend to have the lowest numbers of doctors and other health professionals.

The 'inverse care law'

It has been known since at least 1971 that an 'inverse care law' exists[1]. This 'law' suggests that the greater the need people have for healthcare, the less likely they are to get their fair share, and that this inequity is more pronounced where medical care is most exposed to market forces. Studies in subsequent decades have found evidence to support this idea, not only in terms of general health and care, but in terms of the prevalence of particular conditions, the quality of care and the availability of relevant medical specialists. This remains the situation in the UK despite over 50 years of a nationalised health service intended to provide services according to need.

The 2001 Census was the first to ask every person in England and Wales[2] about their medical qualifications, their occupation and their health status. It thus provides a straightforward but comprehensive source of detailed information with which to explore and illustrate the persistence of an inverse care law across these two countries. For this analysis the countries were divided into

Life in Britain

The latest Census reveals that within the UK people live in very different worlds. For some, resources and amenities abound; for others life is characterised by deprivation and difficulties, especially when their need for support is great.

The 2001 Census marked the bi-centenary of Census taking in the UK. It is the most comprehensive social record of life in this country now available. Since 1801 successive governments have asked the population to assist in the taking of a Census.

This report is one of a series of 10 showing key patterns and inequalities in life in the UK revealed by the 2001 Census. These reports focus on geographical inequalities, highlighting where services and opportunities appear not to be available or accessible to those people and places that need them most.

counties, unitary authorities and former metropolitan authorities[TR]. For each of these areas, data from the Census were available on the number of practising, qualified health professionals, and on indicators of the population's health. There were two health questions on the Census form; one asked whether or not the person has a long-term illness, health problem or disability that limits daily activities or work, and the other asked the person to rate their health over the previous 12 months as 'good', 'fairly good' or 'not good'. For this analysis, the group of people most in need of healthcare was defined as those who reported a limiting long-term illness as well as rating their health as 'not good' over the last 12 months.

This definition does not include all people using health services; it excludes, for example, those needing acute emergency care, pregnant women and new born babies. However, it is a good measure of the general health status of the population. Populations in areas with higher rates of limiting long-term illness tend also to have lower life expectancy[TR]. Although the measures of health used here are self-reported by people when they fill in their Census questionnaire, there is very strong evidence to suggest that they reflect real health problems and are not just detecting differences in people's opinions about their own health.

The 2001 Census therefore facilitates a comparison of the number of health professionals per head of population with a measure of the need for healthcare, for each of the areas across England and Wales. This report therefore asks:

Do areas which have higher proportions of people in poor health also have fewer working health professionals?

Comparing areas

In 2001, 3.9 million people in England and Wales reported both poor health and limiting long-term illness. This is 7.6% of the population.

Table 1 shows the total number of qualified, practising health professionals, and the number per 10,000 population for the whole of England and Wales. The table identifies four different types of health professional. The Census did not differentiate between private or state, hospital or community, nor full- or part-time employment of the health professionals listed in Table 1, so this report simply considers their general geographical availability to those most in need.

Table 1: Qualified, practising health professionals in England and Wales (2001)

Qualified health professionals in practice	Number in England and Wales	Per 10,000 population
Medical doctors	115,239	23
Dental practitioners	20,947	4
Nurses, midwives and health visitors	403,994	79
Other health-associated professionals and therapists	122,209	24
All health professionals	**662,389**	**130**

Note: The population here and throughout this report is total population of all ages. The numbers of health professionals are simply counts of people in the specified occupation; they do not take into account whether they are in full- or part-time employment.

Figure 1 shows the relationship between the concentration (number per head of population) of each of the four groups of health professionals and the proportion of the population with limiting long-term illness *and* poor health. There is an 'inverse' relationship between the two measures. When one decreases the other tends to increase. In general, the concentration of doctors is lower in areas where there is a higher proportion of people in need of medical care. The correlation coefficient for each graph (a measure of the strength of the relationship) is given in the accompanying technical report.

Of all the four groups of qualified medical professionals identified by the 2001 Census, only the concentration of working nurses, midwives and health visitors has a positive relationship with poor health. That is to say, in general the more people there are in need of these services in an area, the more people providing these services tend also to live in that area. However, there remain a number of areas in the North of England and Wales where many people are in need (more than 10% of the population) but there are less than the national average number of nurses per person; for instance in Hartlepool, Redcar and Cleveland, Blackpool, Halton, Stoke-on-Trent, Caerphilly and Torfaen.

Medical doctors are more likely to live in places where people are less likely to be in need of healthcare (thus the graph shows an inverse relationship). This is despite clusters of doctors near large hospitals that tend to be in areas with higher need. The inverse relationship between dentists per head of population and the prevalence of poor health is stronger, and that for 'Others' (which includes mainly private rather than state provision, such as complementary medicine practitioners) is even more so. This finding is in agreement with previous evidence from 1971 suggesting that the inverse care law is most strongly in effect where market forces are strongest.

Long distance commuting will reduce some of these inequalities. For instance, Tables 2 and 3 give figures for the five areas with the highest percentage of people with poor health and limiting long-term illness, and the five areas with the highest number of medical doctors per head of population. In practice some doctors will commute between these areas and some patients travel for treatment to the areas where doctors are concentrated.

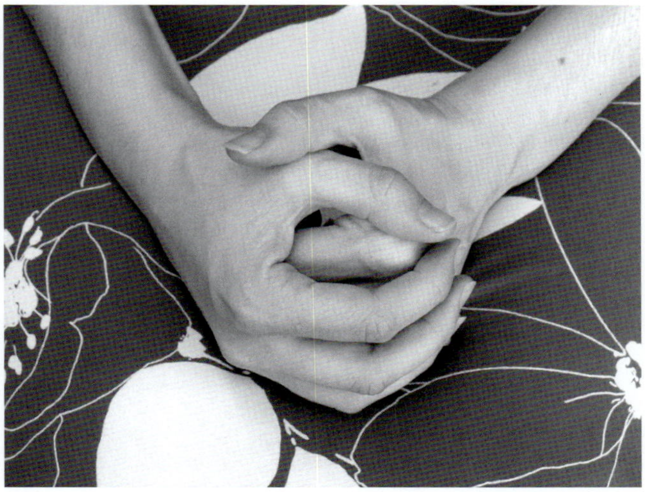

100 years ago

In 1901 there were nearly 33 million people living in England and Wales. There was no National Health Service (NHS), but free healthcare was available for some people at teaching hospitals. For babies born in 1901, life expectancy was then estimated to be 45 for boys and 49 for girls. The 1901 Census returns give 22,698 physicians, surgeons or general practitioners (GPs), of whom 212 were women; 7 doctors per 10,000 population overall compared with 23 today. There were 5,309 dentists – less than 2 per 10,000 population. Health experiences, life expectancy and access to health services would have varied markedly across the country and between social classes in the early 20th century. Although the NHS now exists, inequalities in access to care persist in the early 21st century.

For more information, see 'A century of change: trends in UK statistics since 1900' (www.parliament.uk/commons/lib/ research/rp99/rp99-111.pdf); National Archives (www.nationalarchives.gov.uk); Mohan, J. and Gorsky, M. (2001) *Don't look back? Voluntary and charitable finance of hospitals in Britain, past and present*, London: Office of Health Economics.

Figure 1: The association between the percentage of people in each area with limiting long-term illness (LLTI) and poor health (X-axis), and each of the measures of the four types of health professional in terms of qualified, practising health professionals per 10,000 people (Y-axis)

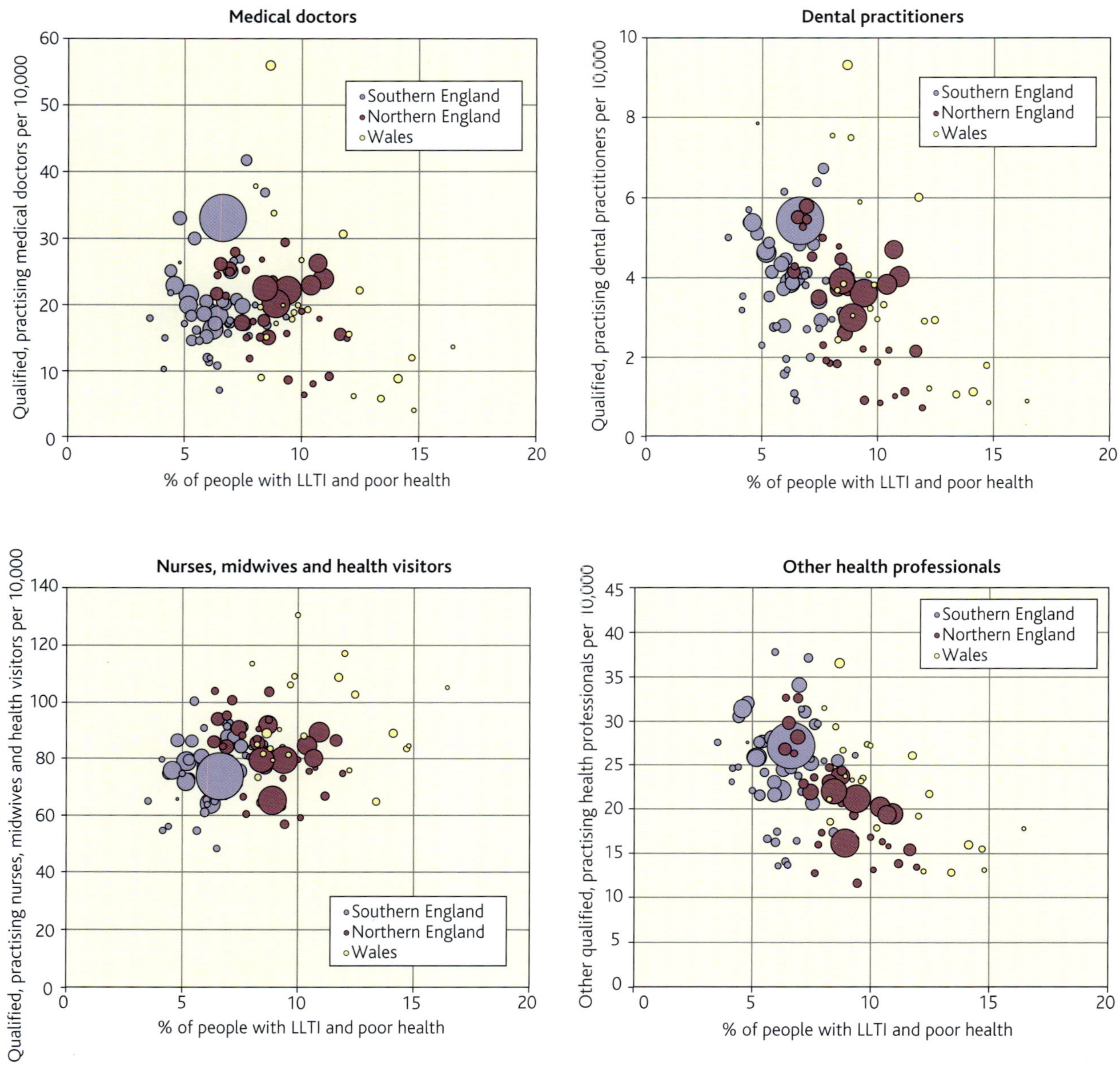

Note: Each circle is a county, unitary or former metropolitan authority, drawn with the area in proportion to the total population in 2001 (the largest circle in each graph represents London, with a population of just over 7 million). Areas in northern England are those that lie west or north of the counties of Gloucestershire, Warwickshire, Leicestershire and Lincolnshire (the Severn-Humber divide).

Table 2: The five areas in England and Wales with the highest percentage of people with poor health and limiting long-term illness (LLTI) (2001)

Area	Qualified medical practitioners per 10,000 population	% of people with poor health and LLTI
Merthyr Tydfil	13.7	16.6
Blaenau Gwent	4.0	14.8
Neath Port Talbot	12.0	14.7
Rhondda, Cynon, Taff	8.9	14.1
Caerphilly	5.8	13.4
England and Wales average	**22.6**	**7.6**

Table 3: The five areas in England and Wales with the highest number of doctors per 10,000 population (2001)

Area	Qualified medical practitioners per 10,000 population	% of people with poor health and LLTI
Cardiff	55.9	8.7
City of Bristol UA	41.7	7.6
Monmouthshire	37.8	8.0
Leicester UA	36.9	8.4
Bath and North East Somerset UA	34.7	5.9
England and Wales average	**22.6**	**7.6**

Note: UA = unitary authority.

The area with the highest concentration of doctors (Cardiff) is close to areas with very low numbers (the Valleys of South Wales), and it is likely that some doctors live in Cardiff and practise in the Valleys. However, although similar situations can be identified elsewhere, it is unlikely to change the overall pattern substantially, especially given the large regional differences apparent in the maps in Figures 2 and 3. In general doctors and patients do not commute hundreds of miles to meet. Furthermore, there is widespread evidence that more affluent and in general more healthy people are better equipped to secure NHS treatment when they need it.

An alternative means to equalise the distribution could be for rates of illness to fall disproportionately in the areas with the poorest health – but that may require greater availability of health services (as well as other resources). Part of the reason for health inequalities existing is that some people in some parts of the country have received more healthcare than others. This is because the better availability of doctors in healthier areas is likely to result in these populations receiving a greater degree of preventative healthcare, so further improving their health, while fewer doctors for populations in poorer health is likely to lead to fewer opportunities for preventative action.

The maps in Figures 2 and 3 make it apparent that ill-health is concentrated in South Wales, the North West and the North East of England. Areas with the best health are those in central southern England. The highest concentrations of doctors are found in London, Oxfordshire, Leicester and the Bristol-Bath-Cardiff area.

Figure 2: The geographical variation in the prevalence of people with poor health and limiting long-term illness (2001)

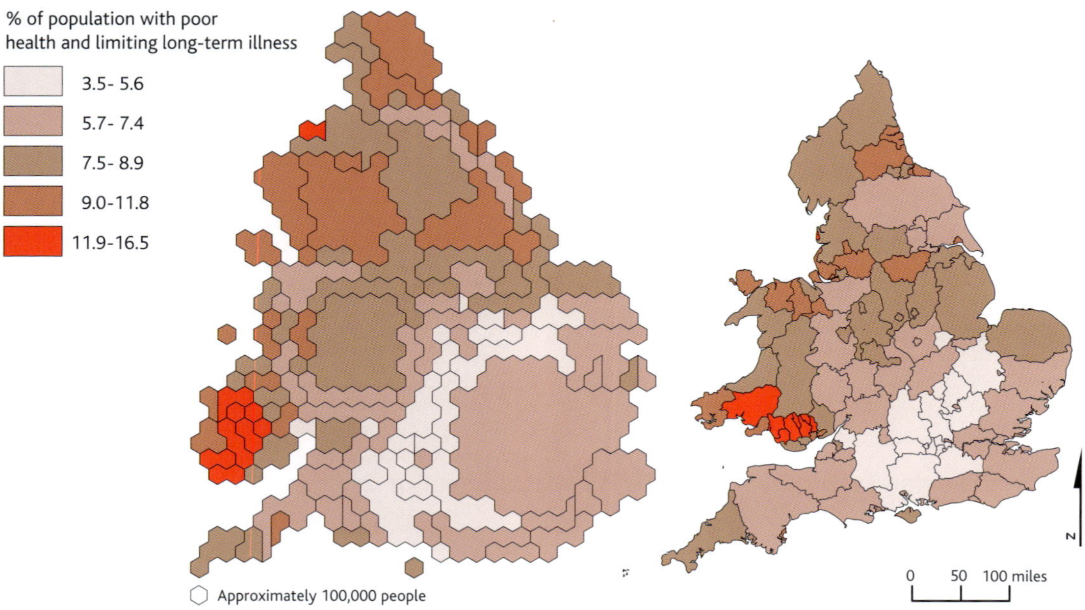

Figure 3: The number of qualified medical practitioners per 10,000 population for each area

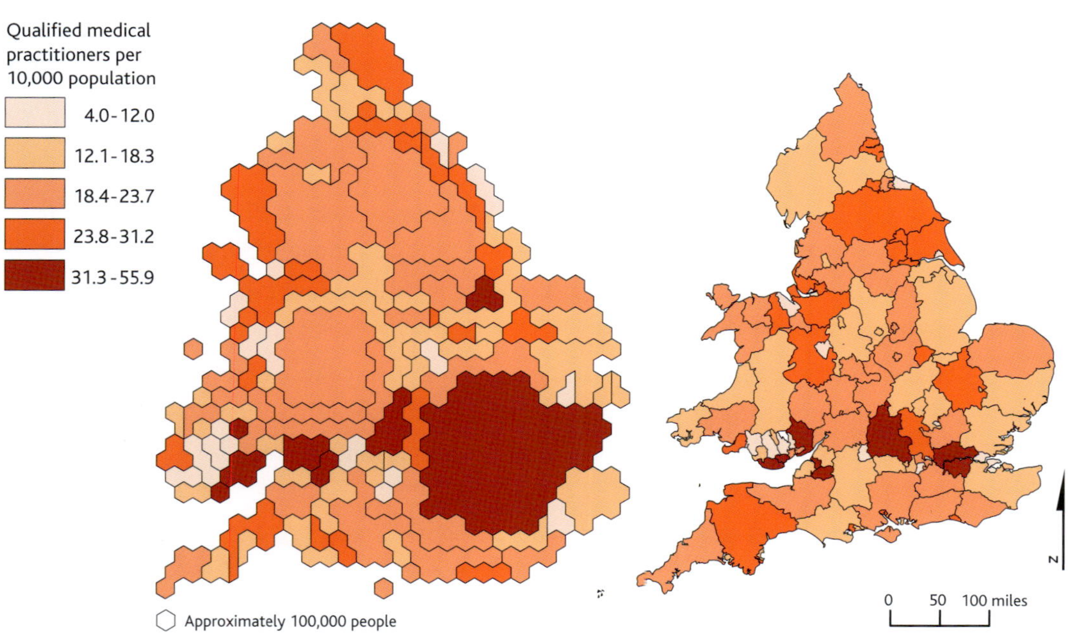

Note: Both maps in each figure represent the same places, shaded identically. The map on the left is a cartogram – each area is shown in proportion to the size of its population in 2001. The largest area is London, since it has the highest population of any of the places[TR]. The map on the right shows the actual boundaries of the areas.

Since 2001

Between September 2001 and September 2003, the NHS in England and Wales recruited an additional 9,700 whole-time equivalent (WTE) doctors and 30,000 WTE nurses[3]. However, the patterns observed in this report do not change quickly, and the current situation is unlikely to be very different from that measured by the Census in April 2001.

Discussion

Despite the intention to provide publicly funded health services in the UK that are delivered in response to need, it is apparent that an inverse care law is still in operation. Populations with greater need for care tend to live in areas with lower numbers of doctors, dentists and other health professionals. Only nurses, midwives and health visitors tend to be concentrated more in areas of higher need. This is likely to reflect the tendency for an inverse care law to be more acute under market forces – there is a greater pool of nurses to be drawn from than of dentists and less scope for nurses to work privately. Also, health service bodies have a duty of care to populations most in need, and provision of nurses, midwives and health visitors is likely to reflect that. The higher status, more powerful, and better paid health professionals are more likely to operate in a national job market and have more control over their location.

In the short term, it may be possible to implement policies that will address the geographic distribution of health professionals. Incentives could be given to draw practitioners to areas with low availability, and to finance that, funding could be reduced in those areas with current relative over-provision. This would have to be explicitly aimed at redressing the distribution of health professionals, as opposed to policies that simply provide more funding in areas of greatest need, such as the deprivation payment scheme for GPs. The alternative is to redistribute those in need of medical services – perhaps one of the elements of current policies aiming to improve access to quality healthcare through increased choice.

The long-term solution would be to have a more sustainable, secure workforce rooted in the areas with greatest need. This may need to be addressed through geographically biasing the intake of medical schools, and even addressing the shortages at an earlier stage in students' education. Part of the explanation of the map of inequalities in health is undoubtedly due to less healthcare being available where it is most needed. Thus the inverse care law can be self-reinforcing; the population's health improves fastest where service provision is best, and that draws yet more provision to those areas.

The Department of Health does not appear to have an effective policy of equalising the availability of care for all (for example, aiming for an even distribution of GPs per head), let alone making it proportional to need. In order to reverse the inverse care law, it would be necessary to instigate an effective policy of encouraging doctors and other health professionals to move towards the areas where people need their services the most. If the UK health service was privately run the persistence of the inverse care law would be understandable and expected; yet it still persists despite a service that is, in theory, provided according to need.

Notes

1 Tudor Hart, J. (1971) 'The inverse care law', *Lancet*, vol 1, pp 406-12.

2 The Census forms for England and Wales asked specifically about people's medical qualifications, while those for Scotland and Northern Ireland did not; this report therefore only considers England and Wales.

3 Department of Health (www.dh.gov.uk/PublicationsAndStatistics/Statistics/fs/en) and National Assembly for Wales (www.wales.gov.uk/keypubstatisticsforwalesheadline/index.htm).

TR Further information on this point is available in the accompanying technical report.

What do we know?

- Healthcare tends to be provided inversely according to need; that is, the people in most need of medical services are least likely to receive their fair share.
- Doctors, dentists and other health professionals, including those mainly providing care in the private market, tend not to live in areas of the greatest health need.

What have we found?

- The 2001 Census demonstrates that an 'inverse care law' is still in operation, despite more than 50 years of provision by the NHS.
- The 'inverse care law' does not seem to apply when we consider nurses, midwives and health visitors – these professionals are more likely to be found in proportion to need (and have the least power to influence the location of their employment).

Other reports in the series

The companion report to this, *In sickness and in health*, shows a strong geographic relationship between the provision of informal care and the need for that care.

1. *Doctors and nurses*
2. *In sickness and in health*
3. *Teachers*
4. *Sons and daughters*
5. *Changing rooms*
6. *A place in the sun*
7. *The office*
8. *Open all hours*
9. *Top gear*
10. *Home front*

Contact details

The reports were prepared by Ben Wheeler, Mary Shaw, Richard Mitchell and Danny Dorling. The authors can be contacted via:
Professor Danny Dorling • Department of Geography • University of Sheffield • Winter Street • Sheffield S10 2TN
e-mail: danny.dorling@sheffield.ac.uk • www.sheffield.ac.uk/sasi

Project funder: Joseph Rowntree Foundation

JOSEPH ROWNTREE FOUNDATION

The POLICY PRESS

In SICKNESS and in HEALTH

Informal care provided by 5.9 million

For the first time, the 2001 Census made visible the work of 5.9 million people providing care and support to others on an informal basis; 1.2 million of these people provide more than 50 hours of care per week. Caring is a phenomenon found all over Britain, and is very strongly related to the need for that care. These findings suggest that people in very different circumstances, rich or poor, young or old, working or not, from deprived or affluent areas, all care for their loved ones in response to those people's needs.

Measuring informal care

> "Informal care is a term which hides a rich variety of human relationships between spouses, between children and parents; between kith and kin, friends and neighbours. Most care without giving thought to the financial cost of caring. It somehow demeans them to reduce their dedication to cash amounts."[1]

The 2001 Census was important in that it was the first to ask about self-reported general health (in addition to a question on limiting long-term illness, which was introduced in 1991) and it also asked about an activity directly related to poor health – the provision of informal care. This additional question in 2001 asked:

Do you look after, or give any help or support to, family member, friends, neighbours or others because of:
- **long-term physical or mental ill-health or disability, or**
- **problems related to old age?**

Possible answers were: No; 1-19 hours a week; 20-49 hours a week; 50+ hours a week.

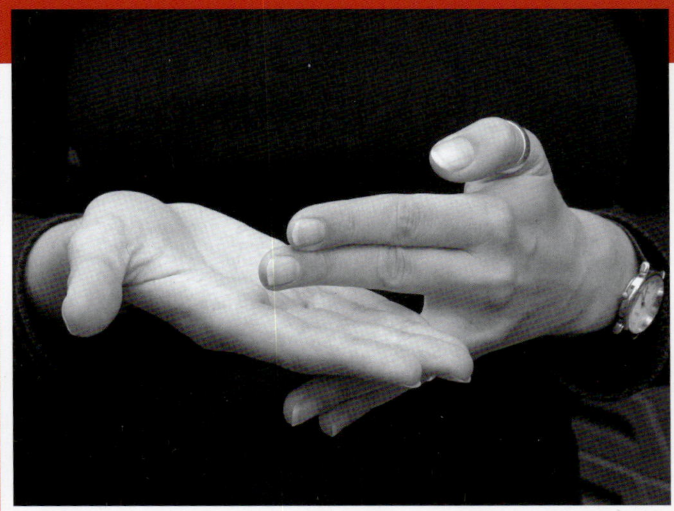

The image above shows British Sign Language for 'access'

Life in Britain

The latest Census reveals that within the UK people live in very different worlds. For some, resources and amenities abound; for others life is characterised by deprivation and difficulties, especially when their need for support is great.

The 2001 Census marked the bi-centenary of census taking in the UK. It is the most comprehensive social record of life in this country now available. Since 1801 successive governments have asked the population to assist in the taking of a Census.

This report is one of a series of 10 showing key patterns and inequalities in life in the UK revealed by the 2001 Census. These reports focus on geographical inequalities, highlighting where services and opportunities appear not to be available or accessible to those people and places that need them most.

This question thus opens a window on people's private lives, revealing the domestic activities and responsibilities of millions of people.

Even though the 2001 Census was the first to measure caring, people have always cared for each other in the domestic setting of the home. However, the concept of 'informal care' emerged in the 1970s, recognising the continuing role of the provision of unpaid care within the home, in the context of the widening role of the welfare state and the National Health Service (NHS) as providers of formal care in the post-war decades. Britain has what has been described as a "mixed economy of welfare, in which the state, voluntary sector, the family and the market have played different parts at different times"[2]. Support for carers is high on the policy agenda and the current Labour government has a National Strategy for Carers.

For this analysis, as with the other reports in this series, the country is divided into counties, unitary authorities and former metropolitan authorities. For each of these areas, data were obtained based on responses to the health and informal care questions described above. Data from both health questions were used; firstly that which asked whether or not a person has a long-term illness, health problem or disability that limits daily activities or work and secondly the self-reported health question which asked the person to rate their health over the previous 12 months as 'good', 'fairly good' or 'not good'. For this analysis, the group of people *most* in need of healthcare has been classified as those who reported a limiting long-term illness as well as rating their health as 'not good' over the last 12 months. Many, but not all, of these people may well be in need of some informal care.

This report uses 2001 Census data to investigate the extent of informal care provision and some of the characteristics of people who provide informal care. It addresses the question:

Do areas with high proportions of people in poor health also have high proportions of people providing informal care?

Findings

In 2001, 4.5 million people in the UK reported that they had both poor health *and* a limiting long-term illness. This is 7.8% of the population. Around 4 million people provide care for 1-19 hours a week, 0.7 million people provide care for 20-49 hours a week and some 1.2 million people reported that they provide informal care for others for 50+ hours a week. This gives a total of 5.9 million people providing some form of informal care each week, 1 in 10 of the population.

Table 1 gives an indication of who makes up this workforce of informal carers. In terms of those providing the greatest amount of care (50+ hours a week),

- one in a hundred carers is under the age of 18;
- around a third are aged 65+;
- six out of ten are women;
- a fifth are in poor health themselves.

Table 1: Numbers and characteristics of informal carers in the UK (2001)

	People caring 1-19 hours a week		People caring 20-49 hours a week		People caring 50+ hours a week	
Characteristics of informal carers	**Number**	**% of total**	**Number**	**% of total**	**Number**	**% of total**
Total	**3,952,571**	**100**	**659,071**	**100**	**1,247,294**	**100**
Young people (aged 5-17)	145,853	4	16,113	2	13,029	1
Older people (aged 65+)	542,772	14	113,037	17	381,519	31
Women	2,247,491	57	396,640	60	754,904	61
Carers with poor health themselves	341,594	9	93,460	14	257,038	21

Some people are therefore looking after themselves as well as providing care for others. Evidence from other surveys suggests that a quarter of carers care for more than one person[3].

A total of 1.2 million people provide informal care 50+ hours a week – that is, providing care that is more than the equivalent of a full-time job (the European Working Directive limits most working hours to 48 a week). This is about the same as the number of people working in the formal, paid sector of the NHS.

The Census also allows us to look at whether people combine informal caring and work (see Figure 1). Of those carers aged 16-74 who do 50+ hours of caring a week, 68% are economically inactive and 32% active. One in six (168,000 people) have a full-time job. Full-time in the Census was 30+ hours a week. One in eight (125,000 people) are permanently sick/disabled themselves, compared to one in five of all carers who classify themselves as having poor health.

Figure 1 indicates that while many people combine caring with full-time or part-time work or with studying, those with greater caring commitments are less likely to be economically active. The responsibility of caring is likely to fall on those with the fewest commitments in the formal labour market, and likewise participating in caring will affect any opportunity of taking up paid work or study. As the box '100 years ago' indicates, many people (especially women) have always had to juggle informal care with earning a wage.

Comparing areas

Figure 2 shows that, looking at areas of the UK, there is a very close relationship between caring (taking the most extreme cases of 50+ hours a week) and the need for care (proportion of people with limiting long-term illness and poor self-reported health). Compare this to the findings shown in the companion report to this, *Doctors and nurses* (Report no 1), which shows an 'inverse care law'. This law indicates that those areas with higher proportions of people in need have fewer doctors than those areas with fewer people in need.

If we assume that within these areas informal care is being provided to the people who need it, informal care seems to be responsive to individual needs and circumstances, impervious to the existence of the market. Whereas care in the formal setting of the market is given in exchange (primarily for wages), informal care can be

100 years ago

In 1901 there was no welfare state; those in need of assistance could look only to 'poor relief' supplied by their parish, or the workhouse. For those who had been in a position to pay their membership dues some limited support in times of hardship came from friendly societies and sick clubs. Hospitals were mainly places of death rather than care – the family was the primary source of care for those who could not afford to pay for a private nurse. B.S. Rowntree's survey of poverty in York carried out in 1899 gives some insight into those in need, and their carers, a century ago.

The standard of life: Life in Class A (Income under 18s weekly for a moderate family)

1. No occupation. Married. Age sixty-four. Two rooms. The man "has not had his boots on" for twelve months. He is suffering from dropsy. His wife cleans schools. This house shares one closet with eight other houses, and one water-tap with four others. Rent 2s 6d....

23. Blind. Age sixty-three. Married. Two rooms. Parish relief. Husband been blind twenty years. Sober. Wife delicate, but earns a few shillings by needle-work and sitting up at night with sick people. This house shares closet with another house. Rent 2s 3½d.

For more information see Rowntree, B.S. (1901) *Poverty: A study of town life*, reprinted by The Policy Press, Bristol, for the Joseph Rowntree Foundation, in 2000.

Figure 1: Percentage of all people providing informal care for different amounts of time in different economic activity categories

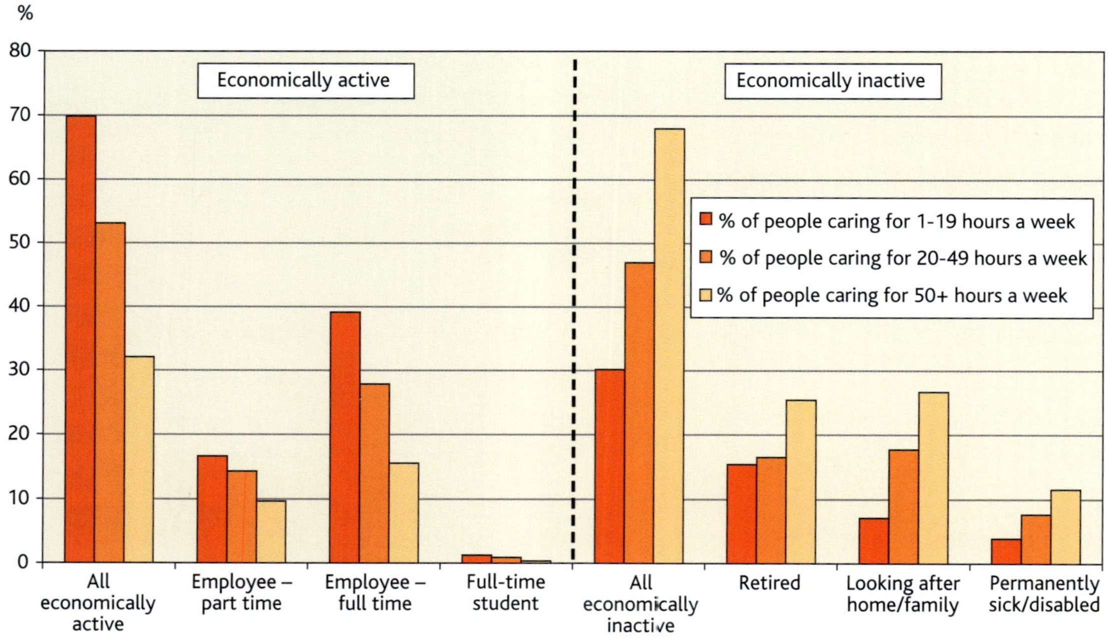

Note: The graph only includes people between the ages of 16 and 74, as Census data on economic activity is limited to this age group. It shows that, for example, about 30% of people caring 1-19 hours a week are economically inactive, while nearly 70% of those caring for 50+ hours a week are economically inactive.

Figure 2: The association between the percentage of the population with poor health and limiting long-term illness (LLTI) (X-axis) in each area and the percentage providing informal care for 50+ hours a week (Y-axis)TR

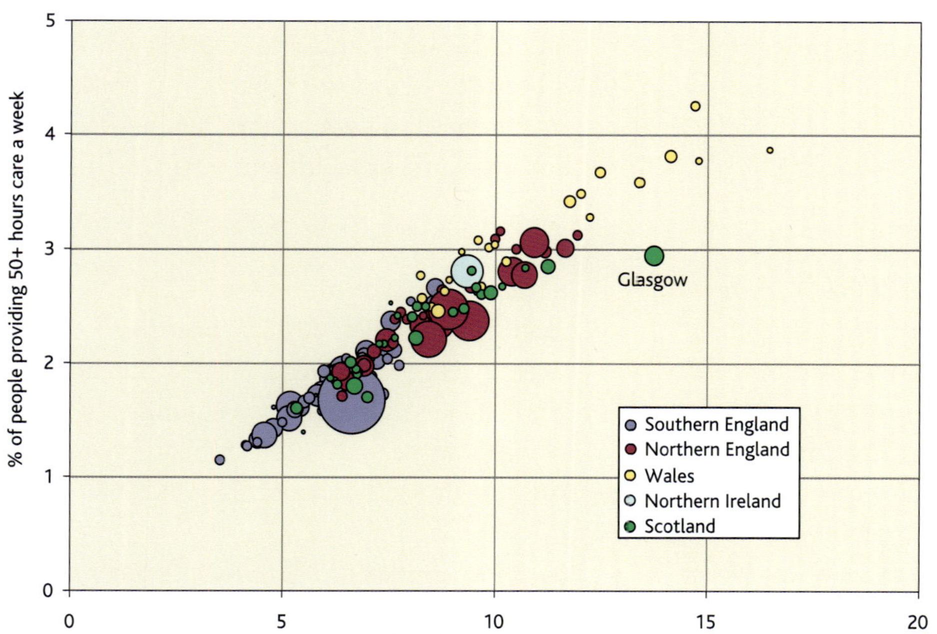

Note: Each circle is a county, unitary or former metropolitan authority, drawn with the area in proportion to the total population in 2001 (the largest circle represents London, with a population of just over 7 million). Areas in northern England are those that lie west or north of the counties of Gloucestershire, Warwickshire, Leicestershire and Lincolnshire (the Severn-Humber divide).

provided through a sense of duty, as an unconditional gift for a loved one, or as part of a complex system of reciprocity between kith and kin which may stretch across generations (caring for an elderly parent because they in turn cared for your spouse as a child; helping a friend who may return the favour in the future). The increased prevalence of divorce and step-families increases the complexity of these family structures and caring relationships. It should also be borne in mind that the standard of care in the formal sector is monitored and regulated, whereas the Census tells us nothing about the type or standard of informal care.

The largest 'outlier' on Figure 2 is Glasgow. Given the percentage of people with limiting long-term illness and poor health here, we would expect just under 4% of the population to be providing 50+ hours of care a week if the pattern was the same as for the rest of the UK. However, the proportion of people providing 50+ hours of care is actually just under 3%. This relative deficit of informal carers may be explained by greater provision of social services in that area, by disproportionate out-migration from Glasgow of a well-educated, young and able subset of the population, or by some other factor.

Table 2 lists the five areas with the highest percentage of people with poor health and limiting long-term illness. Four of these are old mining, iron or steel community areas of South Wales, and the other is Glasgow.

The maps in Figure 3 show in which areas informal carers are more and less prevalent, depicting all people providing informal care for 20+ hours (combining the 20-49 and 50+ hours groups). The lowest rates of informal care provision are found in London, the Home Counties, and other parts of central southern England. The proportion of people providing care, and the proportion of people with limiting long-term illness and poor health increases to the west and north, with the highest rates of both in the Valleys of South Wales, parts of Scotland, and the areas around Tyneside and Merseyside. Both provision of informal care and the prevalence of ill health reflect the classic UK geographical health divide. As Figure 4 illustrates, these patterns are not simply reflecting the distribution of the older population of the UK.

Table 2: Informal carer figures for the five areas with the highest percentage of people with poor health and limiting long-term illness (LLTI) in the UK (2001)

	% of population providing informal care			
Area	% of people with poor health and LLTI	1-19 hours a week	20-49 hours a week	50+ hours a week
Merthyr Tydfill	16.5	6.8	2.0	3.9
Blaenau Gwent	14.8	6.8	1.9	3.8
Neath Port Talbot	14.7	8.0	2.0	4.2
Rhondda, Cynon, Taff	14.1	7.1	1.7	3.8
Glasgow City	13.7	5.5	1.5	2.9
UK average	**7.8**	**6.8**	**1.1**	**2.2**

Figure 3: The geographical variation in the percentage of the population providing informal care for 20+ hours a week

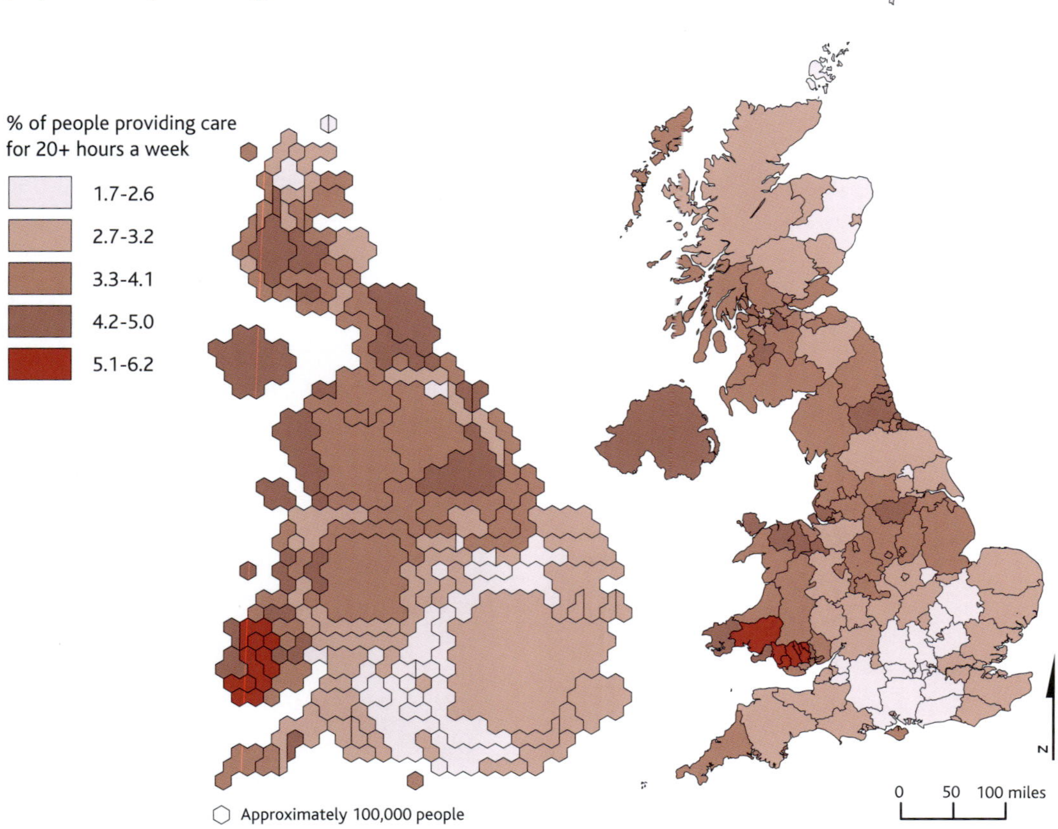

Figure 4: The percentage of the population aged 65+ in each area

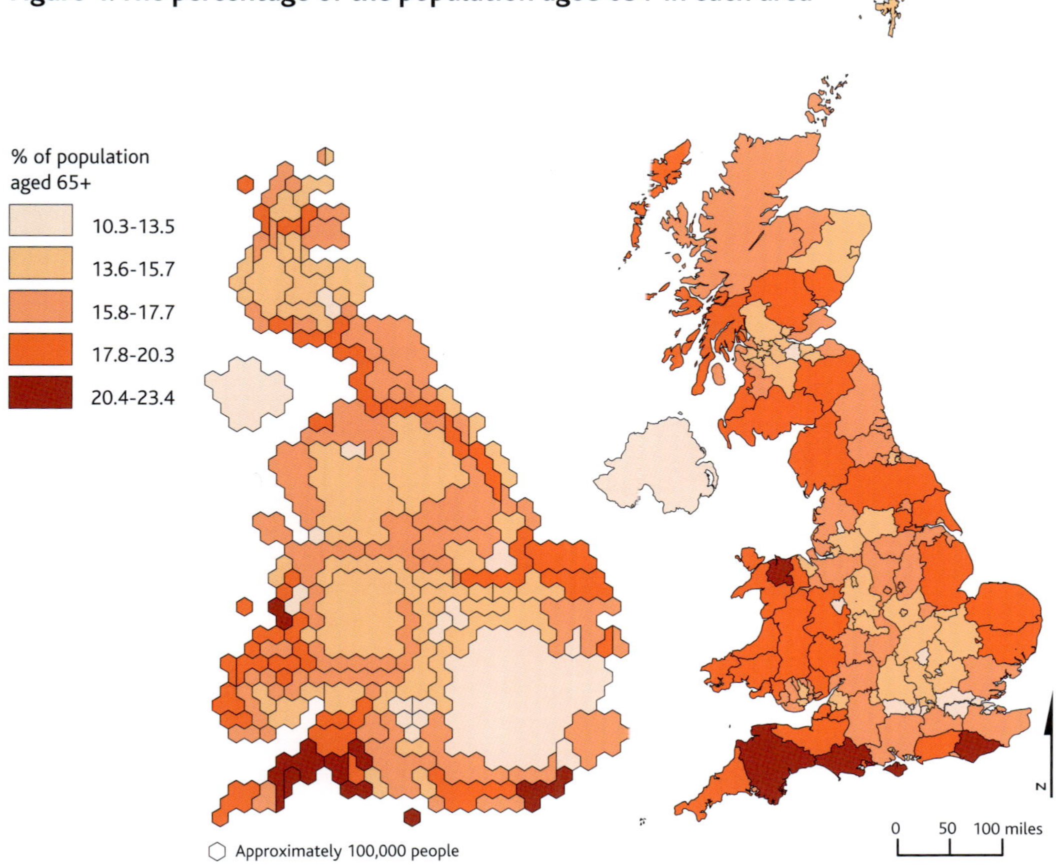

Note: Both maps in each figure represent the same places, shaded identically. The map on the left is a cartogram – each area is shown in proportion to the size of its population in 2001. The largest area is London, since it has the highest population of any of the places[TR]. The map on the right shows the actual boundaries of the areas.

Since 2001

It is unlikely that these patterns have changed very much in the few years since the Census. However, the need for care is likely to increase substantially in the near future. The population is ageing: in 2001, 15.9% of the population were aged 65+ and projections suggest that by 2021 this will have risen to 19.1%, and by 2036 to 24.1%[4]. Between 1991 and 2001, the percentage of people stating that they had a limiting long-term illness rose from 13% to 18% – even though the average age of the population did not change.

Discussion

The activity of caring is based on social relations of friendship, support and social obligation and bound up with notions of reciprocity and mutuality. By and large informal care takes place outside the market. Our geographical analysis of the very close relationship between the provision of and need for care suggests that care can be seen as purely and simply a response to a need.

Those carers providing 35+ hours care a week can in some restricted circumstances claim the Carer's Allowance. For most carers, though, their caring work is unpaid (in monetary terms). Providing care may come at a financial cost with benefits to carers falling short of market wages by a long mark, plus the costs of wages foregone and possibly travel and other costs. However, there may also be benefits for the carer – feelings of personal reward, satisfying a sense of duty, forming a social investment – as well as the more obvious benefits to the person cared for.

Caring is either combined with paid work (most often part time) or means that carers are unable to take on the additional tasks of paid work (two thirds of those who do more than 50 hours of caring a week are 'economically inactive'). At some stage it is possible that policies which focus on increasing the proportion of people in paid work might affect the availability of this pool of 5.9 million carers to provide unpaid care. With the longest working hours in Europe it is likely that, for many people, combining roles as worker and carer presents a substantial, often exhausting, challenge. Moreover, with an ageing population, and given the increase in self-reported limiting long-term illness between 1991 and 2001, the need for carers and the demands on them is likely to increase in the future. However, it could also be argued that further investment by the government in formal services could be specifically aimed at reducing dependence on informal care where it is provided out of necessity due to insufficient professional care.

Notes

1 Royal Commission on Long-Term Care (1999) *Note of dissent*, p 133, cited in Land, H. (2002) 'Spheres of care in the UK: separate and unequal', *Critical Social Policy*, vol 22, no 1, pp 13-32.

2 Offer, J. (1999) 'Idealist thought, social policy and the rediscovery of informal care', *British Journal of Sociology*, vol 50, no 3, pp 467-88.

3 Hirst, M. (2001) 'Trends in informal care in Great Britain during the 1990s', *Health and Social Care in the Community*, vol 9, no 6, pp 348-57.

4 Office for National Statistics, Government Actuaries Department[TR].

TR Further information on this point is available in the accompanying technical report.

What do we know?

- The UK has a mixed economy of welfare – people in need of care are provided with a combination of care from the state, the voluntary sector and the private/family sector – with variations and changes according to needs, and with varying levels of market involvement.
- The 2001 Census was the first to enumerate carers and reported 5.9 million providing care, and 1.2 million providing 50+ hours of care a week.

What have we found?

- This study shows how strongly the provision of informal care is related to the need for that care. In areas where need is high, caring is also high. This is not simply explained by the geographic distribution of older age groups of the population.
- Many carers are themselves ill, some combine caring responsibilities with paid work; those with greater caring commitments are less likely to be in paid work.
- While the provision of informal care is by and large external to the market, changes in work patterns combined with an ageing population may have an adverse impact on the availability of carers.

Other reports in the series

The companion report to this, *Doctors and nurses*, describes the relationship between need for health services and availability of practising health professionals, and finds very different results to those shown here.

1. *Doctors and nurses*
2. *In sickness and in health*
3. *Teachers*
4. *Sons and daughters*
5. *Changing rooms*
6. *A place in the sun*
7. *The office*
8. *Open all hours*
9. *Top gear*
10. *Home front*

Contact details

The reports were prepared by Ben Wheeler, Mary Shaw, Richard Mitchell and Danny Dorling. The authors can be contacted via:
Professor Danny Dorling • Department of Geography • University of Sheffield • Winter Street • Sheffield S10 2TN
e-mail: danny.dorling@sheffield.ac.uk • www.sheffield.ac.uk/sasi

Project funder: Joseph Rowntree Foundation

JOSEPH ROWNTREE FOUNDATION

The POLICY PRESS

TEACHERS

An 'inverse education law'

In this report we investigate the relationship between the proportion of young people without qualifications, and the availability of teachers in areas across England and Wales. An 'inverse education law' seems to exist, where areas with the greatest proportions of unqualified young people have the lowest availability of teachers per head of population. The areas doing best have four times the density of teachers and one third of the rate of young people with no or unknown qualifications when compared to the areas doing worst.

Teachers and qualifications

A person's educational attainment has the potential to be a strong influence on their quality of life and on what kinds of opportunities arise for them. If young people obtain good qualifications, they are more likely to get good jobs with good incomes and then be able to enjoy the associated higher quality of life[1]. To achieve good qualifications is commonly thought to take a combination of the efforts of pupils, their families and their teachers. Without appropriate teaching, young people rarely succeed in obtaining good qualifications.

What are the implications of having no qualifications? Young people who have left school with qualifications are much more likely to be employed than their peers who do not have qualifications. Basic educational qualifications open the door both to higher and further education, and to skilled work. They also open the door to a greater income, as shown in Figure 1, which shows the distribution of people without qualifications and those with a university degree or higher among five income groups. More than half of the working-age adults who have a university degree are in the top income group, whereas less than 1 in 10 of those with no qualifications

Life in Britain

The latest Census reveals that within the UK people live in very different worlds. For some, resources and amenities abound; for others life is characterised by deprivation and difficulties, especially when their need for support is great.

The 2001 Census marked the bi-centenary of census taking in the UK. It is the most comprehensive social record of life in this country now available. Since 1801 successive governments have asked the population to assist in the taking of a Census.

This report is one of a series of 10 showing key patterns and inequalities in life in the UK revealed by the 2001 Census. These reports focus on geographical inequalities, highlighting where services and opportunities appear not to be available or accessible to those people and places that need them most.

Figure 1: Income group and level of qualification[2]

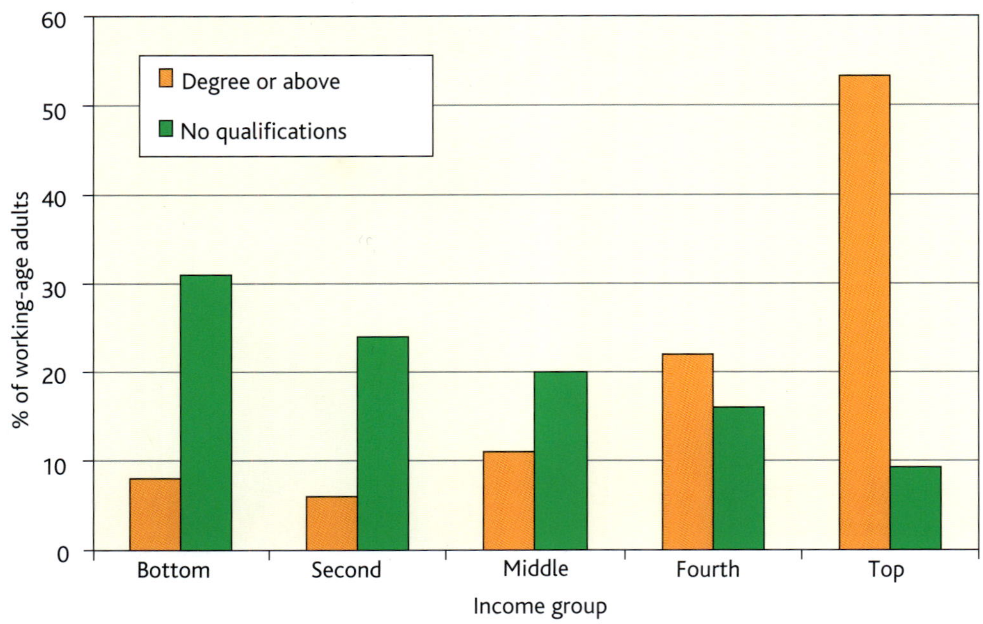

are in that group. In contrast, more than half of those with no qualifications are in either the lowest, or the second lowest income groups. Of course, these are not hard and fast rules; some people with no qualifications go on to earn a great deal of money while others with excellent qualifications struggle to get any kind of job (see *The office*, Report no 7).

In this report, the analysis investigates whether or not there is an 'inverse education law' by comparing the number of young people without qualifications in an area to the number of teachers living and working there. Another report in this series, *Doctors and nurses* (Report no 1), describes an 'inverse care law' that is apparent in the UK – areas with the worst health tend also to have fewer doctors. This seems inappropriate, since a national health service designed to bring about the greatest improvement in the population's health would probably involve having the greatest number of doctors available in places where health is worst. This report investigates whether a comparable situation exists with regard to the geographic distribution of teachers and young people without qualifications.

The 2001 Census asked each person in England and Wales[3] if they had a professional teaching qualification (for teaching in schools). The Census also asked for each person's occupation, which means that it is possible to count qualified teachers who are actually teaching. In addition, the Census asked each person to list their qualifications, with options from no/unknown qualifications, through GCSEs, A-levels and NVQs to higher degrees, making it possible to count young people who have no or unknown qualifications. The analysis presented here divides the country into the same areas used in other reports in the series (counties, unitary authorities, and former metropolitan authorities), and asks:

Do areas where high proportions of young people have no or unknown qualifications tend also to have fewer teachers?

Findings

In England and Wales in 2001 there were 662,000 qualified teaching professionals who were working as teachers at that time; one teacher for every 16 children aged 5-15 (compulsory school ages). However, this takes no account of teachers working part time; using government figures of 438,900 full-time equivalent (FTE) teachers in January 2001 gives a ratio of one full-time teacher for every 24 children in the 5-15 age group.

The 2001 Census also recorded 5.7 million people aged 16-24, one million (17.6%) of whom had no (or unknown[4]) qualifications. Due to the way that ages and qualifications are grouped in Census data releases, this analysis considers the proportion of 17 year olds who are in full-time education and who have no or unknown qualifications. Although these young people are still in full-time education, the system could be deemed to have failed them because they did not obtain standard qualifications at the age of 15/16 with most of their peers. In 2001, of the 427,500 17 year olds who were in full-time education, 29,200 (7%) had no qualifications.

Comparing areas

Figure 2 shows the relationship between the proportion of young people with no or unknown qualifications and the number of qualified teaching professionals per 100 children aged 5-15, for the 109 areas of England and Wales. The graph shows that there is an 'inverse' relationship between these measures; areas with a high proportion of young people with no or unknown qualifications tend to have a lower number of teachers per child aged 5-15. This inverse relationship is statistically significant and fairly strong[TR].

100 years ago

The 1901 Census returns document 230,345 teachers in England and Wales. The ratio of pupils to teachers in state-funded elementary schools was 48.5 pupils for each teacher. Secondary education was not universally available, and even when local education authorities (LEAs) were established in 1902 to provide a post-elementary state education, most pupils would still have had to pay fees. By 1911, still only 7.5% of 12-14 year olds went to secondary school. The legal school leaving age only reached 16 in 1972.

For more information, see the National Archives (www.nationalarchives.gov.uk).

The geography of the two measures can be explored to a greater extent using the maps in Figures 3 and 4. Figure 3 shows the distribution of the young people without qualifications measure, indicating that the areas with the highest proportion of 17 year old students with no or unknown qualifications include a number of towns and

Figure 2: The association between the percentage of 17 year olds with no or unknown qualifications and the number of working, qualified teaching professionals per 100 children aged 5-15 in the 109 areas of England and Wales (2001)[TR]

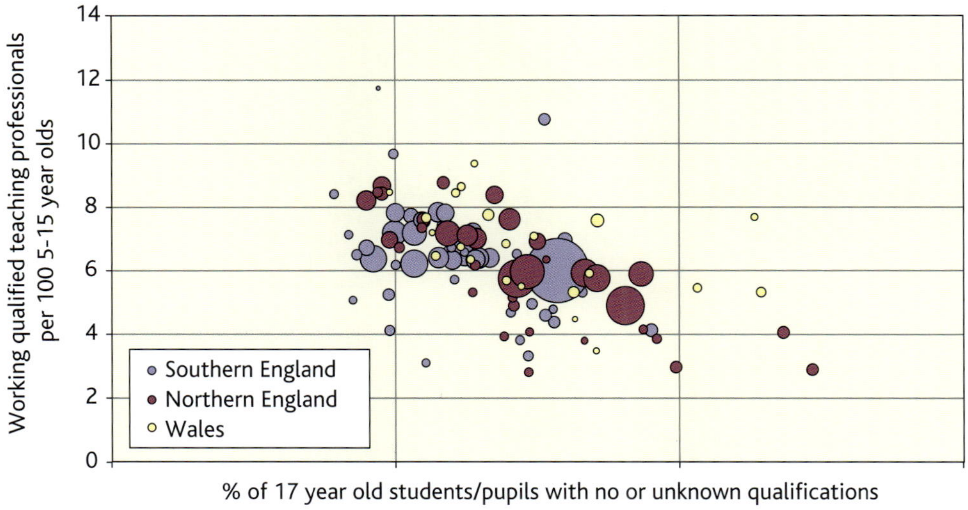

Note: Each circle is a county, unitary or former metropolitan authority, drawn with the area in proportion to the total population in 2001 (the largest circle represents London, with a population of just over 7 million). Areas in northern England are those that lie west or north of the counties of Gloucestershire, Warwickshire, Leicestershire and Lincolnshire (the Severn-Humber divide).

Figure 3: The proportion of young people with no or unknown qualifications in each area

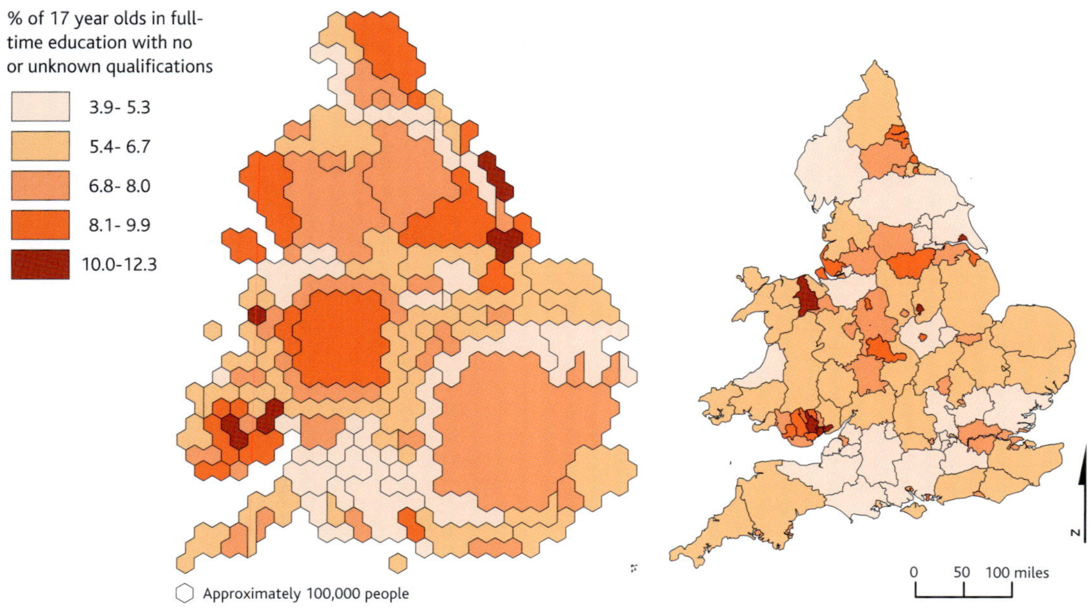

Figure 4: The geographical variation in the number of working, qualified teachers per 100 children aged 5-15

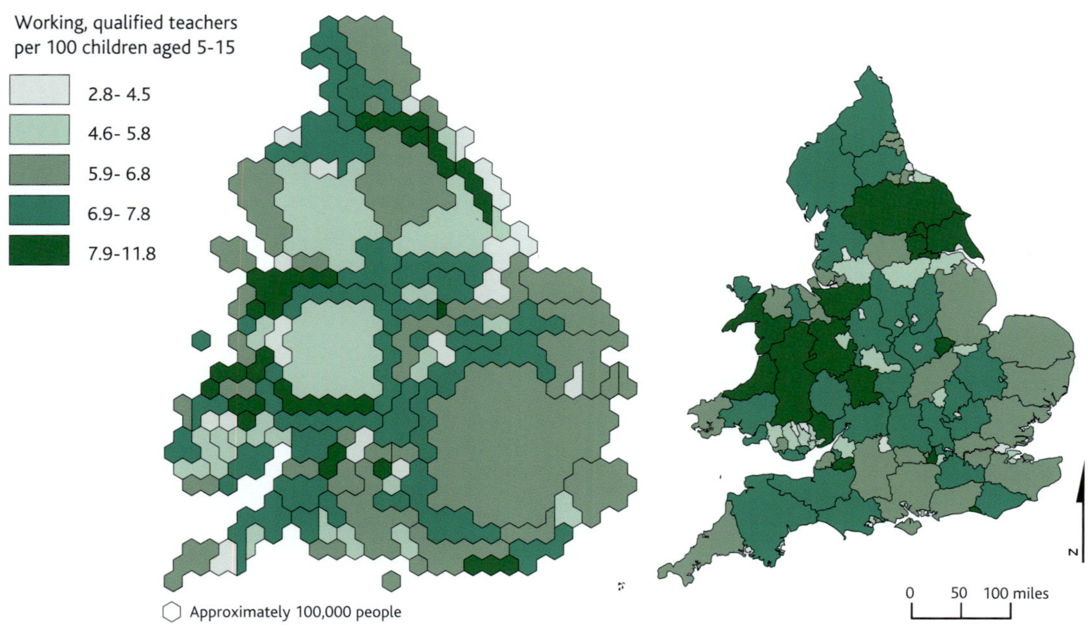

Note: Both maps in each figure represent the same places, shaded identically. The map on the left is a cartogram – each area is shown in proportion to the size of its population in 2001. The largest area is London, since it has the highest population of any of the places[TR]. The map on the right shows the actual boundaries of the areas.

cities in the North and Midlands of England as well as areas of South Wales.

Figure 4 shows the distribution of the 'teachers per 100 children' measure across England and Wales. Along with the areas listed in Table 2, the highest densities of teachers are generally found in mid-Wales, parts of the West Midlands and Yorkshire. The lowest numbers of teachers are found in the Valleys of South Wales, and towns and cities in the East Midlands and the North, such as Hartlepool, Kingston-upon-Hull, Leicester and Nottingham.

Tables 1 and 2 list the five areas with the highest proportion of young people with no or unknown qualifications, and the five with the lowest number of children per teacher. Notice that in Table 1 most of the areas have more children per teacher than the average, but that there is still some variation within the group. Notice too that in Table 2 not all the areas have a particularly low proportion of 17 year olds with no or unknown qualifications despite a higher density of teachers. Although the association demonstrated in Figure 2 is strong, a few areas do not fit the trend observed among most.

Table 1: The five areas with the highest proportion of young people with no or unknown qualifications

Area	% of 17 year old students with no or unknown qualifications	Children aged 5-15 for each working, qualified teacher[a]
Kingston upon Hull	12.3	34.5
Nottingham	11.8	24.4
Caerphilly	11.4	18.9
Denbighshire	11.3	13.0
Newport	10.3	18.2
England and Wales	**6.8**	**15.9**

Table 2: The five areas with the lowest number of children per teacher

Area	% of 17 year old students with no or unknown qualifications	Children aged 5-15 for each working, qualified teacher[a]
Rutland	4.7	8.5
Brighton and Hove	7.6	9.3
Bath and North East Somerset	5.0	10.3
Monmouthshire	6.4	10.6
Shropshire County	5.9	11.4
England and Wales	**6.8**	**15.9**

Note: [a] Note that these figures do not account for teachers working part time; they are based on counts of people working as teachers (full-time equivalents are not available in the Census data).

Since 2001

In January 2001 there were 438,900 FTE teachers in the state-maintained sector in England and Wales; by January 2004, this had risen to 457,200 FTE, an increase of 4%. In England in January 2001 there were 18.3 pupils for every teacher (nursery, primary and secondary); this fell to 17.7 by January 2004. Figures for Wales were similar, reducing from 21.5 to 20.6 for primary schools and 16.6 to 16.5 for secondary schools between 2001 and 2003 (combined figures are unavailable)[5]. It seems fair to say that education and teacher numbers have received a considerable boost in terms of investment and recruitment in recent years. This will not help the thousands of young people who have already left school with no qualifications, although the increasing availability and promotion of 'lifelong learning' and adult education should be of benefit to people who did not get qualifications while at school.

Discussion

The significance of having no qualifications needs to be properly understood. Qualifications are a marker of educational attainment and essentially, the higher the educational attainment, the more likely a person is to have and hold a good job, with a high wage. This is true for both men and women. Education is also an important marker for a better chance of good health in later life, although this is partly because it is so strongly associated with increased wealth.

An alternative perspective comes from reflecting that education is expensive in terms of the investment of time and money by pupils, teachers, administrators, parents and, of course, tax payers. It is meant to benefit both the individual and the wider society of which the educated individual should become a useful member. In our society, qualifications are used to denote the degree of success achieved by both pupil and school. For a child to attend school for 11 years or so and to leave without a formal recognition of what has been achieved must be regarded as very serious. Of course, to get into further and higher education, pupils need qualifications such as GCSEs. The young people focused on in this analysis did not achieve those standard qualifications at the same time as most of their peers, and at the time of the Census, at age 17, did not have any formal qualifications.

The relationship between numbers of teachers and the educational attainment of young people must be considered in order to weigh the significance of these findings. It is a relatively simple equation that says that the more teachers there are per pupil, the smaller a class size ought to be on average. Although the evidence is not entirely straightforward, smaller class sizes have been shown to produce better results from pupils, particularly in the crucial early school years[6]. More teachers might also reflect provision of a wider variety of educational opportunities for a pupil, allowing them a greater chance of finding their own particular aptitudes, honing them, and getting them recognised through a formal qualification.

In England and Wales the LEA is largely responsible for recruiting teachers and evidence suggests that higher expenditure by the LEA (including employing more teachers) is associated with better examination results at LEA level, even after taking poverty in the local community into account[7]. Many of the areas identified by this report as having both a higher proportion of young people who have no or unknown qualifications and a lower number of teachers are poor and deprived. The difficulties in recruiting teachers in these areas are well known[8], so much so that some LEAs are now experimenting with special incentives and assistance to try to attract staff. This analysis supports this approach, and substantial incentive schemes may need to be implemented on a national basis to recruit and retain teachers in areas with the greatest need.

Of course, no incentive schemes will be successful if there are simply not enough teachers trained and available to work in the first place. 'Teacher shortages' has been a familiar headline in recent years in the UK. However, more recent official figures do show a considerable positive shift in attitudes towards teaching as a career and a corresponding rise in applicants. There are also 25,000 more teachers in the classroom than there were five years ago, with the job jumping from 100th place to first in a league table of the most popular career swaps[9].

Teachers are not just there to guide children to success in examinations. They also have important roles as stable figures, role models even, particularly in the often turbulent and difficult lives of children living in deprived areas. Although this report has focused on success in examinations as the key outcome of a good education, greater teacher availability is also likely to be associated with less easily measured benefits such as the provision of extra-curricular activities. The increasing numbers of teachers are to be welcomed and it is hoped that they will be deployed in the areas which need them most – those areas where teacher numbers are lower, which are also those areas that, as this analysis has shown, are those where higher proportions of young people leave compulsory schooling with no formal qualifications.

Notes

[1] Kuh, D., Head, J., Hardy, R. and Wadsworth, M. (1997) 'The influence of education and family background on women's earnings in midlife: evidence from a British National Birth Cohort Study', *British Journal of Sociology of Education*, vol 18, no 3, pp 385-405.

[2] Source: Department for Work and Pensions, *Households Below Average Income 2002/03*, © Crown Copyright 2004.

[3] This report only considers England and Wales, as this question was not asked in Scotland and Northern Ireland.

[4] In this report we have considered people who have 'unknown' qualifications along with those we know not to have any qualifications, since (a) they are grouped together in most Census tables and (b) it seems reasonable to assume that most people who did not tick any boxes for the qualifications question on the Census form had none. In terms of the data available for the analyses presented in this report, the two groups are inseparable.

[5] Data sources: Department for Education and Skills (www.dfes.gov.uk), National Assembly for Wales (www.wales.gov.uk).

[6] Blatchford, P., Bassett, P., Goldstein, H. and Martin, C. (2003) 'Are class size differences related to pupils' educational progress and classroom processes? Findings from the Institute of Education class size study of children aged 5-7 years', *British Educational Research Journal*, vol 29, no 5, pp 708-30.

[7] West, A., Pennell, H., Travers, T. and West, R. (2001) 'Financing school-based education in England: poverty, examination results, and expenditure', *Environment And Planning C: Government and Policy*, vol 19, no 3, pp 461-71.

[8] *Standards and quality in education 2001/02: The annual report of Her Majesty's Chief Inspector of Schools*, London: The Stationery Office.

[9] 'Teaching becomes class act at last', *The Observer*, 11 April 2004[TR].

[TR] Further information on this point is available in the accompanying technical report.

What do we know?

- In the UK, educational attainment is measured by gaining qualifications. The higher the qualifications obtained, the greater a person's chances of getting a good job, with a high income. Educational attainment is also a good predictor of better health.

What have we found?

- There appears to be an 'inverse education law' operating in England and Wales; areas which have fewer teachers per 100 children aged 5-15 have a greater proportion of 17 year olds with no qualifications.

Other reports in the series

The companion report to this, *Sons and daughters*, looks at the extent to which areas with higher proportions of young people with qualifications tend also to have a higher proportion of their parents' generation with good qualifications.

1. *Doctors and nurses*
2. *In sickness and in health*
3. *Teachers*
4. *Sons and daughters*
5. *Changing rooms*
6. *A place in the sun*
7. *The office*
8. *Open all hours*
9. *Top gear*
10. *Home front*

Contact details

The reports were prepared by Ben Wheeler, Mary Shaw, Richard Mitchell and Danny Dorling. The authors can be contacted via:
Professor Danny Dorling • Department of Geography • University of Sheffield • Winter Street • Sheffield S10 2TN
e-mail: danny.dorling@sheffield.ac.uk • www.sheffield.ac.uk/sasi

Project funder: Joseph Rowntree Foundation

JOSEPH ROWNTREE FOUNDATION

The POLICY PRESS

SONS and DAUGHTERS

Education by generation

In England, Wales and Northern Ireland, 16-17 year olds are more likely to obtain good GCSEs and equivalent qualifications if they live in an area where a high proportion of their parents' generation (people generally aged 40-54) are well qualified. Since children's achievement is so strongly related to that of their parents' generation, geographical inequalities in educational attainment across the country are maintained over time. However, this is not the case in Scotland, where there is much less geographical variability in the proportion of young people who have qualifications.

Education and qualifications

Young people who achieve good qualifications at school are the most likely to get a place at university, to get a good degree, and later, to do well in the employment and housing markets. Understanding the circumstances which lead to success in examinations at school is therefore very important. The 2001 Census was the first to ask everyone below the age of 75 to describe all of their qualifications. Before 2001, Censuses only asked whether a person had a university degree or equivalent and, in earlier Censuses, at what age they had left school. It is because qualifications have become more important to life chances in the UK that a more detailed Census question is now justified. The Census tells us about a range of qualifications: academic, vocational and professional.

The young people who have the best opportunities for gaining qualifications are those who grow up in and around the most well-educated families. Recent research shows that one of the best predictors of a child's chances of going to university is the proportion of adults in the child's neighbourhood who have a university degree[1].

Life in Britain

The latest Census reveals that within the UK people live in very different worlds. For some, resources and amenities abound; for others life is characterised by deprivation and difficulties, especially when their need for support is great.

The 2001 Census marked the bi-centenary of census taking in the UK. It is the most comprehensive social record of life in this country now available. Since 1801 successive governments have asked the population to assist in the taking of a Census.

This report is one of a series of 10 showing key patterns and inequalities in life in the UK revealed by the 2001 Census. These reports focus on geographical inequalities, highlighting where services and opportunities appear not to be available or accessible to those people and places that need them most.

The 2001 Census allows us to compare the proportions of young people (16-17 year olds) who have standard qualifications in an area with the proportion of people old enough to be their parents' generation (40-54 year olds) who have high level qualifications. The intent here is not to compare the educational attainment of 40-54 year olds with that of their actual children; this is not possible with Census data[2]. However, it is interesting to investigate how close the geographical connection is between these two measures for different groups of people.

Qualifications, particularly those obtained at school, differ in Scotland from the rest of the UK. This report focuses on the examinations children do around the age of 16. In England, Wales and Northern Ireland this means 'Level 2' qualifications (largely GCSEs)[3]. In Scotland this means 'Group 1' qualifications (largely Standard Grades)[4]. Since the Census was conducted in April 2001, any 16 year olds sitting examinations in the summer of that year would not have these qualifications counted here. For the 40-54 age group, the qualification groupings are more straightforward[5].

Despite the important national differences, it is still possible to assess the relationship between educational attainment of young people and that of their parents' generation within each country of the UK, and to then compare those relationships. This report therefore asks:

To what extent do areas with a high proportion of young people with qualifications tend also to have a high proportion of their parents' generation with good qualifications?

Figure 1: Percentages of 16-17 year olds and 40-54 year olds with qualifications as described in the text

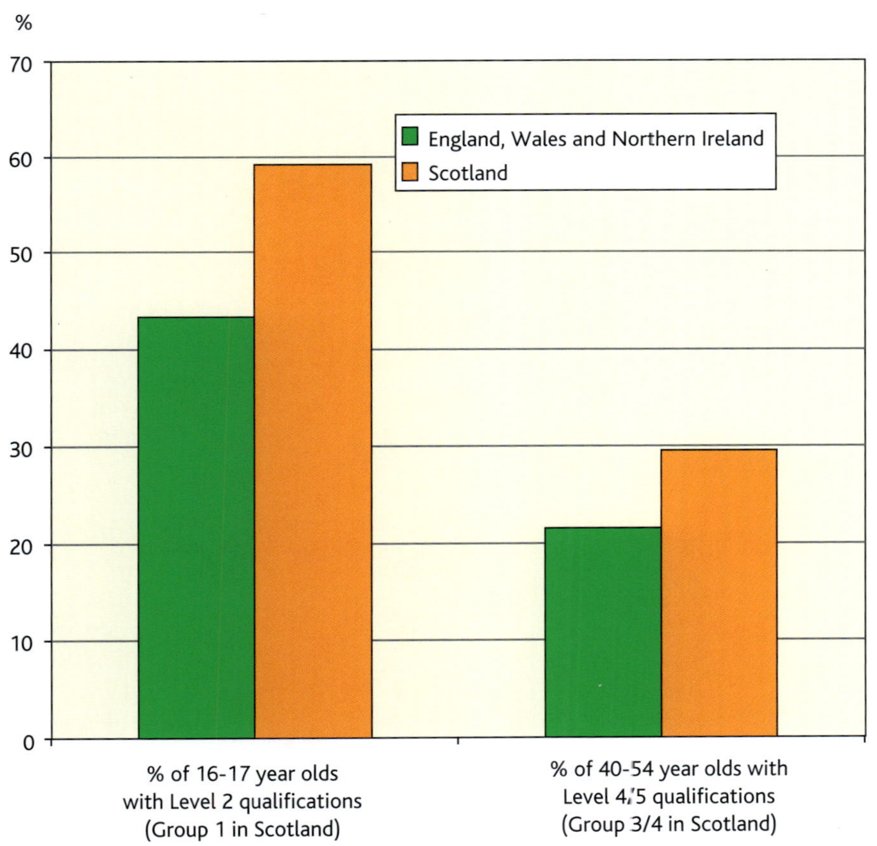

Findings

In England, Wales and Northern Ireland in 2001, a total of 591,000 16-17 year olds had gained Level 2 qualifications and 2.3 million people aged 40-54 had Level 4/5 qualifications (equivalent to university degrees). In Scotland, 75,000 16-17 year olds had Group 1 qualifications and 315,000 40-54 year olds had Group 3/4 qualifications (again equivalent to university degrees). Figure 1 shows the proportions of people within each of these age groups with these qualifications.

Just under one half of 16 and 17 year olds (just over one half in Scotland) have standard qualifications whereas just under a quarter of 40-54 year olds (just over a quarter in Scotland) have high level qualifications. The higher proportion of people with qualifications in Scotland is partly due to the way qualifications are grouped by the Census there. This graph does not necessarily mean that people in Scotland are generally better qualified than elsewhere in the UK (although there is a great deal of evidence that the education system in Scotland is very good).

100 years ago

In 1901, the education sector was in a state of rapid change. Secondary education was generally not provided by the state although some local school boards, which ran elementary schools, had started providing secondary education. That was stopped by a court ruling that said public funds could only be used for elementary education for 5-15 year olds. However, this changed in 1902 when the government set up local education authorities (LEAs) and funded secondary schools – although pupils still had to pay fees and only a wealthy minority could take up the opportunity. Secondary education only became universally available in 1944, but was selective. The school leaving age was raised to 16 in 1972.

For more information see the National Archives (www.nationalarchives.gov.uk).

Comparing areas

Figure 2 illustrates the relationship between the younger and older people's qualifications for each of the 142 counties, unitary and former metropolitan authorities across the UK (the same areas used for each report in this series). This graph shows that in England, Wales and Northern Ireland, areas in which higher proportions of 40-54 year olds have good qualifications tend to also have more 16-17 year olds gaining qualifications. Areas with fewer well-qualified 40-54 year olds tend to have fewer qualified young people. However, as Figure 1 suggests, it is apparent that circumstances are different in Scotland to those in the rest of the UK.

The proportion of each age group with the specified qualifications is higher in most Scottish areas. As before, this may be explained by the different qualifications and their groupings in the Census tables. However, the relationship between the proportion of young people with qualifications and people in their parents' generation with good qualifications is also different in Scotland and this is not because of the ways in which the Census groups qualifications. In Scotland a relationship between qualifications among 16 and 17 year olds and those among their parents' generation is different: there is a much smaller amount of variation in the proportion of young people with qualifications among the Scottish areas than among areas in the rest of the UK (this may be evidence of the high quality of the Scottish education system, or suggests that there is more variation within these areas of Scotland rather than between them). The percentage of 16-17 year olds with standard qualifications ranges only between 56% and 62% in Scotland. In the rest of the UK, the proportion of 16-17 year olds with standard qualifications ranges between 31% and 58%. Thus the educational profile of the younger generation in Scotland is very different, and not related to that of the older generation as it is in England and Wales. Note that, in general, both children and their parents' generation have lower qualifications in Northern Ireland than almost anywhere else in the UK.

Variation in the measures across the UK is illustrated in the maps in Figures 3 and 4. Areas with the lowest proportions of young people with qualifications are in the North of England and South Wales, Glasgow and Dundee. In terms of 40-54 year olds, the areas with most highly qualified people are London and the Home Counties, Edinburgh and central Scotland.

Since 2001

In England in 2000/01, 50% of all 15-year-olds obtained 5 or more GCSEs at grades A* to C. This proportion has been increasing since the late 1980s, and by the end of the 2002/03 academic year had risen to 52.9%[6]. By 2004, 43% of people aged under 30 had attended a university (but not necessarily gained a degree). Achievement of such historically high levels of qualifications, high average school leaving ages and such a high proportion of young people going on to university followed the introduction of near universal comprehensive secondary education during the 1960s and 1970s. The government has set a target for 50% of people aged under 30 to participate in university education by 2010 and although progress is being made towards meeting the target, some children still left school with no qualifications in 2003/04 (6.5% of 15 year old boys and 4.2% of girls achieved no GCSE/GNVQ passes, slight increases from 2002/03)[7].

Figure 2: The association between the percentage of 16-17 year olds with Level 2 qualifications (Group 1 in Scotland) and the percentage of 40-54 year olds with Level 4/5 qualifications (Group 3/4 in Scotland)

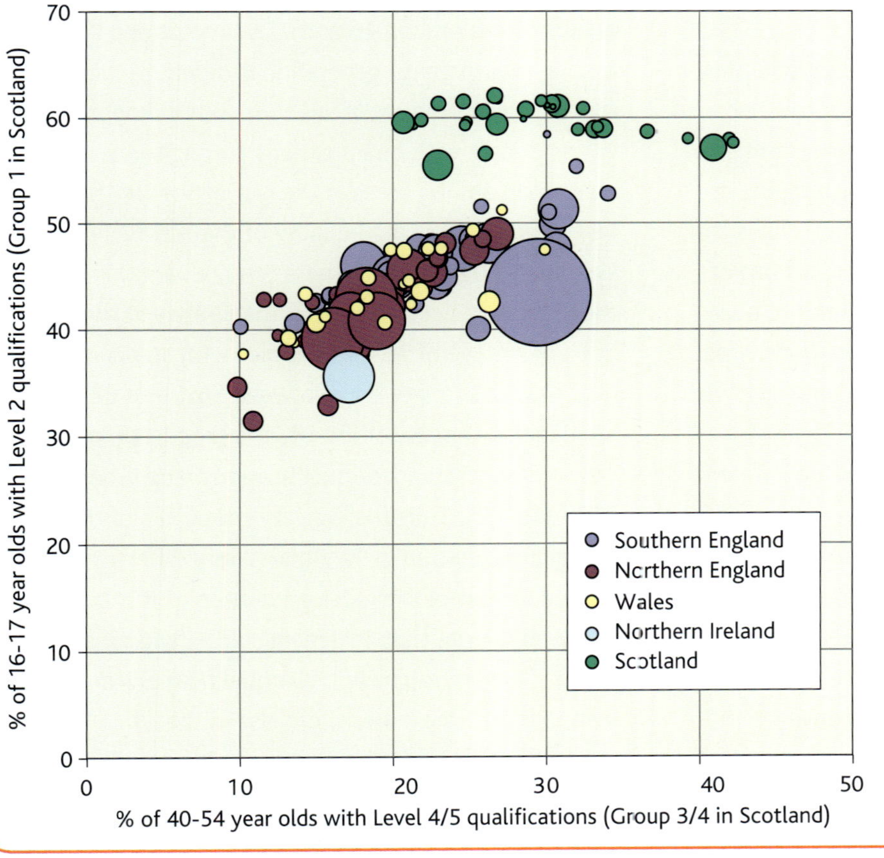

Note: Each circle is a county, unitary or former metropolitan authority, drawn with the area in proportion to the total population in 2001 (the largest circle represents London, with a population of just over 7 million). Areas in northern England are those that lie west or north of the counties of Gloucestershire, Warwickshire, Leicestershire and Lincolnshire (the Severn-Humber divide).

Figure 3: The geographical variation in the percentage of 16-17 year olds with relevant qualifications

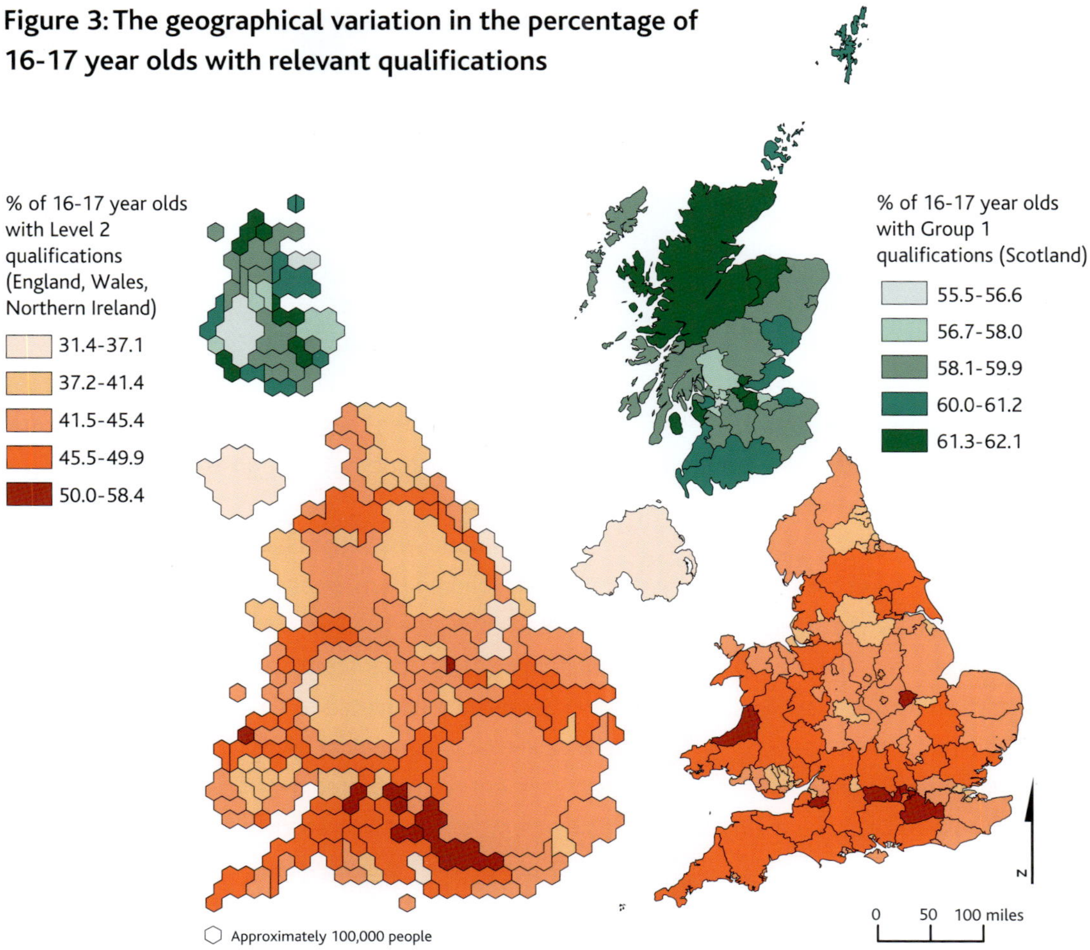

Figure 4: Variation across the country of the proportion of 40-54 year olds with high level qualifications

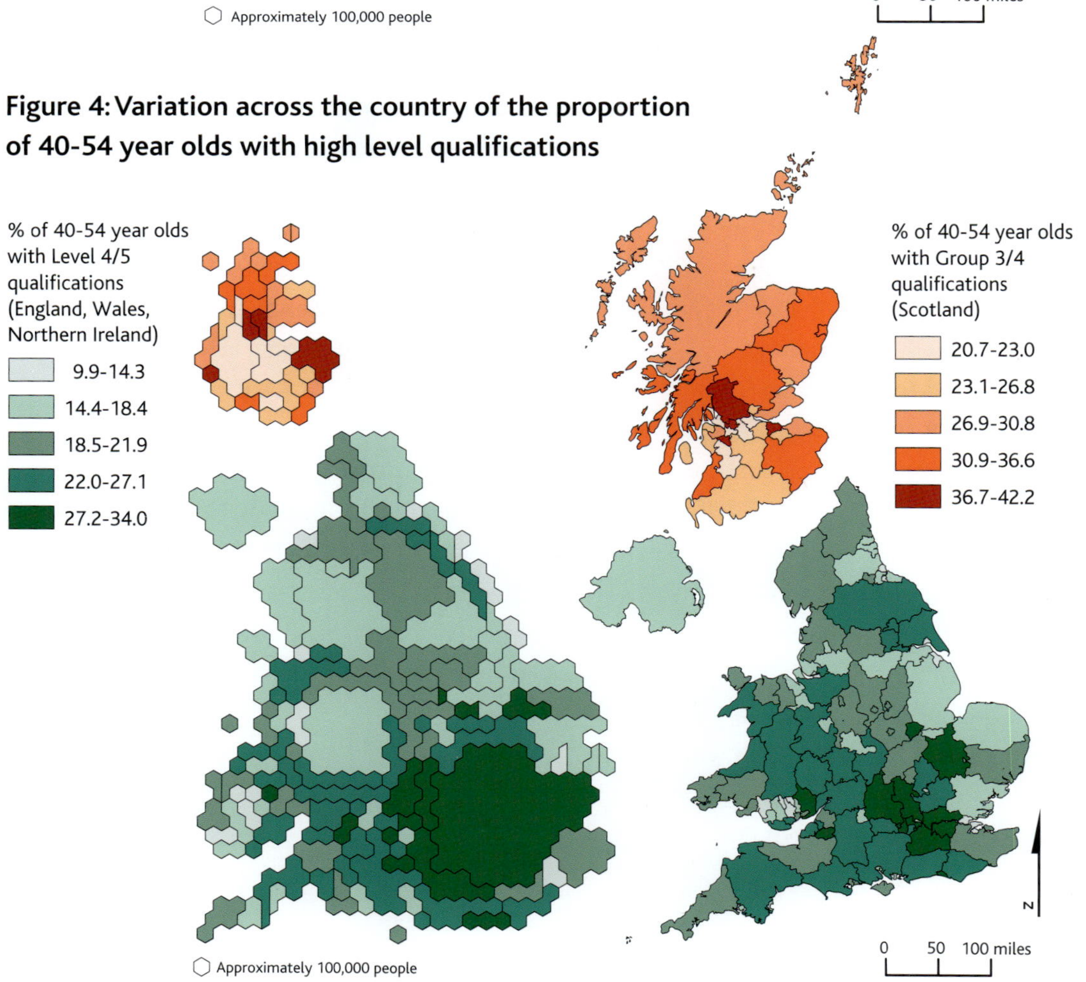

Note: Both maps in each figure represent the same places, shaded identically. The map on the left is a cartogram – each area is shown in proportion to the size of its population in 2001. The largest area is London, since it has the highest population of any of the places[TR]. The map on the right shows the actual boundaries of the areas.

Discussion

The close association between the qualified proportions of 16-17 year olds and people in their parents' generation in the same areas means that the geographical disparities in educational attainment in England, Wales and Northern Ireland are unlikely to change in the near future. This is reinforced in the companion report to this, *Teachers* (Report no 3), by the finding that areas with the best qualified young people also have the greatest availability of teachers. People do move around over their lifetime, but the likelihood is that those who are well-educated will end up living in areas with other well-educated people, working in good jobs (see *Open all hours*, Report no 8). It is no coincidence that these areas tend also to be where the schools with better examinations results are located. These people often then go on to have children who also achieve. Without effective policies to address the situation, the geographical divide between better and less well-educated populations will almost certainly be maintained in the near future.

The social and geographic gap between those who achieve and those who do not might be narrowed by moving 'good jobs' away from London and the South East and increasing the provision of educational and vocational training support in the 'least well qualified' areas. Those parents educated to university level are better placed to give their children the best, to help them with their school work and to pay for help if they think it is needed. As parents with these advantages become more and more concentrated within the South of England, more and more poorer children elsewhere will attend schools in which few of their friends' parents are highly educated.

This report provides some evidence, however, that the Scottish education system may be more effective at enabling young people to achieve qualifications regardless of the kind of neighbourhood they come from. Variation in the proportion of 16-17 year olds with qualifications between areas in Scotland is very much smaller than that among areas across the rest of the UK. In Scotland, the difference between the best and worst areas in terms of the proportion of children getting good qualifications is just 10%. In the rest of the UK that difference is so large that in the best areas children are 90% more likely to receive good qualifications than those in the worst areas. It is often claimed that there has long been a very different attitude towards 'education for all' in Scotland, compared to south of the border. Proportionally, far more children from the poorest parts of Glasgow go on to university than do children from the poorest parts of large English cities. Scotland demonstrates that a child's chances of having qualifications at age 16-17 do not have to be so strongly determined by where they live or by how well educated people in their parents' generation are.

Analysis of non-Census data has shown that outside of Scotland, children from areas where many parents are educated to degree level tend to do better at school than children living in other areas, irrespective of whether their own parents are educated to degree level[1]. Thus it is not the case that geographical inequalities in educational achievement are replicated over time simply because able parents give birth to able children. Neither is it the case that the best educated parents perpetuate these inequalities by helping their children with their education, demanding more of them and so on, as that would not explain why all children in such areas tend to do better. Children learn better in environments where it is easier to learn. As geographical areas become more socially polarised, in particular as people with university degrees become ever more concentrated in the South East of England (see *Open all hours*, Report no 8) we should expect this concentration to be magnified in future inequalities in educational achievement across the country. In the future, educational inequalities might well involve what university a young person attends rather than whether they attend university, or whether they attain postgraduate qualifications. Finally, although the situation in Scotland appears to be quite different, we know that within the large areas that we are studying here, such as Edinburgh and Glasgow, widespread inequalities remain.

Notes

1 Corver, M. (2005) *Young participation in higher education 1994-2001*, Bristol: HEFCE.

2 The data tables released from the Census do not include information about individuals and their families. Therefore, with these data, it is not possible to ascertain the educational achievements of young people and their parents; only the achievements of people around the age of their parents' generation living in the same area can be compared. The assumption is made that the generation of the 16-17 year olds' parents will be largely encompassed by the age group 40-54. Additionally, it is acknowledged that 40-54 year olds in an area may not have children in the same area, in the age range 16-17, or at all.

3 The full listing of qualifications included in Level 2 in England, Wales and Northern Ireland is: 5+ O levels, 5+ CSEs (grade 1), 5+ GCSEs (grade A*-C), School Certificate (Senior Certificate/Advanced Senior Certificate in Northern Ireland), 1+ A levels/AS levels, NVQ Level 2, Intermediate GNVQ.

4 The qualifications included in Group 1 in Scotland are: 'O' Grade, Standard Grade, Intermediate 1, Intermediate 2, City and Guilds Craft, SVQ Level 1 or 2 or equivalent.

5 Levels 4 and 5 in England, Wales and Northern Ireland consist of first and higher degrees, professional qualifications, HNCs, HNDs and NVQ Level 4-5. In Scotland, the same qualifications are grouped into Groups 3 and 4, although Group 3 also includes the RSA Higher Diploma.

6 See Department for Education and Skills (www.dfes.gov.uk)[TR].

7 Dorling, D. (2005) *The human geography of the UK*, London: Sage Publications.

TR Further information on this point is available in the accompanying technical report.

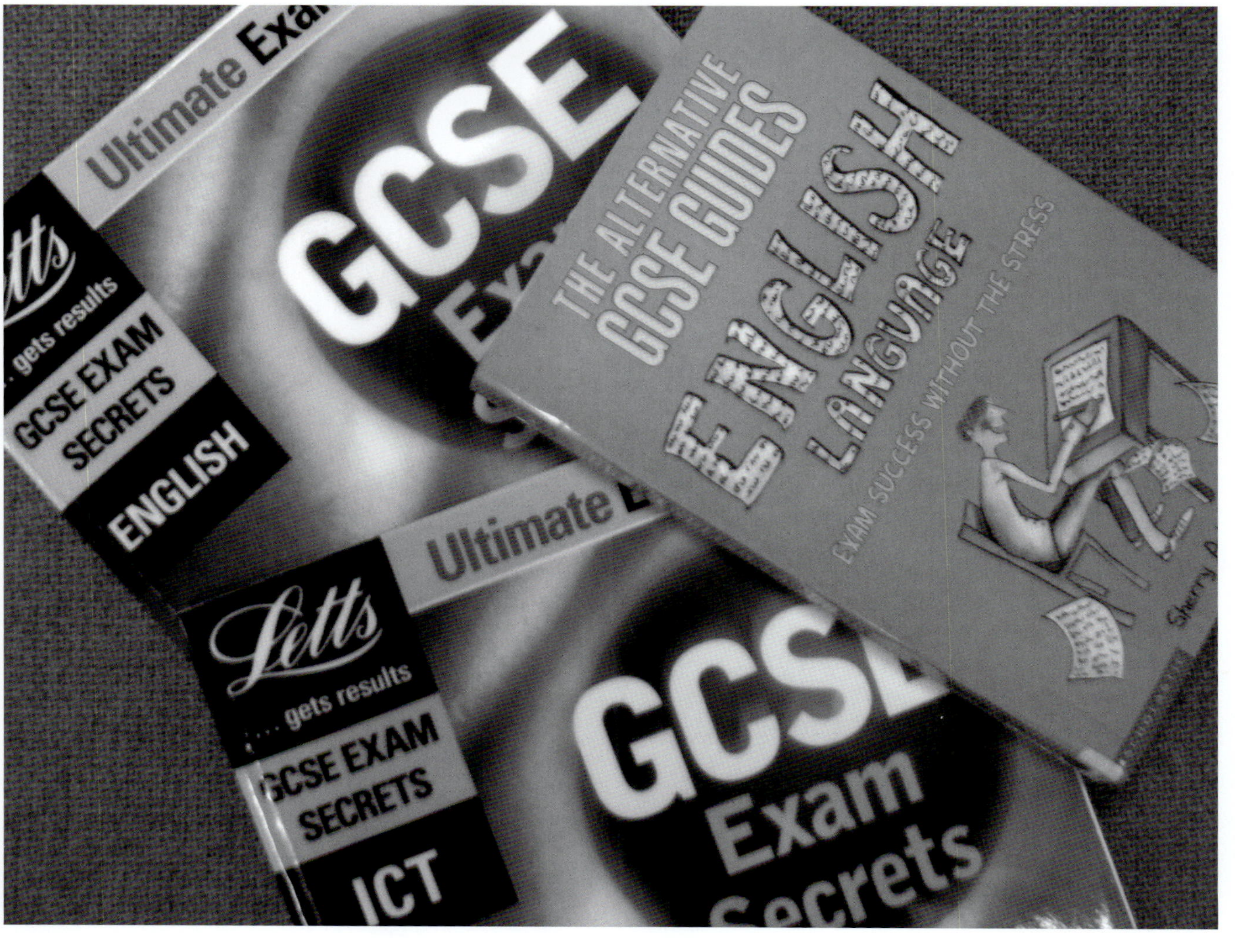

What do we know?

- Good qualifications at an early stage in life lead to an increased likelihood that a person will be able to obtain a good job and other opportunities.

What have we found?

- In England, Wales and Northern Ireland, 16-17 year olds are more likely to obtain good GCSEs and equivalent qualifications if they live in an area where a high proportion of people in their parents' generation (people aged 40-54) are well qualified. Since the children's achievement is so strongly related to that of their parents' generation, inequalities in educational attainment across the country are maintained over time.
- This is not the case in Scotland, where there is much less geographical variability in the proportion of young people who have qualifications.

Other reports in the series

The companion report to this, *Teachers*, looks at whether areas with higher proportions of young people with no or unknown qualifications also tend to have fewer teachers.

1. *Doctors and nurses*
2. *In sickness and in health*
3. *Teachers*
4. *Sons and daughters*
5. *Changing rooms*
6. *A place in the sun*
7. *The office*
8. *Open all hours*
9. *Top gear*
10. *Home front*

Contact details

The reports were prepared by Ben Wheeler, Mary Shaw, Richard Mitchell and Danny Dorling. The authors can be contacted via:
Professor Danny Dorling • Department of Geography • University of Sheffield • Winter Street • Sheffield S10 2TN
e-mail: danny.dorling@sheffield.ac.uk • www.sheffield.ac.uk/sasi

Project funder: Joseph Rowntree Foundation

JOSEPH ROWNTREE FOUNDATION

The POLICY PRESS

CHANGING ROOMS

Space to live

In the UK, people's experience of how much space they have to live in varies markedly. Some people have more space than they may need, others have too little, and overcrowding and under-occupancy of houses vary geographically across the UK. Areas in which more households are overcrowded do not also tend to contain larger numbers of homes that are underoccupied. Solving housing shortages *within* areas in the UK is not simply a matter of converting larger houses to flats and somehow 'redistributing' rooms. Overcrowding and underoccupancy of homes vary widely geographically between different, but often neighbouring, parts of the UK.

Overcrowding and households in low occupation

Decent housing is a basic human right. Most of us spend the majority of our 24-hour day at home, either awake or asleep. The physical and social environment offered to us by our homes can have a range of impacts on our health and well-being[1]. Since the beginning of the 20th century, governments and local authorities have recognised that quality housing is essential and have made efforts to ensure that everyone has a warm, dry place to live where children can grow up safely. In the UK today, however, the quality of the housing we each enjoy varies enormously. One of the key indicators of housing quality employed in the UK is the relationship between the number of people who share a dwelling and the size of that dwelling, usually measured in terms of the number of rooms it has. As the distribution of people around the UK continually shifts and changes, with notable recent expansion in the cities and especially in the South East of England, the pressure on the housing supply has become notable. Plans to build new housing developments, even new towns, to satisfy the changing and growing demands

Life in Britain

The latest Census reveals that within the UK people live in very different worlds. For some, resources and amenities abound; for others life is characterised by deprivation and difficulties, especially when their need for support is great.

The 2001 Census marked the bi-centenary of census taking in the UK. It is the most comprehensive social record of life in this country now available. Since 1801 successive governments have asked the population to assist in the taking of a Census.

This report is one of a series of 10 showing key patterns and inequalities in life in the UK revealed by the 2001 Census. These reports focus on geographical inequalities, highlighting where services and opportunities appear not to be available or accessible to those people and places that need them most.

for larger or smaller, cheaper or more exclusive housing make headlines in regional and national media. In this report we take two groups of people to illustrate and compare the current housing experiences of UK residents as recorded at the 2001 Census.

The first group are those defined as living in an 'overcrowded' house. That is to say, there are more people sharing the same dwelling than is recommended. Living in an overcrowded house is associated with physical and mental health problems[1]. Not having enough space can be very stressful. The government actually lays down occupancy standards that specify in a complex way exactly how many people should be living in a dwelling according to its size and number of bedrooms[2], but for this study we have taken a more simple definition of overcrowding. This group might be taken as representing those who have less space than they need. The second group are those defined as living in an 'underoccupied home'. That is to say, that there are very few people living in a dwelling, given the size of that dwelling. This group might be taken as representing those who have more space than they need.

The 2001 Census asked each household for details of their dwelling, including the number of rooms available to the household. The actual question asked by the Census was:

How many rooms do you have for use only by your household?

- ***Do not count*** **bathrooms, toilets, halls or landings, or rooms that can only be used for storage such as cupboards.**
- ***Do count all*** **other rooms, for example kitchens, living rooms, bedrooms, utility rooms and studies.**
- **If two rooms have been converted into one, count them as one room.**

Other questions in the Census establish the number of people living in the household. Using the number of people, and the number of rooms, the Census provides a count of *the number of people per room* for each household in the UK. Using this information we can compare the proportion of households that are overcrowded and those that are underoccupied in an area and this provides a picture of housing occupancy across the country. For this analysis, overcrowded households were defined as those with more than one person per room, or more simply, households in which there are more people than rooms (using the definition of 'rooms' above). This is a reasonable and simple definition of overcrowding. The analysis defines underoccupation as households with just one or two people living in dwellings of eight or more rooms. This is a quite generous definition of under-occupancy, but it does reflect the growing desire for space in our homes.

This report compares the proportions of overcrowded and underoccupied homes for 142 areas across the UK – counties, unitary authorities and former metropolitan authorities, as used in the other reports in this series. The analysis addresses this question:

Do areas where a higher proportion of households are overcrowded tend also to have a lower level of underoccupied homes?

Findings

There were 24.5 million households recorded in the UK at the 2001 Census. Just under half a million (1.9%) had more people than rooms and, by our definition, are overcrowded. Although this seems a very small proportion, it is still a very large number of households. About 1 million households (4.3%) had one or two people living in eight or more rooms, that is to say, they were underoccupied. There are therefore more than twice as many households that have more space than they might need than there are overcrowded households. Much is written about the growing gap between rich and poor in the UK, and while overcrowding is not always an indicator of poverty (but it often is), the size of the richer, underoccupied group relative to the overcrowded group is surprising. Many people in the UK have grown wealthier through the housing market and housing is now a main component of many people's overall assets.

It is interesting to consider the number of people, especially children, who might be living in overcrowded/underoccupied homes. However, in order to calculate these figures, different definitions need to be used, since the Census tables used to produce the figures in the remainder of this report only include numbers of households. Figure 1 shows the number of people aged under 18 and 18+ living in households by occupancy rating (the alternative overcrowding/under-occupancy definition[TR]). These graphs show that children and young people aged under 18 are more likely to live in overcrowded housing than people aged 18+. Both graphs also show that there are far more people living in underoccupied property than in overoccupied property; there is no overall shortage of space.

Comparing areas

Figure 2 illustrates the relationship between the two groups of households across the 142 areas of the UK. This graph demonstrates an 'inverse' relationship; areas with a high rate of overcrowding (high percentage of households with more people than rooms) tend also to have a lower rate of underoccupied homes[TR].

Conversely, areas in which there are higher levels of underoccupied homes tend also to have low levels of overcrowded homes. The circles on the graph form a curve. This curve tells us that the relationship between overcrowding and underoccupancy is not entirely straightforward. There are many places where about 1% of households are overcrowded, but these areas have a variety of levels of underoccupancy. There are also a good number of areas that have a very low level of underoccupancy, but where the proportion of households which are overcrowded varies widely.

100 years ago

The 1901 Census recorded 6.3 million inhabited houses in England and Wales, with an average of 5.2 people per house. Overcrowding at this time was classified as having more than two people per room, and 8.2% of the population lived in overcrowded houses according to this definition. However, there was wide variation across the country, with the highest rate – 36% – in Jarrow.

For more information see the National Archives (www.nationalarchives.gov.uk).

Figure 1: Number and % of people in households by occupancy rating

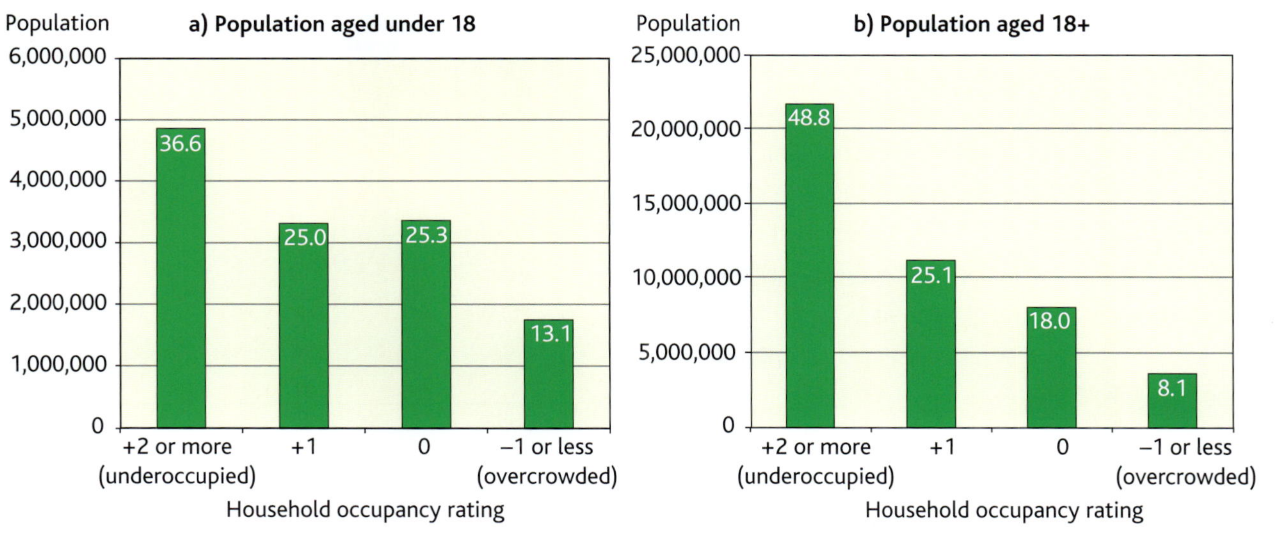

Figure 2: The overcrowding and underoccupation measures associated across the 142 areas[TR]

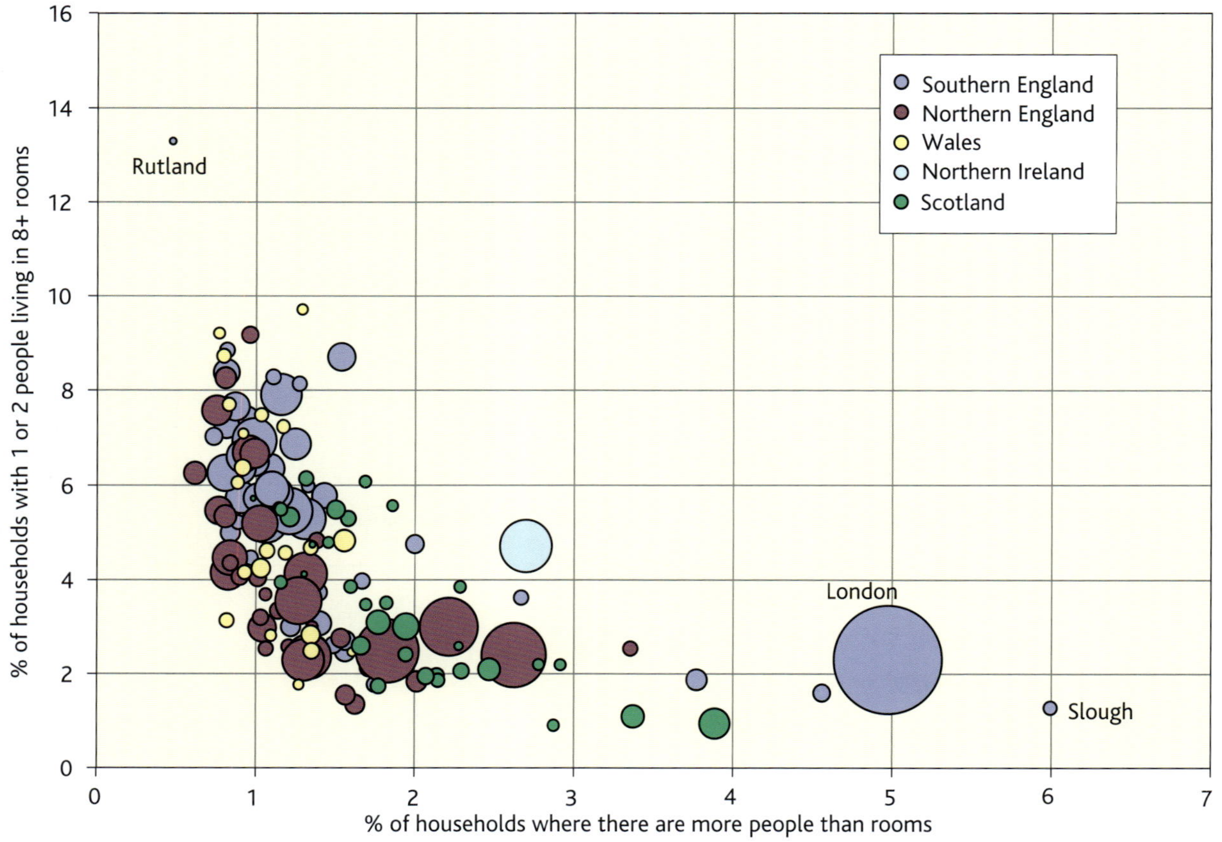

Note: Each circle is a county, unitary or former metropolitan authority, drawn with the area in proportion to the total population in 2001 (the largest circle represents London, with a population of just over 7 million). Areas in northern England are those that lie west or north of the counties of Gloucestershire, Warwickshire, Leicestershire and Lincolnshire (the Severn-Humber divide).

Table 1 tells us more about the places that have the highest levels of overcrowding. The 'top five' all have levels of overcrowding of at least twice the national average and Slough has a level that is more than three times as high. All these areas also have levels of underoccupancy that are about half (or less) the national average. This shows clearly that the overcrowding cannot simply be solved by dividing up larger properties in the same area so that there is a more equal distribution of rooms to people. However, most of the areas with high overcrowding do seem to neighbour areas with high levels of underoccupancy, as can be seen by comparing the maps in Figures 3 and 4.

Table 1: The five areas of the UK with the highest rates of overcrowded households (more people than rooms) (2001)

Area	% of households overcrowded	% of households underoccupied
Slough	6.0	1.3
London	5.0	2.3
Luton	4.6	1.6
Glasgow City	3.9	0.9
Leicester	3.8	1.9
UK	**1.9**	**4.3**

Table 1 highlights London's position near the top of the overcrowding league. Figure 2 shows that this is part of a very interesting pattern for southern England as a whole. The largest circle on Figure 1 is London and its position suggests a very high level of overcrowding and low level of underoccupancy. This is no real surprise. House prices in London mean that many people have to live in one or two rooms, small flats or share household spaces. Indeed very few people can afford to have eight or more rooms. Most of the other circles denoting areas in southern England are at the opposite end of the graph suggesting that these are areas that have very low levels of overcrowding and among the highest levels of underoccupancy. This pattern is made clearer by Figures 3 and 4.

The map in Figure 3 shows the geographic distribution of the overcrowding measure. Areas with the highest prevalence of overcrowded households tend to be around London and parts of the South East of England, cities in the North and Midlands of England and southern Scotland, particularly Glasgow. The map in Figure 4 shows that the areas with the highest rates of underoccupancy are around the Home Counties, parts of South West England, Wales and North Yorkshire. The areas with the lowest prevalence of underoccupation are cities in the North and Midlands of England, and southern Scotland.

Look at South East England and the Welsh border areas on each map. These are areas that have both particularly low levels of overcrowding and particularly high levels of underoccupancy. These are also the places where, we are told, demand for housing (particularly affordable housing) has reached crisis point. Home builders are asking for planning regulations to change so that they can 'meet demand'.

Other patterns are also interesting. Scotland, particularly Glasgow and its environs, seems to do particularly badly in terms of overcrowding. This may well be due to a combination of particular kinds of housing stock there (tenement flats, which tend to have fewer, though sometimes large, rooms) as well as acknowledged levels of poverty, although new housing development is slowly improving in the city. Cities with high student populations are also highlighted to an extent on the overcrowding map. Students tend to overcrowd to keep housing costs low.

Perhaps not surprisingly, the UK's rural areas tend to have a relatively high level of underoccupancy when compared to the cities. More space and a larger housing stock contribute to this. However, it is worth noting that larger properties are always relatively more expensive, preventing younger and poorer rural dwellers from entering the housing market there. Conversions of existing larger properties in the countryside might help ease a perceived rural housing shortage, but that shortage may not be indicated well by our overcrowding measure.

Since 2001

In 2004, the government announced plans to demolish 400,000 houses in the North of England, and to build hundreds of thousands of new homes in the South East and East of England[3,4]. Much of the housing in the North being demolished is empty, and is in some cases being knocked down in order to stimulate 'failing' housing markets – areas where house prices have fallen drastically. Simultaneous massive building programmes are under way in the South due to low availability of housing, particularly lack of affordable housing for key public sector workers, and in an attempt to cut house prices.

Figure 3: Geographical variation in the percentage of households with more people than rooms (2001)

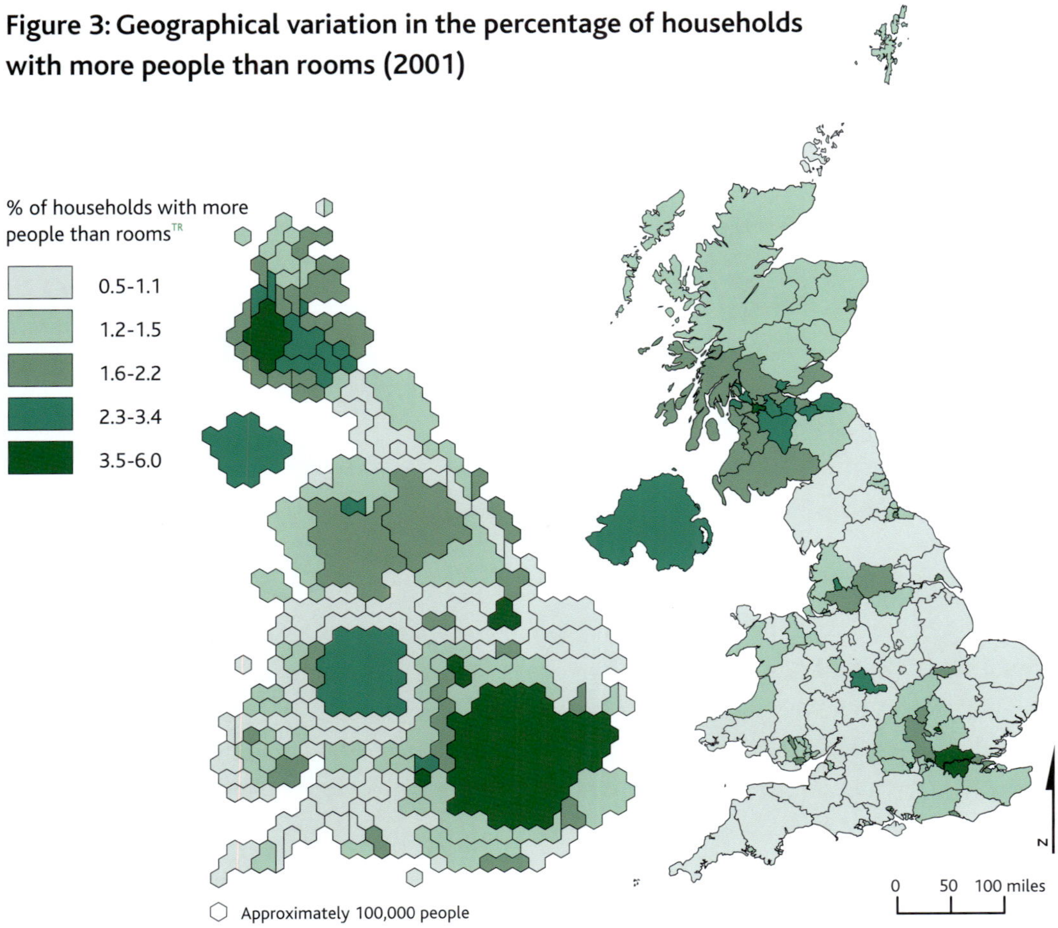

Figure 4: The percentage of households consisting of 1 or 2 people living in a dwelling with 8+ rooms across the UK (2001)

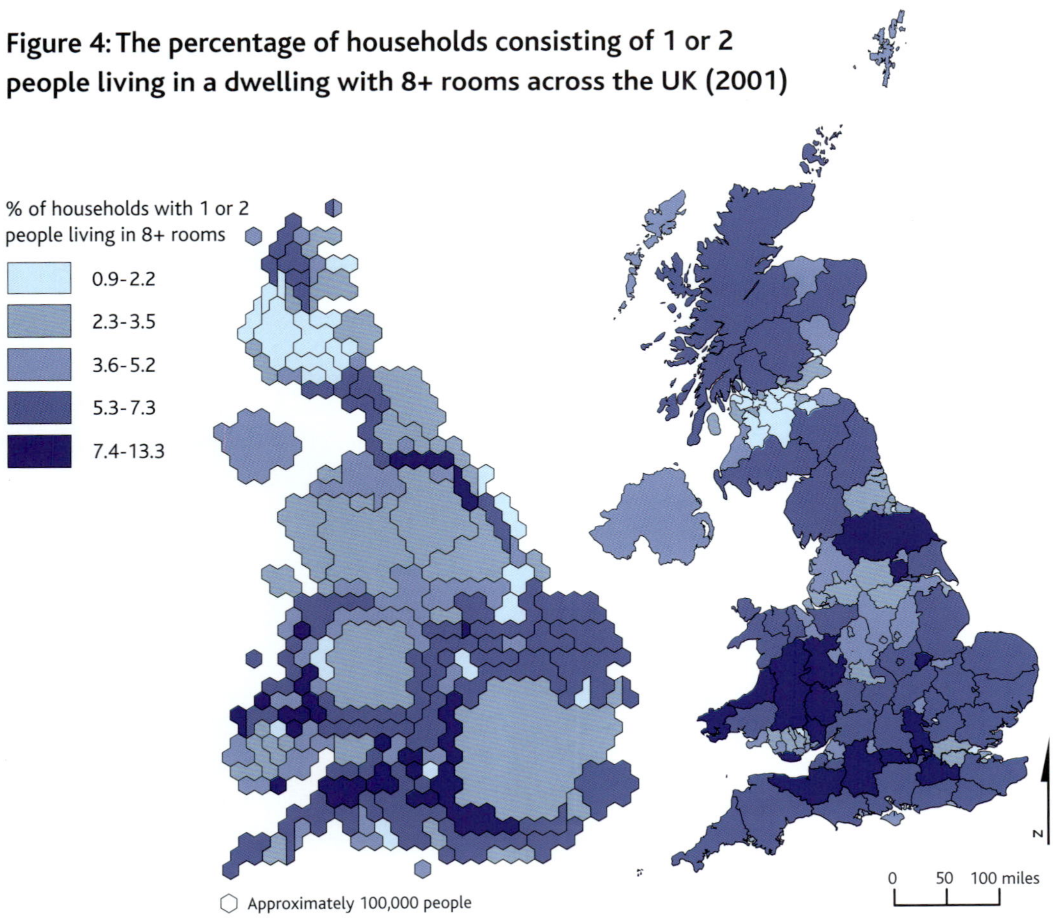

Note: Both maps in each figure represent the same places, shaded identically. The map on the left is a cartogram – each area is shown in proportion to the size of its population in 2001. The largest area is London, since it has the highest population of any of the places[TR]. The map on the right shows the actual boundaries of the areas.

Discussion

The analyses have shown that in the UK people's experience of space in their houses varies markedly. Some people have more space than they need. Others have too little space. Figure 2 shows that areas in which more households are overcrowded do not also tend to contain larger numbers of households that are underoccupied. Figures 3 and 4 show that often these contrasting areas neighbour each other. Solving housing shortages *within* areas in the UK is not simply a matter of converting larger houses to flats and somehow 'redistributing' rooms. This analysis conveys that there is a broad geographical divide in terms of housing experience. However, there may also be variation among groups of people defined by other, non-geographic criteria, for example by ethnicity. Such variations are complex, and are likely to be changing over time.

Some areas have more home space than they need, others do not have enough. Consequently, suitable and affordable housing is often not available where it is most needed, but this shortage can have different manifestations, and it is often available nearby. London is the fastest growing city in the country. Many young people are flocking there, but the city's housing stock is already overcrowded. Although the population of Glasgow is falling slowly, its housing stock is not suitable for the needs of many of its people. It is outdated, in poor condition and cramped in some parts of the city, small but too expensive in others. In a number of rural areas there are plenty of larger properties, currently occupied by one or two people. These are often too expensive and too big for younger families trying to stay in the communities they grew up in.

The intention of this analysis is not to imply that people in households that have been classified as 'underoccupied' are doing something wrong. In many cases these will be family houses where children have grown up and moved away. The ageing and affluent population of the rural South, for example, want to stay where they are and enjoy their environment. The problem is that this distribution of housing is not compatible with the needs of the UK as a whole and certainly represents a serious social inequality with consequences for the health, wealth and well-being of other groups in society.

This analysis intends to show the geographical divide between people who live in overcrowded conditions and those who live in relatively spacious accommodation. These two groups tend to live in different areas in the UK and this represents a persistent and growing spatial and social inequality.

Notes

[1] Shaw, M. (2004) 'Housing and public health', *Annual Review of Public Health*, vol 25, pp 397-418.

[2] The 1985 Housing Act (sections 324-6 and 358-64).

[3] 'Prescott to raze 400,000 homes', *The Observer*, 22 August 2004.

[4] 'Plan to "blitz" east of England with 500,000 homes backed', *The Independent*, 16 October 2004[TR].

[TR] Further information on this point is available in the accompanying technical report.

What do we know?

- Many households in the UK experience overcrowding, which is associated with poor physical and mental health.
- Many households in the UK have plenty of space, with eight or more rooms per person not uncommon in many areas.

What have we found?

- Areas in which more households are overcrowded do *not* also tend to contain larger numbers of households that are underoccupied.
- Solving housing shortages *within* areas in the UK is not simply a matter of converting larger houses to flats and somehow 'redistributing' rooms.
- Overcrowded areas often geographically adjoin areas where there appears to be surplus space.

Other reports in the series

The companion report to this, *A place in the sun*, describes the location of holiday and second homes and compares this to households which may be having difficulty getting into the housing market.

1. *Doctors and nurses*
2. *In sickness and in health*
3. *Teachers*
4. *Sons and daughters*
5. *Changing rooms*
6. *A place in the sun*
7. *The office*
8. *Open all hours*
9. *Top gear*
10. *Home front*

Contact details

The reports were prepared by Ben Wheeler, Mary Shaw, Richard Mitchell and Danny Dorling. The authors can be contacted via:
Professor Danny Dorling • Department of Geography • University of Sheffield • Winter Street • Sheffield S10 2TN
e-mail: danny.dorling@sheffield.ac.uk • www.sheffield.ac.uk/sasi

Project funder: Joseph Rowntree Foundation

JOSEPH ROWNTREE FOUNDATION

The POLICY PRESS

A PLACE in the SUN

185,000 empty holiday homes

The 2001 Census recorded 185,000 unoccupied holiday homes and second residences in the UK. These properties are mostly found in rural areas, particularly around the National Parks. However, these areas are also more likely to contain larger than average numbers of households that are renting their home from a private landlord. It is probable that many of these tenants would be homeowners were they able to purchase rather than rent. The challenges to people wanting to buy their own home in these areas probably include lack of available, affordable properties, due in part to the growing prevalence of second homes. The Census counts of empty holiday and second residences may well be an underestimate.

Empty houses

The prevalence of second residences/holiday homes in some areas has been recognised as one contributing factor to the difficulties faced by people trying to take the first step onto the property ladder[1,2]. A 2002 study of all local authority areas in England found that the areas with the least affordable 'entry-level' housing were, perhaps predictably, in central London, but also in the rural South West of England[3].

Put simply, without large numbers of additional dwellings being built, the more people in areas of high demand who own second or third homes, the harder it will be for local people and people from outside the area to live and move there. Often second properties are empty for most of the year, although increasingly people rent out their second or third homes. In the long term it is currently financially advantageous in the UK to buy your property rather than to rent. Given this, an excess of people in middle age renting in an area may be an indicator of where property is too expensive and in too short a supply

Life in Britain

The latest Census reveals that within the UK people live in very different worlds. For some, resources and amenities abound; for others life is characterised by deprivation and difficulties, especially when their need for support is great.

The 2001 Census marked the bi-centenary of census taking in the UK. It is the most comprehensive social record of life in this country now available. Since 1801 successive governments have asked the population to assist in the taking of a Census.

This report is one of a series of 10 showing key patterns and inequalities in life in the UK revealed by the 2001 Census. These reports focus on geographical inequalities, highlighting where services and opportunities appear not to be available or accessible to those people and places that need them most.

to buy. In some areas there is a short supply of affordable homes because of the high demand to live there (such as London) but in other areas short supply is due to the demand to holiday there (often from London). The Censuses let us examine the geographies of both second homes and private renting.

The 2001 Census recorded not only information about people living in the UK, but also about houses and dwellings – even if they were empty at the time. Data from the Census includes counts of 'household spaces'[4] that were unoccupied second residences or holiday homes (these are distinct from unoccupied, vacant dwellings). The Census authorities rely on a high degree of compliance from those filling in the forms and/or the abilities of their enumerators to identify such homes and so the figures are most probably an underestimate. The Census also obtains information on tenure from householders who are occupying each property – that is, whether they own their home outright, have a mortgage, or rent their home, and if they rent it, who they rent it from. This report investigates the possibility that people living in areas where there are many second residences and holiday homes might have a hard time making the move from renting property to owning their own home.

In this analysis, people who might want to buy their own home but who do not are considered to be those households where the 'Household Reference Person' (HRP) is aged 35-74 and the home is rented from a private landlord. The HRP is defined specially in the Census[5], but can also be understood as the 'breadwinner'. In recent decades private renting by such age groups had been declining and was relatively rare. It has risen more recently as house prices have increased; the numbers of people in households with a mortgage has subsequently fallen. Younger age groups are excluded from this analysis in order to discount the student population, who are often private renters. Figures from the Census on these households and the prevalence of unoccupied second residences/holiday homes are compared across 142 areas: counties, unitary authorities and former metropolitan authorities (the same areas used for all reports in this series). The report therefore asks the question:

In areas where there are many households that might be having difficulty getting into the housing market, are there unusually large numbers of second residences/holiday homes?

Findings

The 2001 Census recorded 25.5 million household spaces in the UK, of which 185,000 (0.7%) were unoccupied second residences or holiday homes. There were 16.8 million households where the HRP was aged 35-74, and 1.3 million (8%) of these households rented their home from a private landlord[6].

Figure 1 illustrates the economic activity of the HRP by housing tenure. Private renters have a similar pattern of economic activity to homeowners, although they are slightly more likely to be unemployed, looking after home/family or permanently sick/disabled than homeowners. These older private renters have a very different pattern of economic activity when compared to those renting from the social sector and so the Census would appear to suggest that at these ages the choice or constraint to rent privately rather than buy is not determined mainly by the economic position of the household. It is more likely to be the nature of the areas they are living in which most influences such decisions and constraints.

Comparing areas

Figure 2 shows the relationship between the two measures for the 142 areas across the UK. The association is not very clear to see, since most areas have a relatively low proportion of second/holiday homes – less than 1% in most cases. However, the association is positive[TR]; areas with higher proportions of holiday homes and second residences tend to have higher percentages of households that may be unable to buy a home.

Table 1 highlights the five areas with the highest prevalence of the privately renting households measure. Note that all are found on the coast. Table 2 similarly lists the five areas with the highest prevalence of unoccupied

Figure 1: Economic activity of the Household Reference Person (HRP) aged 35-74 by tenure, UK (2001)

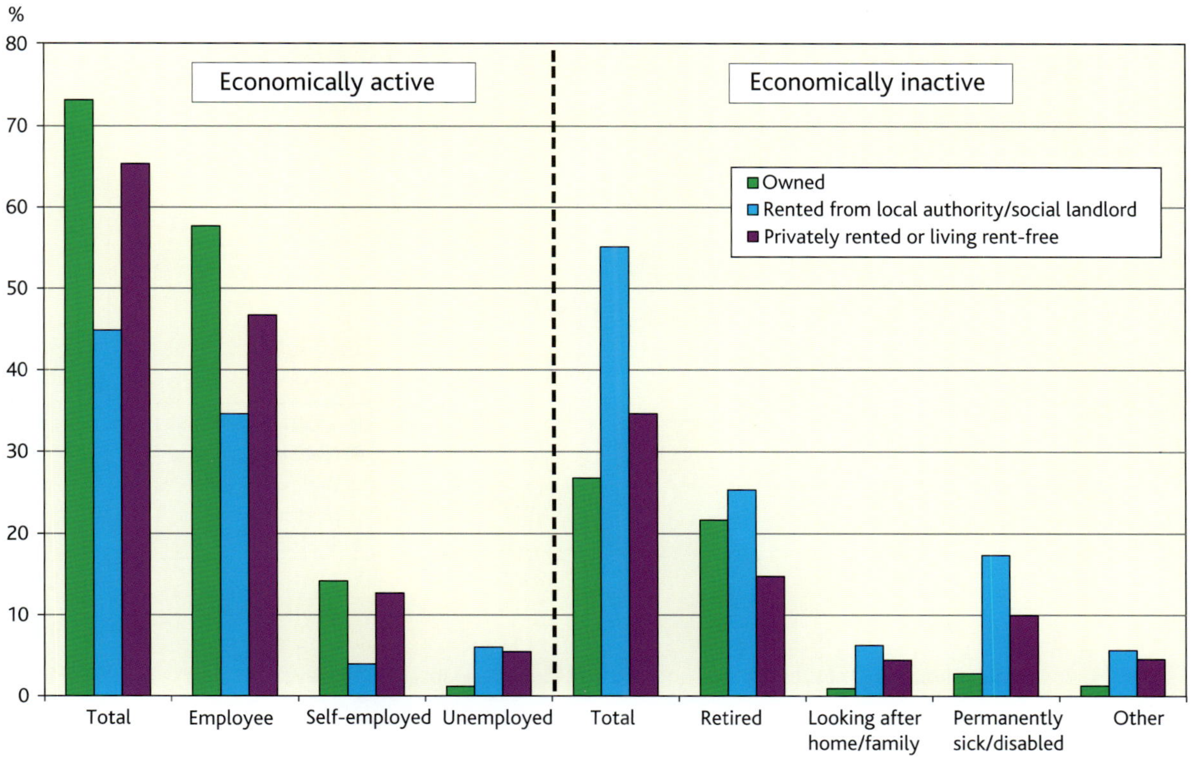

holiday homes/second residences. The geography of these measures is further illustrated in the maps in Figures 3 and 4. It can be seen that the highest percentages of the privately renting measure are generally found in coastal resort areas and the Scottish borders. Similarly, Figure 4 shows that the highest prevalence of second residences and holiday homes are to be found in coastal areas and the Scottish Highlands and Islands. Many of the areas with lots of second residences are in proximity to National Parks: Cairngorms National Park (Highland, Perth and Kinross); Loch Lomond and the Trossochs (Argyll and Bute); Lake District (Cumbria); Yorkshire Dales and North York Moors (North Yorkshire); Snowdonia (Gwynedd); Pembrokeshire Coast (Pembrokeshire); Exmoor; and Dartmoor (Devon).

Since 2001

The 2003 Local Government Act allowed local authorities in England and Wales to reduce the 50% council tax discount on second homes to 10%, and many authorities have taken this opportunity[7]. Similarly, in August 2004, the Scottish Executive announced that it would also

100 years ago

Most people rented their home from private landlords in 1901. Mortgages were not widely available, and it was only in the last decade of the 19th century that legislation was passed allowing local authorities to buy land and build council housing. Poorer people tended to spend a greater proportion of their money on housing. A study by Maud Pember Reeves in Lambeth in 1913 found that while the wealthiest families would spend approximately one eighth of their income on rent, rates and taxes, these expenses could cost a working-class family up to one third of their income.

For more information see the National Archives (www.nationalarchives.gov.uk); Pember Reeves, M.S. (1913) *Round about a pound a week*, reprinted in 1988 by Virago Press, London.

Figure 2: The association between the prevalence of second homes and households who might be having difficulty buying a house

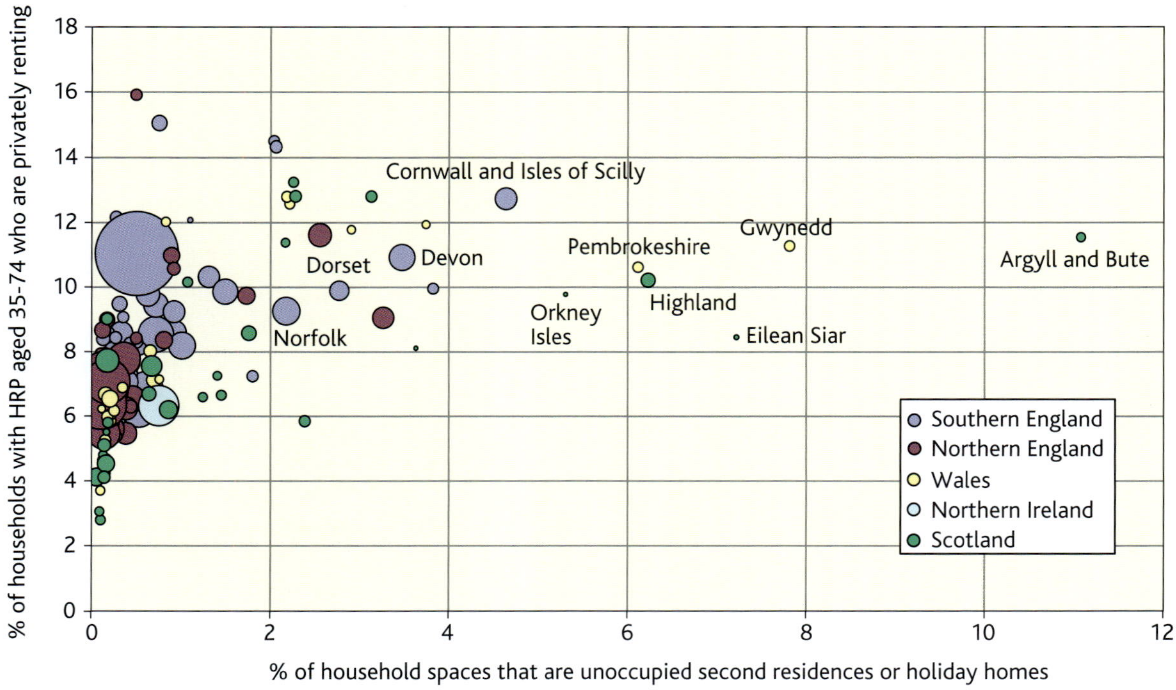

Note: Each circle is a county, unitary or former metropolitan authority, drawn with the area in proportion to the total population in 2001 (the largest circle represents London, with a population of just over 7 million). Areas in northern England are those that lie west or north of the counties of Gloucestershire, Warwickshire, Leicestershire and Lincolnshire (the Severn-Humber divide).

Table 1: The five areas of the UK with the highest percentage of privately renting households with Household Reference Person (HRP) aged 35-74 (2001)

Area	% of households with HRP aged 35-74 that are privately renting	% of household spaces that are unoccupied second residences/ holiday homes
Blackpool	15.9	0.5
Brighton and Hove	15.0	0.8
Torbay	14.5	2.0
Bournemouth	14.3	2.1
Scottish Borders	13.2	2.3
UK	**8.0**	**0.7**

Table 2: The five areas of the UK with highest rates of second residences and holiday homes (2001)

Area	% of households with HRP aged 35-74 that are privately renting	% of household spaces that are unoccupied second residences/ holiday homes
Argyll and Bute	11.5	11.1
Gwynedd	11.3	7.8
Eilean Siar	8.5	7.2
Highland	10.2	6.2
Pembrokeshire	10.6	6.1
UK	**8.0**	**0.7**

Figure 3: The percentage of households with Household Reference Person (HRP) aged 35-74 that are privately renting

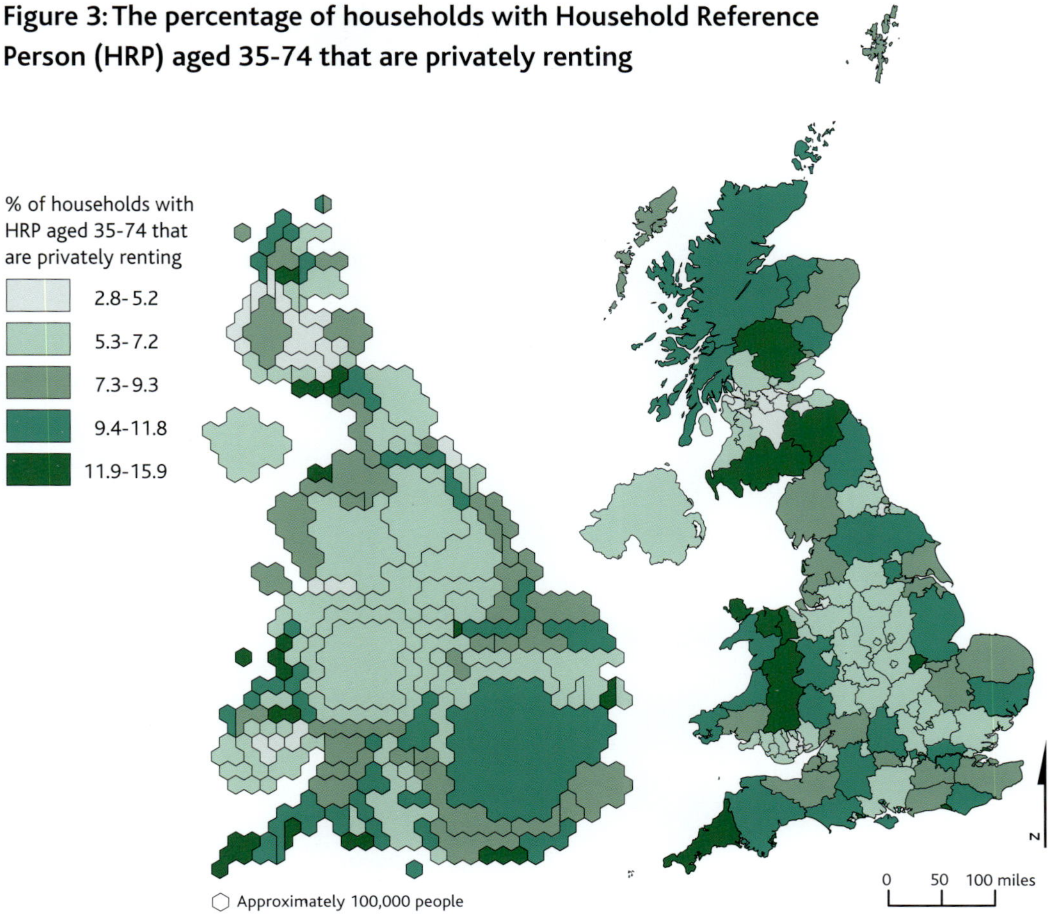

Figure 4: The percentage of household spaces that are unoccupied second residences or holiday homes

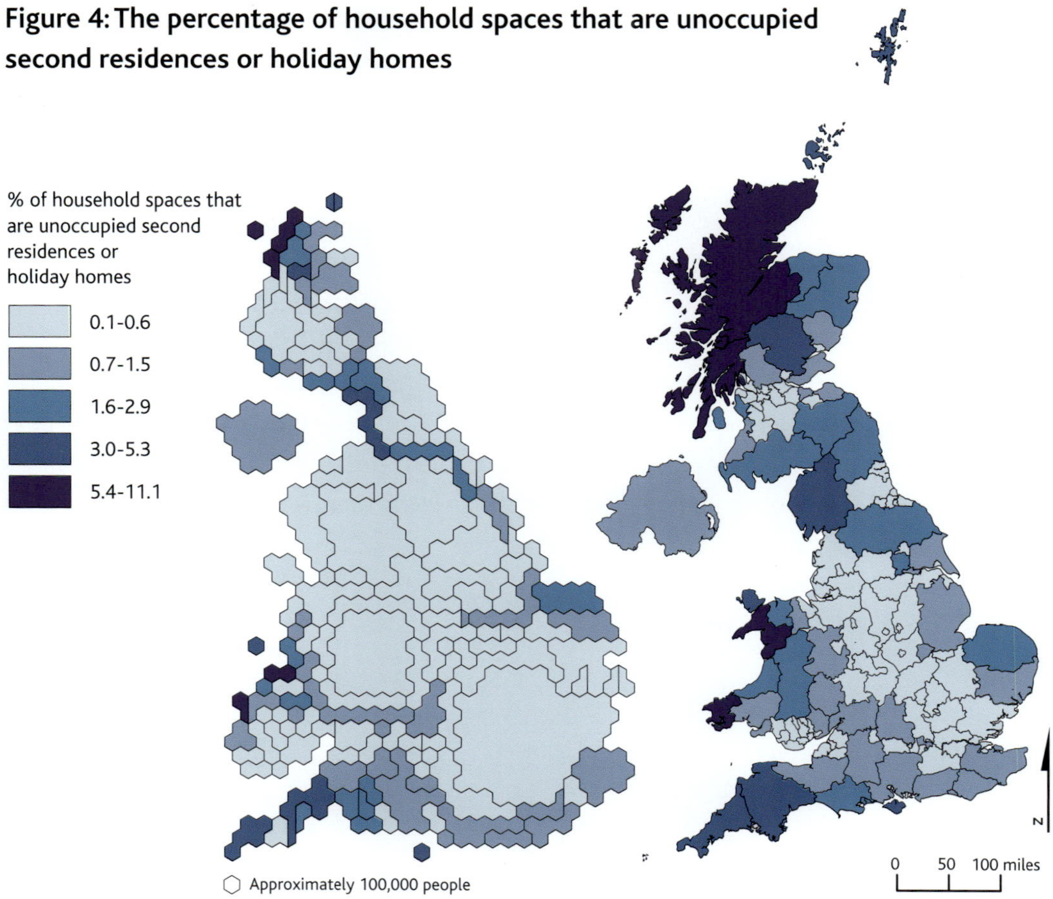

Note: Both maps in each figure represent the same places, shaded identically. The map on the left is a cartogram – each area is shown in proportion to the size of its population in 2001. The largest area is London, since it has the highest population of any of the places[TR]. The map on the right shows the actual boundaries of the areas.

allow councils to reduce the discount to 10%, and that the extra revenue generated would be ring-fenced for new, affordable housing[8]. However, the housing market continued to boom between 2001 and the summer of 2004, latterly most strongly in more peripheral areas[9]. Simultaneously, inequalities in wealth rose with the richest tenth of the population holding a majority of all wealth in the country by the end of the period as opposed to just under half in the mid-1990s[10]. Thus there are now more people, mainly living in London and the Home Counties, who can afford holiday and second homes in remote areas. It is almost certainly the case that fewer local people there will be able to afford to buy a home – more will rent as tenure patterns begin to slowly move in the direction of those of the past.

Discussion

In the distant past private renting was the tenure of the majority of the population. As home ownership grew and as council homes were built private renting declined, rapidly becoming the minority tenure, often most associated with rural areas and tied properties for agricultural labourers. Then, as university student numbers rose, private renting rose most in the cities with growing universities; subsequently private renting became more popular among young professionals as well as being a necessity for increasing numbers of poorer people as the social rented sector contracted. Its rise now in rural areas is not a reflection of a revived agricultural sector in the UK. Rather it reflects the shortage of property available, the very high prices of that which is available, and the limited availability of social housing. Part of the reason for such lack of availability is the increased popularity of such areas and the lack of subsequent home building in such places where building is often strictly controlled to preserve the local environment. The increased popularity of such areas has, however, also led in many cases to people buying their holiday home or second home there.

Rising income inequalities in the UK have led to a growing number of more affluent people being in a position where they can now afford to buy two or three properties rather than one. Simultaneously it has increased the numbers who cannot afford to buy at all and thus between the Censuses of 1991 and 2001 there was no increase in the numbers of people in owner-occupation (and a decline among younger owner-occupiers), a fall in the numbers housed by the state and a rise in private renting. Part of that rise was due to the continued expansion of the universities, but this is not the reason for the rise at ages over 35. Rather it is almost certainly older people and couples finding that they cannot afford to buy. This is particularly acute in rural areas, especially those where the number of second and holiday homes has increased – many of which may be rented out and so do not appear as such in the Census.

London is a notable exception to the rule, with a high prevalence of private renting in the older age group, but a low prevalence of second homes. However, London does contain many second homes belonging to people who spend their weekends in another home in the country, but may label the London abode as their primary residence.

This report has demonstrated clear patterns, and the results are not like many reported in the rest of this series; the key problematic areas highlighted are rural and it is unusual to find rural areas high up in a list of those that are losing out due to some kind of inequality. Areas with increasing prevalences of second homes are likely to become harder for full-time residents to live in, as the decline in demand for shops and services leads to reduction in their availability. Furthermore, as it becomes harder and harder to afford to live in the most popular rural areas, fewer poorer people are found there. Instead, more highly paid professionals such as doctors choose to live there, schools tend to perform better than average and so these areas improve rapidly in most league tables – not because the places have changed, but because the types of people living there – or simply holidaying there – are changing.

Notes

1. Satsangi, M., Higgins, M., Pawson, H., Rosenburg, L., Hague, C., Bramley, G. and Storey, C. (2001) *Factors affecting land supply for affordable housing in rural areas*, Edinburgh: Scottish Executive Central Research Unit/The Stationery Office.
2. Gallent, N., Mace, A. and Tewdwr-Jones, M. (2003) 'Dispelling a myth? Second homes in rural Wales', *Area*, vol 35, no 3, pp 271-84.
3. Wilcox, S. (2003) 'Affordability differences by area for working households buying their homes', Joseph Rowntree Foundation *Findings* No 573, May (www.jrf.org.uk).
4. A 'household space' is the space a household might be expected to occupy within a dwelling – usually the whole dwelling.
5. The 'Household Reference Person' (HRP) replaces the 'Head of Household' of previous Censuses. If the household includes more than one adult, the HRP is defined in terms of socio-economic activity and age. For example, if the household includes one adult in full-time employment and one adult in part-time employment, the person in full-time employment is the HRP. If both adults work part time, the older is the HRP. Further rules exist to designate the HRP in more complex situations.
6. The Census tables used here aggregate households privately renting and those living rent-free. The totals that this includes for England, Wales and Scotland (separate figures for Northern Ireland are unavailable) were: privately renting: 2.29 million households, living rent-free: 0.52 million households.
7. 'Second homes' large discount ends', BBC News, 1 April 2004 (http://news.bbc.co.uk).
8. 'Councils given discretion on holiday home tax', Scottish Executive news release, 5 August 2004 (www.scotland.gov.uk).
9. 'House prices: the boat comes in for homeowners in seaside towns', *The Independent,* 30 August 2004.
10. Paxton, W. and Dixon, M. (2004) *State of the nation: An audit of injustice*, Interim report for the Institute for Public Policy Research (www.ippr.org/research/index.php?current=41).

TR Further information on this point is available in the accompanying technical report.

What do we know?

- Large numbers of second homes and holiday residences in some areas appear to contribute to a restrictive housing market for local people.

What have we found?

- Areas of the UK with high numbers of holiday homes tend also to have much higher than usual numbers of older households (where the 'head of household' is aged 35+) that are renting from a private landlord.
- Most of these areas are in the more rural parts of the UK or by the coast.
- In every area where more than 4% of dwellings are second or holiday homes, the percentages of the older population now renting privately are among the highest in the country.

Other reports in the series

The companion report to this, *Changing rooms*, compares the prevalence of overcrowding and underoccupancy of homes across areas of the UK.

1. *Doctors and nurses*
2. *In sickness and in health*
3. *Teachers*
4. *Sons and daughters*
5. *Changing rooms*
6. *A place in the sun*
7. *The office*
8. *Open all hours*
9. *Top gear*
10. *Home front*

Contact details

The reports were prepared by Ben Wheeler, Mary Shaw, Richard Mitchell and Danny Dorling. The authors can be contacted via:
Professor Danny Dorling • Department of Geography • University of Sheffield • Winter Street • Sheffield S10 2TN
e-mail: danny.dorling@sheffield.ac.uk • www.sheffield.ac.uk/sasi

Project funder: Joseph Rowntree Foundation

JOSEPH ROWNTREE FOUNDATION

The POLICY PRESS

The OFFICE

Qualifications, locations and top jobs

High-status jobs are not evenly distributed across the country. Most jobs falling into the top levels of the government's socio-economic classification are found in London and the South East of England. In areas where there are relatively few of these jobs available, people with good qualifications are more likely to have a job in the lower levels of the socio-economic classification. Therefore, it seems that the place in which someone lives can sometimes be a more important influence on their prospects of a well-rewarded job than their qualifications.

Class and qualifications

Obtaining a qualification such as a degree is expensive, with an average student in England and Wales estimated to be over £12,000 in debt on leaving higher education[1]. Since this is an average, many students will leave university with higher levels of debt than this. The assumption is that a degree will lead to a financially well-rewarded job, so making the cost of obtaining a higher qualification a worthwhile investment. In this report, data from the 2001 Census is used to investigate the likelihood of someone with high-level qualifications working in a well-paid job, and the availability of those jobs across the UK.

The National Statistics Socio-economic Classification (NS-SEC) is the official way in which people are now grouped by class in the UK. It provides an indication of a person's life chances just as previous social class groupings have done before, but has now been validated and used for the first time nationally following the 2001 Census. People in higher levels of NS-SEC are likely to be paid more, be better educated, have better health, and live longer than those in lower levels[2,3]. Details of the classification scheme are given in the box overleaf.

Life in Britain

The latest Census reveals that within the UK people live in very different worlds. For some, resources and amenities abound; for others life is characterised by deprivation and difficulties, especially when their need for support is great.

The 2001 Census marked the bi-centenary of census taking in the UK. It is the most comprehensive social record of life in this country now available. Since 1801 successive governments have asked the population to assist in the taking of a Census.

This report is one of a series of 10 showing key patterns and inequalities in life in the UK revealed by the 2001 Census. These reports focus on geographical inequalities, highlighting where services and opportunities appear not to be available or accessible to those people and places that need them most.

NS-SEC

The National Statistics Socio-economic Classification is the replacement for the Registrar General's 'social class' classification. It places people into a socio-economic category based on their occupation and certain characteristics of the work that they do (whether they are an employer, self-employed or an employee; whether or not they are responsible for supervising others; and the number of employees at the place of work). The highest group is NS-SEC 1, 'Higher managerial and professional occupations', and the lowest is NS-SEC 7, 'Routine occupations'. The NS-SEC classes are listed below with the population in 2001, examples of occupations and relative risk of death.

	NS-SEC	Population 2001[5]	Examples of occupations[3]	Relative risk of death (%)[6]
1	Higher managerial and professional occupations	3,182,614	Doctors, directors of large organisations, clergy	70
2	Lower managerial and professional occupations	6,990,083	Journalists, nurses, school teachers	94
3	Intermediate occupations	3,532,894	Travel agents, police officers (sergeant and below)	99
4	Small employers and own account workers	2,626,067	Farmers, taxi drivers, hotel managers	86
5	Lower supervisory and technical occupations	2,687,927	Train drivers, electricians, bakers	102
6	Semi-routine occupations	4,393,965	Scaffolders, traffic wardens, dental nurses	113
7	Routine occupations	3,410,122	Building labourers, waiters, cleaners	126

The 2001 Census asked questions to establish each person's class according to the NS-SEC, and also asked which qualifications were held by each individual. These qualifications are grouped into 'levels', where the highest is Level 5, which includes higher degrees and NVQ level 5[4]. Data from the Census therefore gives information on people's highest level of qualification, and also the type of occupation that they have. Using these data, it is possible to ascertain, for example, the number of people with high level qualifications working in jobs at the top (or bottom) of the socio-economic classification.

In order to assess variations in the degree to which people with good qualifications have well-paid, high-status jobs, the UK was divided up into 142 areas, as for the other reports in this series. These areas consist of counties, unitary authorities and former metropolitan authorities. The report uses these data to address the question:

Where fewer jobs in the top socio-economic classes are available, are highly qualified people less likely to have one of these jobs (that is, in some places is location more important than qualifications)?

Findings

In the UK in 2001, 8.3 million people[7] had one of the highest level qualifications. Figure 1 illustrates how these people were distributed across the NS-SEC. A total of 6.4 million, around three quarters, of these people had an occupation classified in NS-SEC groups 1 to 4. Therefore, about a quarter of people with high level qualifications did not have what might be considered (especially by them) to be a 'good' job. In some cases, this was because the person was still a full-time student studying for yet more qualifications (340,000 people). However, 630,000 people with these qualifications worked in jobs in NS-SEC 5 to 7, lower level jobs, many of which are routine or semi-routine and unlikely to make use of their qualifications. While some people may choose to work in such jobs, the majority are likely to be employed in such work because a job that would use their qualifications is unavailable. A further 68,000 had never held a job, and 54,000 were long-term unemployed. Most of the remainder of those with high level qualifications but unclassified by NS-SEC were retired.

Overall, 11.4 million people held an occupation in NS-SEC 1 or 2 in 2001. This means that 20% of the population were employed in the top two socio-economic groups of occupations. However, this figure varied across the country from around 10% to 33% of the local population of each area studied in this report.

Comparing areas

Figure 2 illustrates how the two measures are related to each other for all of the 142 areas described in the accompanying technical report. The graph shows that areas with a high availability of good jobs (that is, areas with a high proportion of their population in NS-SEC 1 or 2) tend to have higher proportions of their well-qualified population working in good jobs[TR].

The graph in Figure 3 is the inverse relationship, and shows that in areas with low availability of good jobs, people with good qualifications are more likely to be working in jobs in NS-SEC 5 to 7 (routine, semi-routine and lower supervisory/technical jobs).

Northern Ireland is the only area that falls far from the line associating all of the other areas in both graphs. While the country has an average percentage of its population in socio-economic groups 1 and 2, it has an unusually high proportion of its highly qualified population in classes 1 to 4 (85% where we would expect around 75% if it matched the pattern in other areas). This could be explained by substantial out-migration of well qualified people from Northern Ireland to other parts of the UK if unable to find a good job at home. The outlier to the right of the graph in Figure 3 is the Shetland Islands, where employment circumstances may be expected to be different to the remainder of the UK given the remoteness of the islands.

100 years ago

The first official classification of occupations into 'social grades', later referred to as 'social classes', was developed by Dr T.H.C. Stevenson and first used in the Registrar General's Annual Report for 1911 (published in 1913). The original uses of the class scheme included comparisons of fertility rates and infant and occupational mortality. Stevenson's classification included three basic groups – upper, middle and working classes – but with further division into eight including separate groups for people working in agriculture, mining and textiles. These three specific industries were incorporated into other classes in 1921 making the classification appear similar to that used to map London by Charles Booth in the 1890s. The classification system remained fairly similar until the end of the 20th century. The 2001 Census was the first to classify occupations using a major revision to the social class scheme, the 'National Statistics Socio-economic Classification', as described elsewhere in this report.

For more information see Dorling, D., Mitchell, R., Shaw, M., Orford, S. and Davey Smith. G. (2000) 'The ghost of Christmas past: health effects of poverty in London in 1896 and 1991', *BMJ*, vol 321, pp 1547-51; Rose, D. and O'Reilly, K. (1998) *The ESRC review of government social classifications*, London: Office for National Statistics; Rose, D. (1995) *Official social classifications in the UK*, Surrey: University of Surrey Social Research Update 9 (www.soc.surrey.ac.uk/sru/SRU9.html).

ACCOUNTANT

Figure 1: The distribution of people with high level qualifications in the UK in 2001 (Level 4 or 5 in England, Wales and Northern Ireland; Group 4 in Scotland) across the NS-SEC

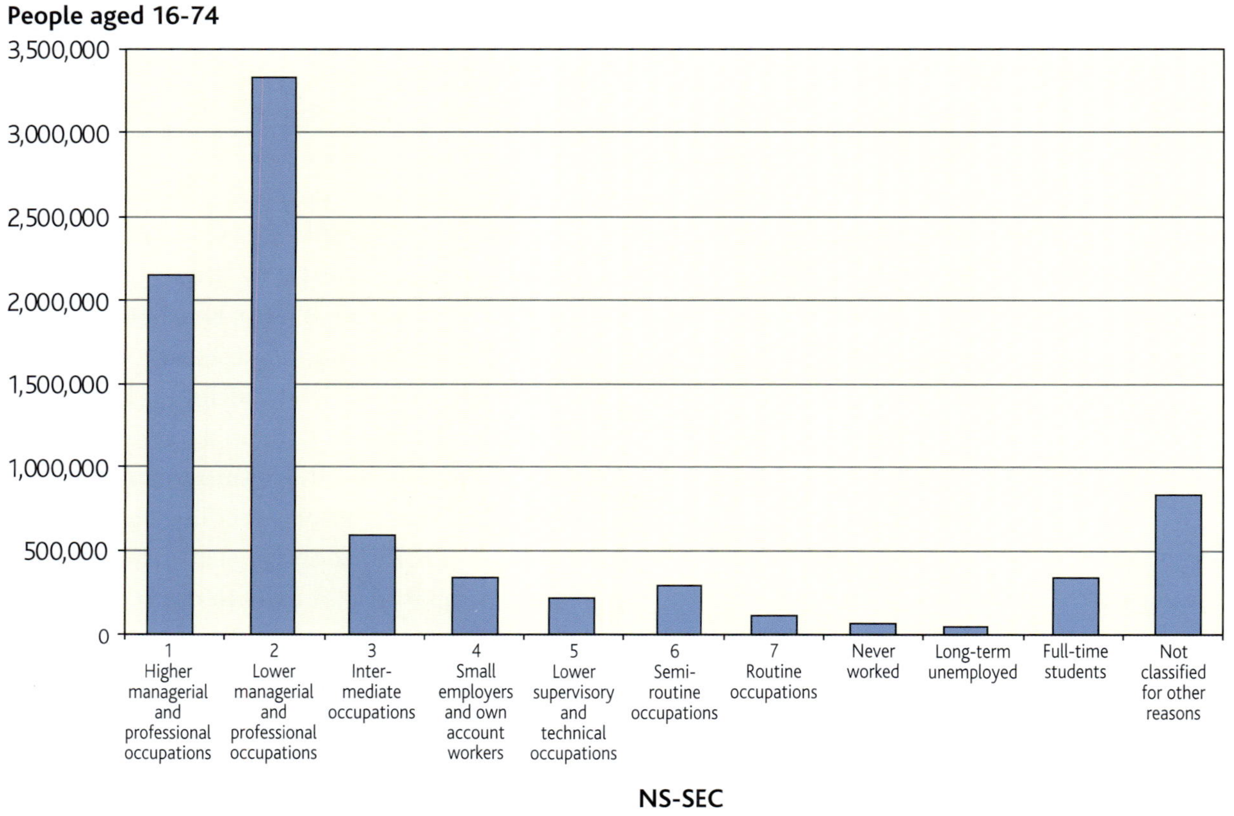

The maps in Figure 4 indicate that the greatest degree of 'under-employment' (high proportions of highly qualified people in relatively poor jobs) exists in the far South West of England, some towns and cities in the English Midlands and North East, and Scotland. The maps in Figure 5 suggest that the areas with the highest availability of top-level jobs (those in NS-SEC 1 and 2) are London and the Home Counties and some parts of southern Scotland.

Since 2001

In the 2000/01 academic year, 431,000 new higher education qualifications (first and postgraduate degrees, HNDs etc) were awarded by UK institutions to UK residents. In 2001/02 this figure was 443,000, and in 2002/03 the number of new qualifications was 469,000[7]. Thus in the few years since the Census, an additional 1.3 million high level qualifications have been obtained. There is no information on where in the country these graduates have ended up. However, the distribution of opportunities to work in top jobs continues to be disproportionately weighted toward London and the South East. The Association of Graduate Recruiters reported that just 8% of new graduate vacancies in summer 2004 were in Scotland, Wales and Northern Ireland; 40% were in London and 11.3% in the South East[8].

Discussion

In this report we are not arguing that all people with high qualifications should hold the best rewarded jobs, nor that people with low qualifications should be poorly rewarded. In fact it is debatable whether the three years that so many people now spend at university do equip them to work in many of the jobs most move on to. Universities are educational institutions, not training schemes. Similarly it is debatable whether many of the people currently largely debarred from securing particular jobs due to lack of university degrees could not do those jobs.

Figure 2: The association between the percentage of people with high level qualifications with a job in the top four NS-SEC classifications (X-axis) and the percentage of all people in the area with a job in the two highest socio-economic classifications (Y-axis), UK (2001)[TR]

Figure 3: This graph has the same Y-axis as that in Figure 2, but here the X-axis is the percentage of people with good qualifications working in the lowest three categories of the socio-economic classification

Note: Each circle is a county, unitary or former metropolitan authority, drawn with the area in proportion to the total population in 2001 (the largest circle represents London, with a population of just over 7 million). Areas in northern England are those that lie west or north of the counties of Gloucestershire, Warwickshire, Leicestershire and Lincolnshire (the Severn-Humber divide).

Figure 4: The percentage of people with high level qualifications in an occupation in the lowest three socio-economic classifications in each area (NS-SEC 5-7)

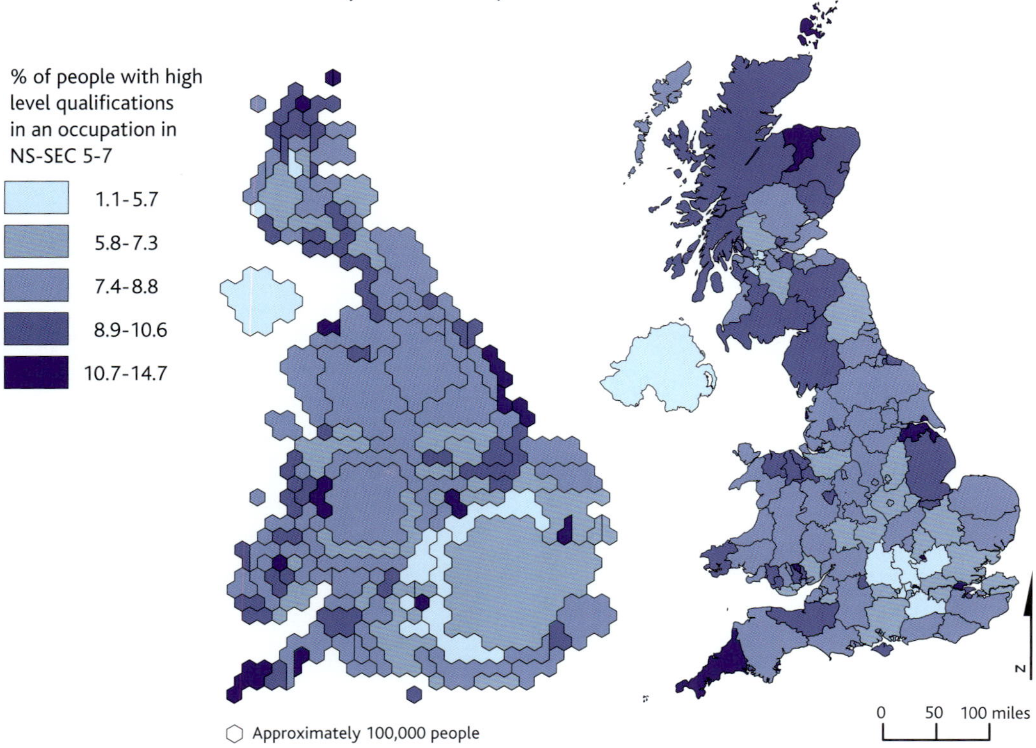

Figure 5: Geographical variation in the proportion of the population working in jobs in the top two socio-economic classes (NS-SEC 1-2)

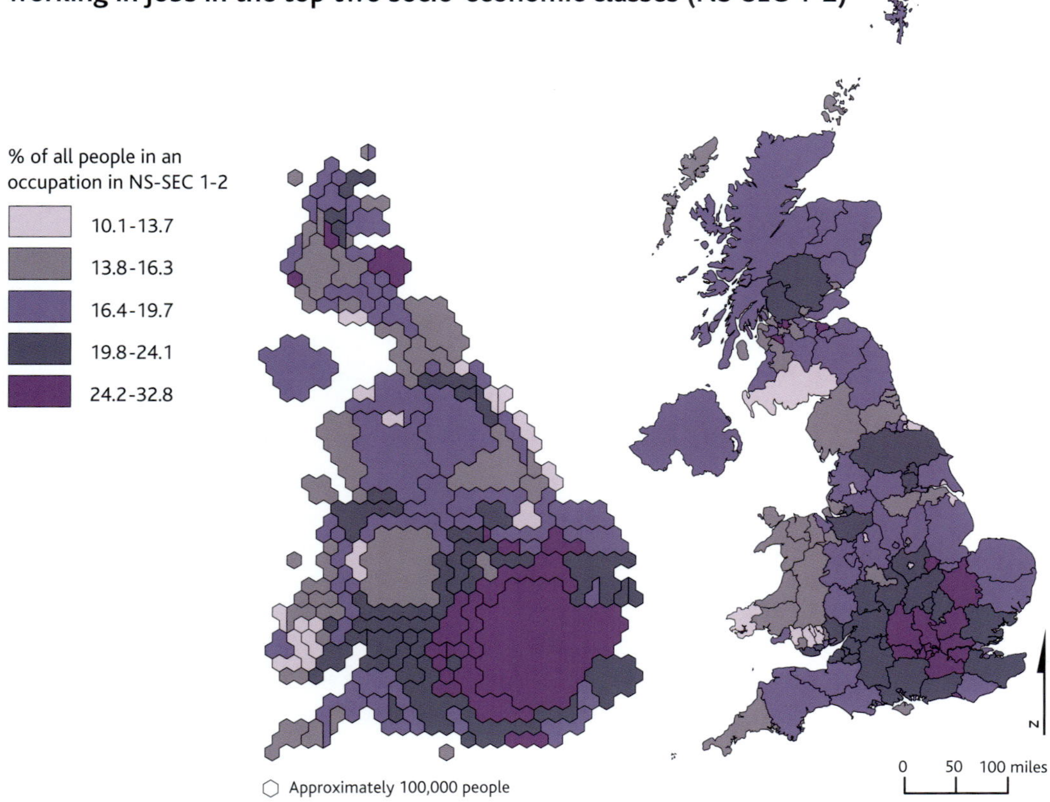

Note: Both maps in each figure represent the same places, shaded identically. The map on the left is a cartogram – each area is shown in proportion to the size of its population in 2001. The largest area is London, since it has the highest population of any of the places[TR]. The map on the right shows the actual boundaries of the areas.

This report shows very clearly that people with the equivalent qualifications to university degrees are most likely to secure well-paid employment in the South of England, particularly around London and outside of the South only in a few areas such as the capitals of Cardiff and Edinburgh. People with high qualifications who remain in much of the rest of Northern England, Wales, Scotland and Northern Ireland are far less likely to secure well-paid employment, and are up to three times more likely to be working in lower status occupations. Given this it is hardly surprising that university graduates continue to concentrate in the South.

There is an inverse relationship between the proportions of people with well-rewarded jobs in an area and the proportions of graduates working in poorly rewarded employment. The UK employment playing field slopes steeply to the South, drawing graduates towards London and leaving those on the higher slopes far more often in poorly rewarded occupations. Thus, even when graduates remain or move northwards they are unlikely to reduce regional divisions in the UK, in say house prices, as their spending power is on average lower. Even for occupations rewarded roughly equally irrespective of location (see related reports in this series, *Doctors and nurses*, report no 1 and *Teachers*, report no 3) the higher paid are more likely to move southwards – partly because they can afford to live there.

This inequality in the provision of well-rewarded jobs will only be altered when there are more such jobs available outside of the South East and fewer in the South East. The two areas outside of the South East which have currently bucked the trend are the capitals of Wales and Scotland. It is possible that further devolved government, if taken far enough, could begin to reverse this trend.

Notes

[1] 'UK student debt rises to £14bn', BBC News (http://news.bbc.co.uk, accessed 29 July 2004).

[2] Rose, D. and O'Reilly, K. (eds) (1997) *Constructing classes: Towards a new social classification for the UK*, Swindon: ESRC/ONS.

[3] Drever, F., Doran, T. and Whitehead, M. (2004) 'Exploring the relation between class, gender, and self rated general health using the new socioeconomic classification. A study using data from the 2001 census', *Journal of Epidemiology and Community Health*, vol 58, pp 590-6.

[4] In England, Wales and Northern Ireland, the highest level qualifications are Levels 4 and 5, which include first and higher degrees, NVQ Level 4 or 5, HNC and HND. In Scotland, the highest level is Group 4 qualifications, including first and higher degrees, and professional qualifications. There is therefore some inconsistency between countries; any substantial differences would be apparent in the comparisons of areas.

[5] Only people aged 16-74 were asked the questions on occupation and qualifications, so people outside this age range are excluded here.

[6] The relative risk of death was the chances of men classified by their occupation in 1981 dying in the period 1986-90. The national average was 100%. Thus, after allowing for differences in age distribution men in NS-SEC class 7 were 1.8 times more likely to die in a given period as compared to men in class 1 (126/70=1.8). The NS-SEC classification includes more people in the top and bottom categories and thus this ratio is slightly smaller than that found for men classified at the extremes of the Registrar General's classification over the same period (130/66=1.97). See Fitzpatrick, R., Bartley, M., Dodgeon, B., Fifth, D. and Lynch, K. (1997) 'Social variations in health: relationship of mortality to the interim revised social classification', Chapter 7 in Rose and O'Reilly (1997) as above.

[7] Higher Education Statistics Agency (www.hesa.ac.uk).

[8] 'Graduates' starting pay "rising"', BBC News (http://news.bbc.co.uk, accessed 14 July 2004).

[TR] Further information on this point is available in the accompanying technical report.

What do we know?

- People in higher socio-economic groups tend to have better life chances and live longer than people in lower socio-economic groups.
- The government is keen to encourage more people to obtain qualifications in the higher levels of the Census classification (mostly degrees).
- Having good qualifications is one way that a person can obtain a job in the higher socio-economic classifications.

What have we found?

- The proportion of highly qualified people working in jobs at the bottom of the socio-economic classification is highest in areas where the availability of good jobs is lowest.
- The highest availability of jobs at the top of the socio-economic spectrum is in London and the South East of England.
- In some places, location can be more important than qualifications in determining whether or not someone can get a good job.

Other reports in the series

The companion report to this, *Open all hours*, looks as whether areas with higher levels of unemployment also have high numbers of people working long hours.

1. *Doctors and nurses*
2. *In sickness and in health*
3. *Teachers*
4. *Sons and daughters*
5. *Changing rooms*
6. *A place in the sun*
7. *The office*
8. *Open all hours*
9. *Top gear*
10. *Home front*

Contact details

The reports were prepared by Ben Wheeler, Mary Shaw, Richard Mitchell and Danny Dorling. The authors can be contacted via:
Professor Danny Dorling • Department of Geography • University of Sheffield • Winter Street • Sheffield S10 2TN
e-mail: danny.dorling@sheffield.ac.uk • www.sheffield.ac.uk/sasi

Project funder: Joseph Rowntree Foundation

JOSEPH ROWNTREE FOUNDATION

The POLICY PRESS

OPEN all HOURS

'Work-rich' or 'work-poor'?

The UK can be divided into relatively 'work-rich' and 'work-poor' areas. In the former, the people who are in work are more likely to be working very long hours, which may affect their well-being. In the latter areas, where unemployment is higher, those in work are less likely to be working long hours and many people do not work at all. This geography of work matters not only because *not* being in work is known to have adverse effects on people, but also because working long hours can be associated with worse health, lower productivity and difficulties balancing the demands of home and work. While some jobs associated with long hours need to be located in particular parts of the country (agriculture, for example), many others could be more evenly distributed across the UK, making the demand for labour more even. This would help reduce the stark differences between the lives of the 'work-rich' and the 'work-poor'.

Employment, unemployment and working hours

Although the UK has not quite reached full employment, as pledged by Gordon Brown in 1999, unemployment is markedly lower today than in recent years. Getting people into work has been a cornerstone of the Labour government's approach to tackling poverty and other wider societal ills. Perhaps because so many more of us are in work, concern is turning towards issues of 'work–life balance'. Concern has grown that many of us are working too many hours in a week and that this might be damaging our physical and mental health and family life. Opinions differ as to what 'long hours' actually means, but typically working more than 48 hours a week is thought to constitute 'too much'. The government brought in Working Time Regulations (WTR) on 1 October 1998, which say

Life in Britain

The latest Census reveals that within the UK people live in very different worlds. For some, resources and amenities abound; for others life is characterised by deprivation and difficulties, especially when their need for support is great.

The 2001 Census marked the bi-centenary of census taking in the UK. It is the most comprehensive social record of life in this country now available. Since 1801 successive governments have asked the population to assist in the taking of a Census.

This report is one of a series of 10 showing key patterns and inequalities in life in the UK revealed by the 2001 Census. These reports focus on geographical inequalities, highlighting where services and opportunities appear not to be available or accessible to those people and places that need them most.

that workers cannot be forced to work for more than 48 hours a week on average.

Despite more people being in employment, unemployment is still a feature of contemporary UK. A little less than 5% of the working-age population was unemployed in the summer of 2004[1]. There are now, for the first time, two groups of people for whom work might be considered a particular problem – those who cannot get a job, and those who spend too much time doing the job they have. One obvious question is whether people who are working very long hours could conceivably work less by letting other people who are not in work share the load, but this depends on where the over-worked and unemployed, and their jobs, are located, and the work that people do.

In this report, data from the 2001 Census are used to explore and compare these two groups. The 2001 Census asked every individual about their employment status (that is to say, whether they were working or not), and also asked them to state the number of hours that they worked. The actual question asked was as follows, and unfortunately only relates to a person's main job:

How many hours a week do you usually work in your main job?
- **Answer to the nearest whole hour**
- **Give average for last four weeks.**

For this analysis, data from the Census were used to calculate the number of people who were unemployed, along with the number of people working long hours (counted as those working more than 48 hours a week). Because of the way that the Census asks about working hours, the long hours group does not include people who do 49 or more hours spread over more than one job, which means people who have two or even three jobs are not included in this group although they ought to be. The analysis was restricted to people aged between 30 and 54. This is because it can be hard to tell the employment status and circumstances of many people in younger and older age groups. They can be students, or semi-retired, and including them may confuse the picture. Although the Census does not, in this case, represent a perfect picture of working life in the UK, it does at least give some indication about whether, and for how long during the day or night, people are working, rather than adhering to complex government definitions of work and working hours.

As for the other reports in this series, the UK was divided into 142 areas: counties, unitary authorities and former metropolitan authorities. The distributions of the unemployed and those working long hours across these areas of the country can then be compared. The report asks this question:

In areas where there is a higher level of unemployment, do the people who are working tend to be working long hours?

Findings

The 2001 Census revealed that 2.95 million people aged 30-54 worked for 49 or more hours a week. This equates to 18% of the working population in that age group in the UK. Figure 1 illustrates the distribution of working hours among people in this age group, showing that most employed people work between 31 and 48 hours per week that equates to a typical 'full-time job'. Those working 30 hours per week or less are classified as working part time by the Census. Part-time employees are more likely to be women – 79% of those employed part time were women, as opposed to 35% of those working full time[TR]. We also know that managers, professionals and operative and assembly workers are those occupations most likely to be working long hours. Among women who work long hours, two thirds are in managerial and professional occupations (23% and 40% respectively). The sectors with a particularly high incidence of long-hours working are construction, transport, communication and agriculture, forestry and fishing. The incidence of long-hours working is higher in the private sector than the public sector. The UK has a reputation as a long-hours culture. In fact, average working hours in the UK are about middle of the range across all EU member states when all employees (full-time and part-time employees) are included. However, the UK position is affected by the fact that the UK employs a high proportion of part-time women workers. Just over one fifth (22%) of UK men working full time

Figure 1: Hours worked per week for people aged 30-54, UK (2001)

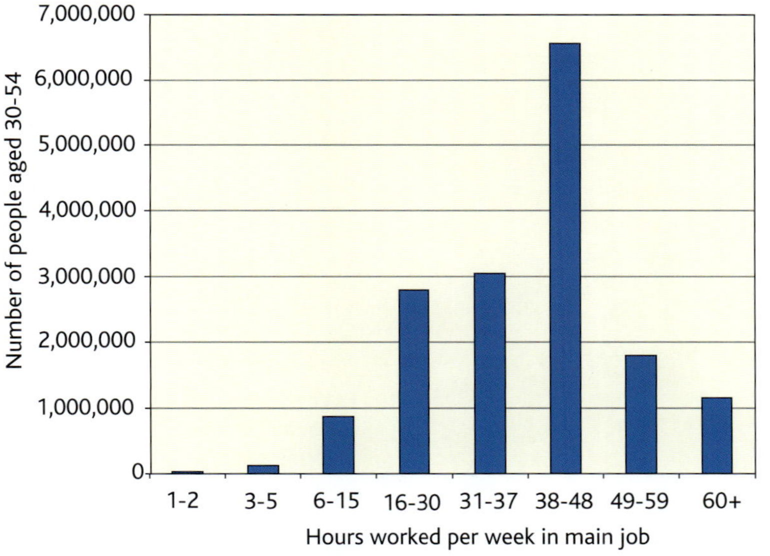

work long hours compared with an average of one tenth (11%) across the other EU member states[2].

About 740,000 people aged 30-54 were unemployed in 2001 – 3.5% of this age group. These people are of particular concern since they are also the most likely to be unemployed on a long-term basis[3].

Comparing areas

This series of reports is about comparing the 'worlds' in which people live in the UK. Figure 2 does this by illustrating the relationship between the percentage of employed people aged 30-54 who are working long hours, and the percentage of people aged 30-54 who are unemployed for the 142 areas of the UK. The figure demonstrates that there is an 'inverse' association between the two measures[TR]. That is to say, areas where larger numbers of the working population work long hours tend also to have low unemployment rates. Figure 2 also shows some differences in this general pattern for different parts of the UK, and these are highlighted by the maps in Figures 3 and 4.

In general, unemployment is higher in the North East of England, Scotland and parts of the English West Midlands, than in southern and central UK (Figure 3). This is reflected in Figure 2 where southern England

100 years ago

Employment circumstances in 1901 were very different to those 100 years later. Most jobs were in sectors such as manufacturing, agriculture and mining, and the workforce included children. The Factory Act of 1891 had raised the minimum age at which a child could legally work from 10 to 11. However, the time around the turn of the century marked the beginning of the de-industrialisation of the UK, with substantial increases in 'white-collar' jobs. For example, the proportion of males aged 10 and over working in agriculture dropped from 24% in 1851 to 10% in 1901. Between 1891 and 1901, the proportions of men employed in telecommunications grew by 53%, in local government by 37% and working as merchants, agents and buyers by 37%.

For more information see the National Archives (www.nationalarchives.gov.uk).

Figure 2: The percentage of people working long hours versus the percentage of people who were unemployed (2001)

Notes: Each circle is a county, unitary or former metropolitan authority, drawn with the area in proportion to the total population in 2001 (the largest circle represents London, with a population of just over 7 million). Areas in northern England are those that lie west or north of the counties of Gloucestershire, Warwickshire, Leicestershire and Lincolnshire (the Severn-Humber divide).

dominates the bottom right-hand end of the range of circles – denoting lower unemployment levels. The position of these circles also denotes markedly higher proportions of long working hours for employed people in the South. Not only are you more likely to be working here, but if you are working, you are more likely to be working long hours. Typically, just over one in five working people aged 30-54 and living in the South are working more hours than the government recommends. However, Figures 2 and 4 show that it is not residents of London who are dominating this long-hours group. The largest circle on Figure 2 is London and it manages to have both quite a high level of unemployment *and* quite a high level of residents working long hours. Figure 4 shows the geography of long-hours working, with a range of different types of areas showing higher levels of long-hours workers. This may reflect different occupations prevalent in different areas. The high rates in the areas around, but not in, London may be associated with commuters working long hours in well-paid jobs in the city. The high rates in mid-Wales and more rural parts of England and Scotland are more likely to be associated with jobs in agriculture, fishing and long shift-based industries such as oil.

Since 2001

Although *The Working Time Regulations* (1998) dictate that workers cannot be forced to work for more than 48 hours a week on average, a survey in 2002 found that the proportion of people working long hours was increasing and had risen from one in eight working more than 60 hours a week in 2000, to one in six in 2002[4]. Meanwhile, the overall official unemployment rate has changed little since 2001; the seasonally adjusted rate based on the Office for National Statistics Labour Force Survey was 4.9% in 2001 and 4.8% in 2004[5]. Accompanying these developments has been an increase in the amount of attention being paid to work–life balance, with numerous government departments taking a keen interest in reducing working hours and making it easier to combine work and family life[6].

Figure 3: Variation in unemployment rates across the 142 areas of the UK (2001)

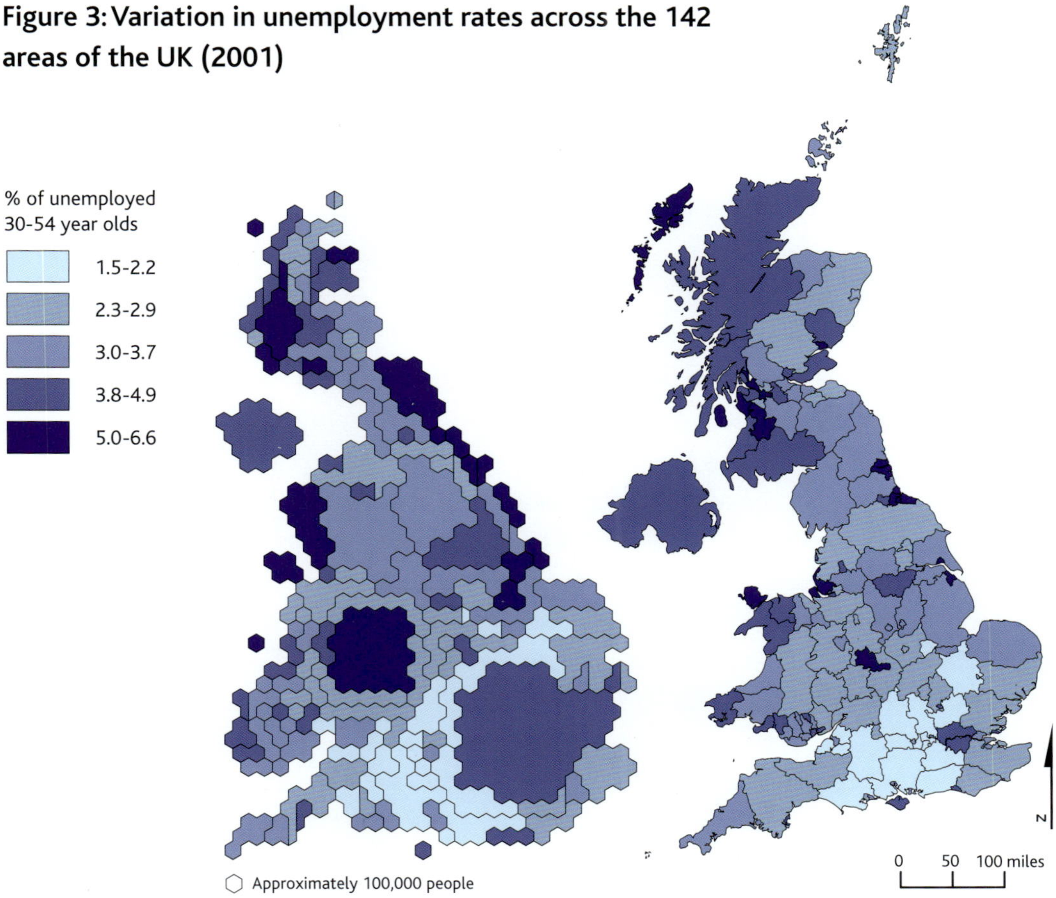

Figure 4: The percentage of employed 30-54 year olds who work long hours across the UK

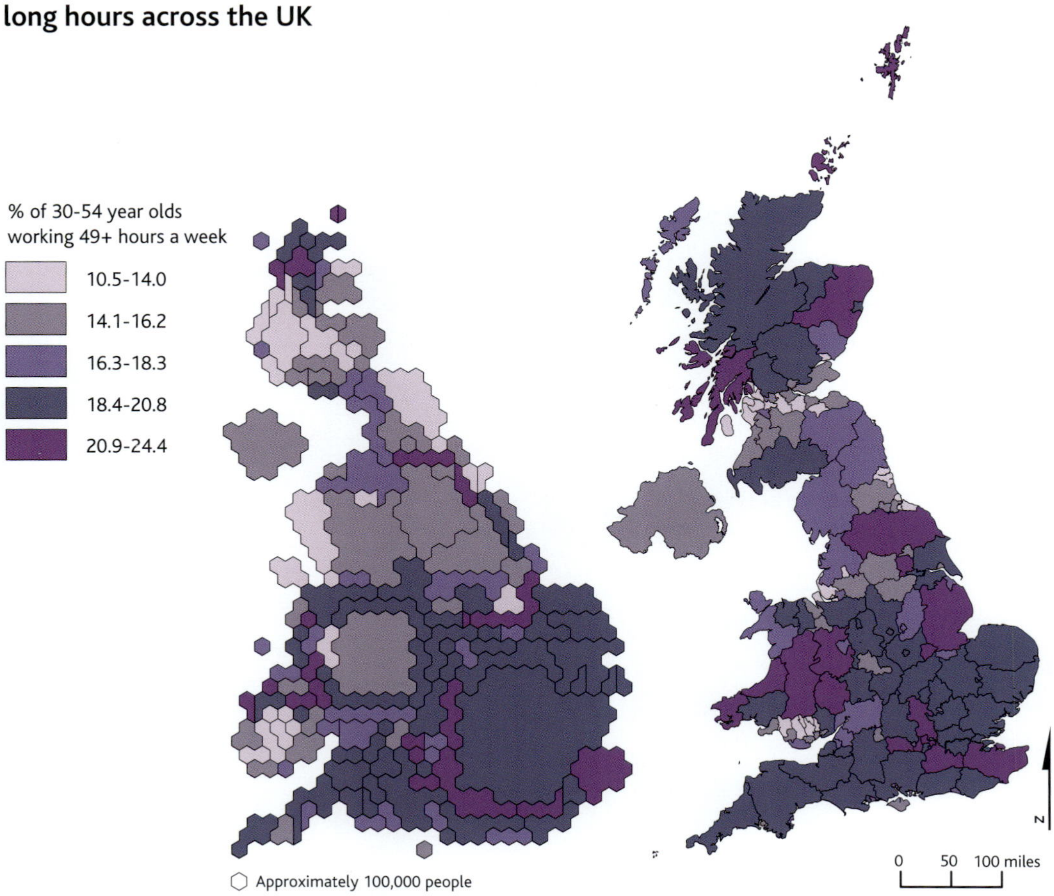

Note: Both maps in each figure represent the same places, shaded identically. The map on the left is a cartogram – each area is shown in proportion to the size of its population in 2001. The largest area is London, since it has the highest population of any of the places[TR]. The map on the right shows the actual boundaries of the areas.

Discussion

This analysis shows that in general, where higher levels of the population are unemployed those who are working are less likely to be working very long hours. What does this mean? First of all, it prompts us to think about employment as a spectrum, rather than as a simple distinction between 'working' and 'not working'. We know that unemployed people who return to work are more likely to work part time and to earn less as a result. Essentially, the areas in which there is greater unemployment and lower rates of long-hours working are those areas in which there is a generally lower demand for labour. There is, literally, less work to be done and hence less money to be earned. People are more likely to not be working, or to be working part time. It is not the characteristics of the people, but of the places that determines this. In other places, there is more work to be done and hence more people are employed, and more of the employed work longer hours. However, it must be recognised that manual and non-manual workers give significantly different reasons for long-hours working. The reasons for long-hours working vary. Some people choose to work longer, because they are directly rewarded for it, but others have to, or want to, 'get the job done'. For some people, for example nurses and police officers, overtime is an essential and traditional way to top up wages. In managerial and professional positions, long hours may not be directly rewarded, but benefits may be indirect, such as improvement of promotion prospects.

Does this geography of 'work' matter? Long hours at work are thought to have several impacts on workers and their families. Although not conclusive, some recent evidence suggests that long hours are bad for productivity and that reductions increase both employment and productivity (more people work, and those who work, work better when they are not tired)[2]. There are associations between long-hours working and health problems, such as poor mental health and cardiovascular disease. Other (similarly disputed) research shows that long hours take a toll on family life[7]. There is overwhelming evidence that unemployment is bad for the health of the unemployed and that their families and communities suffer from the effects of the resulting poverty[8,9]. The government's Social Exclusion Unit recently stated that "Living in an area where there are many other workless people can damage a person's life chances – especially those of children and young people"[10]. The maps in this report show that the UK is divided into areas where there is relatively less work and relatively more work (in terms of both jobs and hours). Unemployed people are unemployed, to some extent, because their local labour market cannot provide them with a suitable job. People who work long hours do so because there is a job to be done which demands more of their time (and may or may not directly reward them for it).

So, if the UK can be divided into relatively 'work-rich' and 'work-poor' areas, and in the former there is more work to do than is good for us, and in the latter there is not enough work, the geographic redistribution of work would seem a possible route to solving the problem. Look again at Figure 4 and the areas in which those in work are more likely to work long hours. Some of these areas contain jobs that are geographically specific – jobs in oil and agriculture and other primary industries cannot easily be moved. Jobs in banking, the Civil Service, IT and the media are not as location specific, especially given the availability of telecommunications. To redress the contrasting worlds of 'work' and 'no work', a deliberate process aimed at evening out the demands for labour across the UK and hence redistributing the benefits of a sensible workload, might help to ease the gap between different parts of the country. However, as numerous attempts to redistribute the Civil Service from London have shown, there is more than rationality at play.

CRAFTSMAN/GARDENER

Notes

1 Incomes Data Services (2004) (www.incomesdata.co.uk/statistics/statempl.htm).

2 Kodz, J. (2003) *Working long hours: A review of the evidence. Volume 1 – Main report*, Employment Relations Research Series No 16, Institute For Employment Studies, Department for Trade and Industry, November.

3 Begum, N. (2004) *Characteristics of the short-term and long-term unemployed*, Labour Market Trends, London: Office for National Statistics, April.

4 'UK working hours rise sharply' (http://news.bbc.co.uk, accessed 29 August 2002).

5 ONS Time Series MGSX Labour Force Survey (www.statistics.gov.uk/statbase/tsdtimezone.asp, last updated 9 August 2004).

6 www.dti.gov.uk/work-lifebalance/

7 Department for Education and Employment (2000) *Work-Life Balance 2000 Baseline Survey*, London: Department for Education and Employment.

8 Bartley, M. (1994) 'Unemployment and ill health: understanding the relationship', *Journal of Epidemiology and Community Health*, vol 48, pp 333-7.

9 Saunders, P. (2002) *The direct and indirect effects of unemployment on poverty and inequality*, SPRC Discussion Paper No 118, Social Policy Research Centre, University of New South Wales (www.sprc.unsw.edu.au/dp/DP118.pdf).

10 Social Exclusion Unit (2004) 'Jobs and enterprise in deprived areas' (www.socialexclusionunit.gov.uk).

TR Further information on this point is available in the accompanying technical report.

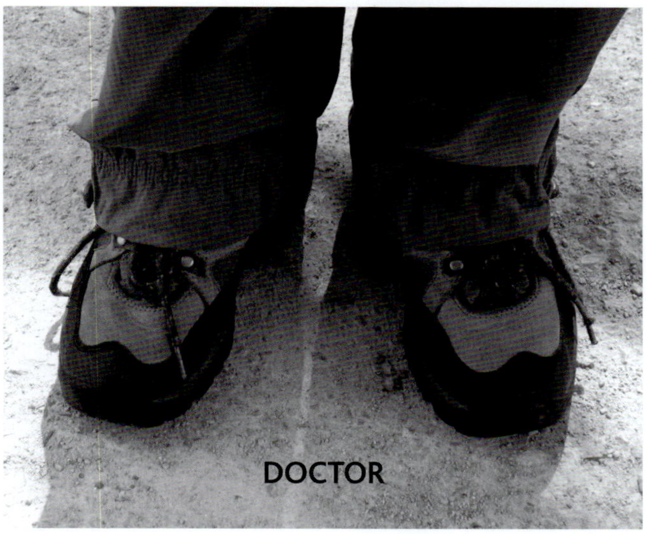

What do we know?

- Unemployment has been either falling or stable in recent years, and any fall has been accompanied by a rise in the numbers of people working very long hours.
- Both not working and working too much have been found to be associated with worse health. Working long hours may damage productivity and work–life balance.
- Not everyone works longer hours to get more money in their next pay packet. Some reap the rewards later on, some are committed to their work, some have to work to 'get the job done', and some have to work long hours in order to afford to be able to live where they do.

What have we found?

- There is a geographical divide in the UK between 'work-rich' areas and 'work-poor' areas. This divide is mainly regional rather than local.
- Areas with higher unemployment rates tend also to have lower proportions of long-hours working among those who do have a job.
- Encouraging the relocation of jobs from those parts of the country which have more work than can be done by the workforce within the recommended maximum of 48 hours a week towards areas in which there is currently more labour available than work to occupy it might help to reduce differences in experience of work (and incomes earned) across the UK.

Other reports in the series

The companion report to this, *The office*, looks at whether in areas where fewer good jobs are available, highly qualified people are likely to be working in lower grade jobs.

1. *Doctors and nurses*
2. *In sickness and in health*
3. *Teachers*
4. *Sons and daughters*
5. *Changing rooms*
6. *A place in the sun*
7. *The office*
8. *Open all hours*
9. *Top gear*
10. *Home front*

Contact details

The reports were prepared by Ben Wheeler, Mary Shaw, Richard Mitchell and Danny Dorling. The authors can be contacted via:

Professor Danny Dorling • Department of Geography • University of Sheffield • Winter Street • Sheffield S10 2TN

e-mail: danny.dorling@sheffield.ac.uk • www.sheffield.ac.uk/sasi

Project funder: Joseph Rowntree Foundation

JOSEPH ROWNTREE FOUNDATION

The POLICY PRESS

TOP GEAR

Too few or too many cars?

Access to cars may be a better indication of wealth than is often assumed, given what is revealed by the 2001 Census. There is a geographical divide in Britain based on access to cars. Two groups of households are compared in this report: those who might need a car but do not have one, and those who may have more cars than they actually need. The report shows first that the number of households in these two situations in the UK is roughly equal (at about one million households in each group). It then shows that the two groups of households tend to live in very different places, but not perhaps where we would expect.

Access to a car

> "Motoring used to be a pleasurable activity, but it wouldn't be considered that now", Susie Haywood, spokesperson for the RAC says. "It's a necessity. And the car is the most valuable household good."[1]

Of course, not everyone would agree with the RAC that having a car is essential. The green lobby and public transport enthusiasts would strongly disagree. However, there can be few who would disagree that having a car can make life easier. Travel by car is, on average, quicker than by public transport, apart from in the most highly congested inner-city areas or on long distance journeys. A recent survey of London motorists revealed that 85% said they could not adjust to life without a car. While car ownership continues to rise, the proportion of households without cars in the UK has fallen steadily from 48% in 1970 to 27% in 2000[2].

Car ownership is strongly associated with income and wealth. Only 5% of households in the highest income group do not have a car but 52% have two or more

Life in Britain

The latest Census reveals that within the UK people live in very different worlds. For some, resources and amenities abound; for others life is characterised by deprivation and difficulties, especially when their need for support is great.

The 2001 Census marked the bi-centenary of census taking in the UK. It is the most comprehensive social record of life in this country now available. Since 1801 successive governments have asked the population to assist in the taking of a Census.

This report is one of a series of 10 showing key patterns and inequalities in life in the UK revealed by the 2001 Census. These reports focus on geographical inequalities, highlighting where services and opportunities appear not to be available or accessible to those people and places that need them most.

cars, while 65% of households in the bottom income group do not have a car. Statistics about what people who have cars actually do with them are revealing. In 1998/2000, people in households with cars made 28% more trips to visit family and friends, and 45% more trips for other leisure activities, than those without cars[2]. Although these activities might themselves be associated with having more money and leisure time, it does seem that cars are useful for leisure and for social interaction and integration. These are things the government is particularly keen to encourage.

This report is not about the pros and cons of having a car, or whether it is environmentally acceptable to have one. Instead, it looks at differences between those who may need a car but have none, and those who have access to more cars than they might really need. In 2000, the proportion of households with two or more cars (28%) was higher than the proportion without a car for the first time. As a recent BBC report stated: "Not long ago the two-car household was the last word in suburban affluence. But changing lifestyles and a fall in car prices have given rise to what used to be seen as an American phenomenon: the three- and four-car family"[3]. The group without access to a car is shrinking and as such it increasingly contains some of the poorest people in society. As our society becomes ever more car-oriented, the relative disadvantage of those without a car continues to grow.

The 2001 Census asked the question:

> **How many cars or vans are owned, or available for use, by one or more members of your household? Include any company car or van if available for private use.**

The report uses the answers to this question to compare the two groups of households. Of course, who 'really needs' a car and the number of cars a household needs are quite subjective issues. The report chooses to represent the group who need a car but do not have one as households which have dependent children but which do not have access to car. The focus on those with children reflects the fact that trying to bring them up without access to a car can be a real struggle. This is not to argue that car access is absolutely essential, but as Dieleman et al observe with dry understatement, "travelling with young children by public transport, by bicycle or on foot is tiresome" (p 524)[4]. It is a reasonable assumption that families with children who do not have access to a car represent a group likely to need one.

The report chooses to represent the second group – those who have more cars than they might really need – as households that have three or more cars. In the UK four out of five households can walk to their nearest food store, three quarters of households can walk to their nearest Post Office and a third can walk to their nearest shopping centre within 13 minutes. A further three out of five households are within 26 minutes of their nearest shopping centre by bus[5]. Despite this proximity to the things we need, 'three or more cars' has been chosen as the cut off. This is because it is easy to see how the modern working family – with or without children – might need two cars to get to and from work, school and the shops. It is harder to see how three cars might be a real necessity. Of course, within this group there will be some households that have three or more adults who all have a legitimate claim on the use of a car. As will be seen later on, the report does explore this possibility.

The report finds out how many households there are in these two groups across the UK, and for each of 142 areas: counties, unitary authorities and former metropolitan authorities. It addresses the question:

> **Do areas with many households that may need a car tend to also have many households that have more cars than they might really need?**

Findings

There were 24.5 million households in the UK at the time of the 2001 Census. Figure 1 shows the numbers of households in each of the two groups. It shows that overall, about 5% of households (1 in 20) have dependent children and no access to a car. The number of households with more than three cars is about the same.

Figure 1: UK households that might need a car and households that might have more cars than needed (2001)

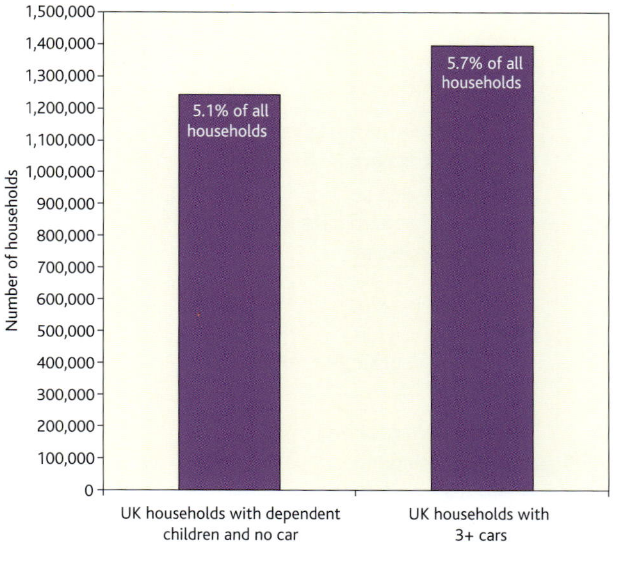

The Census gives a lot of information about these two groups of households. Of the 1.2 million households with dependent children and no car, nearly two out of three are lone-parent households. Other research has shown that working women are more likely to need a car, both in order to get to work and to be able to combine work with childcare and other household commitments. It would be hard to argue that having a car and the means to run it would not be helpful to a lone parent – whether in employment or not.

The Census also tells us that nearly two thirds of households that have three or more cars contain just two or fewer employed people. Furthermore, one in five of the households with three or more cars consists of just one person or a couple; not even enough people to drive all their cars at the same time. Only around a third (about half a million) has dependent children. One popular argument for multiple car ownership is that people who live in rural areas are totally reliant on a car to get around and that therefore most adults in these areas need access to a car. So it is important to look at where these two contrasting groups of households tend to live.

Comparing areas

Figure 2 shows that areas with a high percentage of households with three or more cars tend also to have a low percentage of households with dependent children and no car. This is an 'inverse' relationship; when one group of households decreases, the other increases.

Figures 3 and 4 illustrate where these types of households tend to live. The most striking thing about these maps is that they show just how many households without access to a car *and* who have dependent children live in the rural parts of the UK, most especially in the North of England and in Scotland. The rural South and West of England seem to have the lowest proportions of households that might need a car but do not have one. Figure 3 maps households with more cars than they might really need and the pattern is largely the 'inverse' of Figure 2. Perhaps the most striking thing about Figure 3 is that the areas with the highest ownership of three

100 years ago

In the early part of the 20th century, modes of transport and the need for travel to access shops and services were vastly different. In 1904 there were only 23,000 cars on the roads in Britain. In 2001, the number of private and light goods vehicles registered was 26.4 million. In London in 1904 the average off-peak travel speed for motorised transport was 12 mph. In central London during the period 2000-03 the average was less than 10 mph at all times. A hundred years ago cars would have been perceived as a luxury rather than a necessity, and lack of ownership would not necessarily have led to impediments to accessing goods and services.

For more information see 'A century of change: trends in UK statistics since 1900' (www.parliament.uk/commons/lib/ research/rp99/rp99-111.pdf); National Archives (www.nationalarchives.gov.uk); Department for Transport (www.dft.gov.uk).

Figure 2: The association between the percentage of households with 3+ cars in each area (X-axis) and the percentage of households with one or more dependent children and no car (Y-axis)

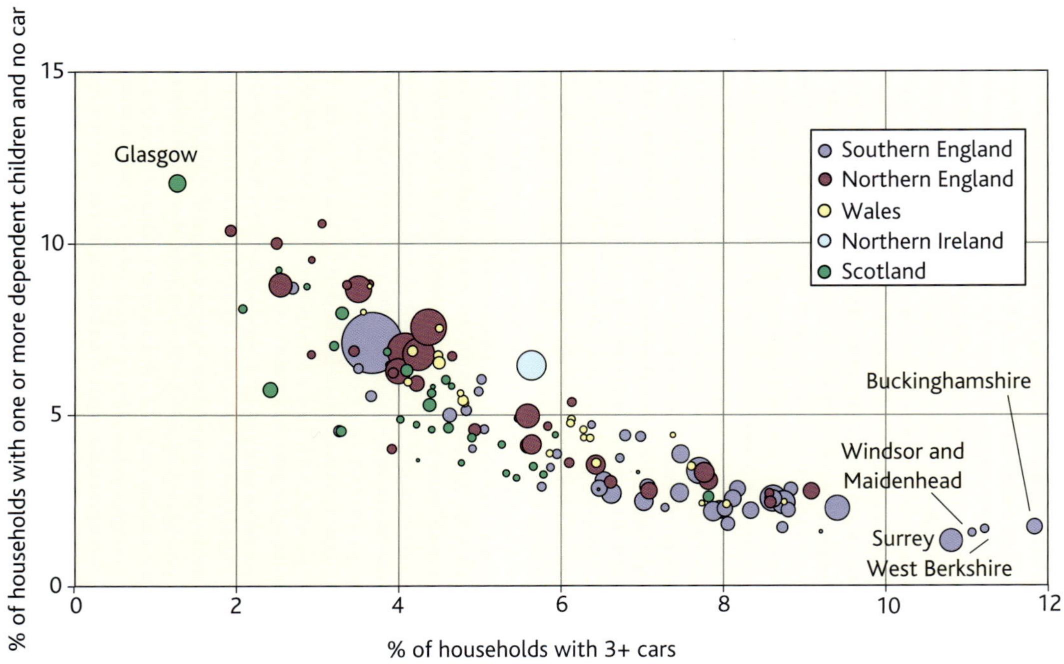

Note: Each circle is a county, unitary or former metropolitan authority, drawn with the area in proportion to the total population in 2001 (the largest circle represents London, with a population of just over 7 million). Areas in northern England are those that lie west or north of the counties of Gloucestershire, Warwickshire, Leicestershire and Lincolnshire (the Severn-Humber divide).

or more cars tend not to be deprived, remote agricultural areas where multiple vehicles may be vital. They are the wealthy areas to the west of London.

Tables 1 and 2 list the five areas with the highest percentage of households with dependent children and no car, and the five areas with the highest proportion of households with three or more cars. Table 1 suggests that those without a car but who might need one are often living in poorer urban areas. The places listed in Table 2 include some areas with rural populations, but certainly not those that could be thought of as at all remote.

Since 2001

Between 2001 and the end of 2003, the number of private and light goods vehicles (mostly cars) registered increased by 1.3 million to 27.7 million. There is no evidence for any change in the distribution of cars by household over this time, and the patterns observed here are unlikely to change quickly.

Discussion

Cars are so much a part of our society that not having access to one is generally taken to indicate not having enough money, as opposed to having made an ideological choice, especially for the parents of dependent children. Of course some people may have made that choice and others, especially older people, do not have a car because they no longer drive. However, as our society becomes ever more oriented to the car user, with out-of-town shops and supermarkets, the consequences of not having one grow larger.

As stated at the outset, this report is not about the pros and cons of having a car or whether it is right to have one (or two, or three...). Its aim is to contrast people at the opposite ends of a socio-economic spectrum to focus on the relationship between relative poverty, relative affluence, and geography. This report and the others in the series demonstrate that people from opposite ends of the socio-economic spectrum tend to be geographically separate as well as financially separate. They are

Figure 3: The percentage of households with dependent children and no car in each area in 2001

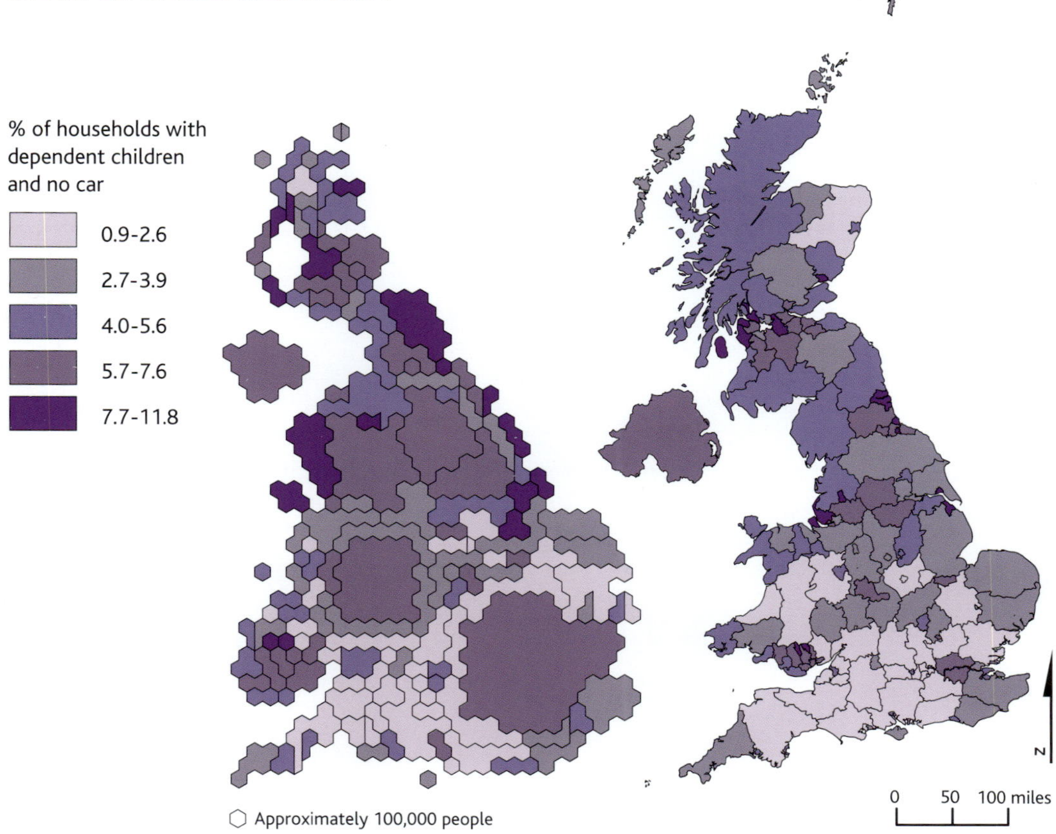

Figure 4: The geographical variation in the percentage of households with 3+ cars in 2001

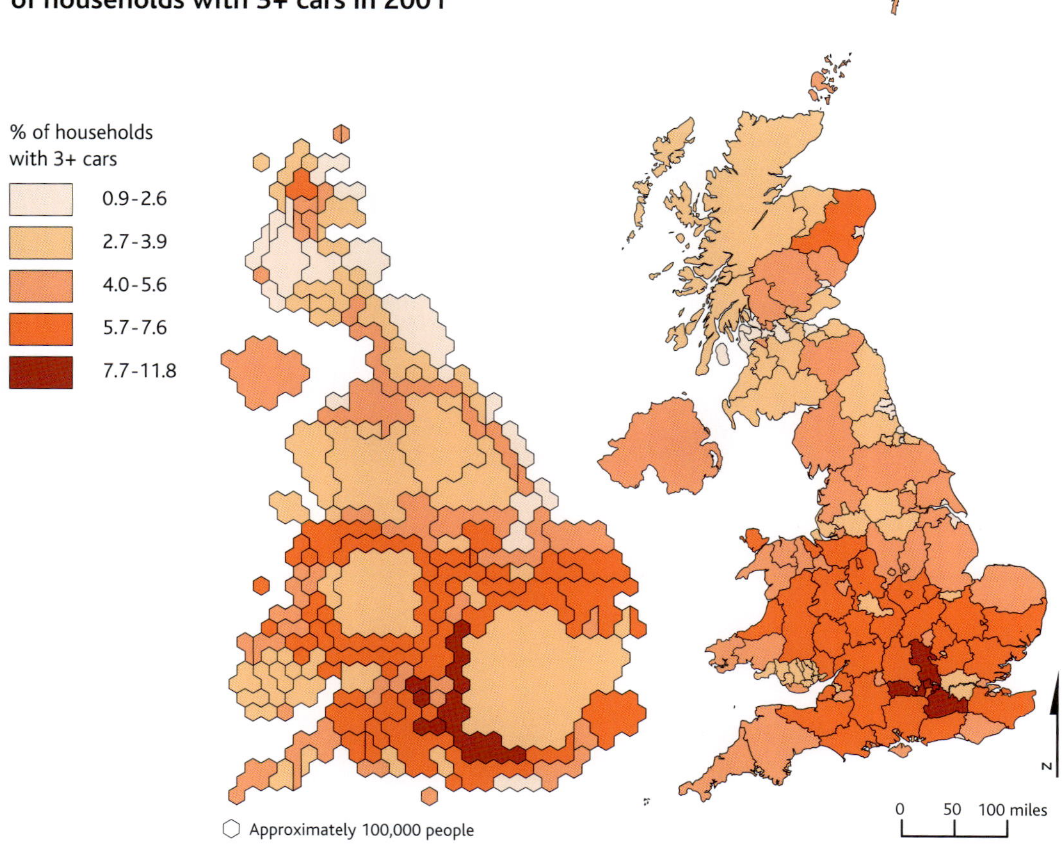

Note: Both maps in each figure represent the same places, shaded identically. The map on the left is a cartogram – each area is shown in proportion to the size of its population in 2001. The largest area is London, since it has the highest population of any of the places[TR]. The map on the right shows the actual boundaries of the areas.

increasingly from 'different worlds'. Curiously, the number of households 'in need of a car' is roughly equal to the number of households 'with more cars than they need'; indeed, it could be said that the number of people who have more than they need is about equal to those who need more. If we permit society to get ever more car-oriented, yet still want the number of cars to stay equal or even to fall, the issue of their distribution could be addressed. Policies which make it easier for a household with a real need for a car to get one, but which make it much more difficult for a household to move from two to three, or even three to four cars might contribute to holding the overall number of cars at a steady rate, while addressing the growing divide between 'car-haves' and 'car-have-nots' in the UK. Of course, reducing reliance on cars altogether might be the better solution.

Society as a whole does not lack the resources to allow everyone a more equal chance of a happier, easier and healthier life but the distribution of those resources is unequal. That inequality is etched into the geography of the UK.

Table 1: The five areas of the UK with the highest percentage of households that have dependent children and no car (2001)

Area	% of households with 3+ cars	% of households with dependent children and no car
Glasgow City	1.3	11.8
Middlesbrough UA	3.1	10.6
City of Kingston-upon-Hull UA	1.9	10.4
Nottingham UA	2.5	10.0
Hartlepool UA	2.9	9.5
UK average	**5.7**	**5.1**

Table 2: The five areas of the UK with the highest percentage of households that have 3+ cars (2001)

Area	% of households with 3+ cars	% of households with dependent children and no car
Wokingham UA	12.2	0.9
Buckinghamshire County	11.8	1.7
West Berkshire UA	11.2	1.7
Windsor and Maidenhead UA	11.1	1.5
Surrey	10.8	1.3
UK average	**5.7**	**5.1**

Note: UA = unitary authority.

Notes

1 'Public transport "can ease jams"' (http://news.bbc.co.uk, accessed 13 April 2004).

2 Department for Transport, Local Government and the Regions (2001) *Focus on personal travel: 2001 edition*, London: The Stationery Office, December.

3 'Rise of the four-car family' (http://news.bbc.co.uk, accessed 5 November 2004).

4 Dieleman, F.M., Dijst, M. and Burghouwt, G. (2002) 'Urban form and travel behaviour: micro-level household attributes and residential context', *Urban Studies*, vol 39, no 3, pp 507-27.

5 *Social Trends 31* (2001) London: The Stationery Office.

TR Further information on this point is available in the accompanying technical report.

What do we know?

- Car access is generally increasing in the UK and in 2000, for the first time, the proportion of households with two or more cars (28%) was higher than the proportion without a car.
- Some consider car access 'essential' for modern life, especially for those with dependent children and for those living in rural areas.

What have we found?

- About 5% of UK households have dependent children, but no access to a car.
- About 5% of UK households have three or more cars (but just one third of this group have dependent children).
- The number of UK households without a car, but arguably in need of one, is therefore about the same as the number of households in the UK with access to more cars than they might really need.
- The geography of these two groups means that they are largely physically separated from each other. They live, literally, in different worlds.

Other reports in the series

The companion report to this, *Home front*, looks at whether areas that have lots of families with no working parents tend to also have lots of young carers.

1. *Doctors and nurses*
2. *In sickness and in health*
3. *Teachers*
4. *Sons and daughters*
5. *Changing rooms*
6. *A place in the sun*
7. *The office*
8. *Open all hours*
9. *Top gear*
10. *Home front*

Contact details

The reports were prepared by Ben Wheeler, Mary Shaw, Richard Mitchell and Danny Dorling. The authors can be contacted via:
Professor Danny Dorling • Department of Geography • University of Sheffield • Winter Street • Sheffield S10 2TN
e-mail: danny.dorling@sheffield.ac.uk • www.sheffield.ac.uk/sasi

Project funder: Joseph Rowntree Foundation

JOSEPH ROWNTREE FOUNDATION

The POLICY PRESS

LIFE IN BRITAIN Using millennial Cen

HEALT

In 2001, 4.5 million people in the UK had both a limiting long-term illness and rated their general health as 'poor'. Areas with high rates of poor health tend to have fewer doctors and dentists, but more people providing informal care and support, than areas with lower rates of poor health.

The 2001 Census reveals the continuation of an 'inverse care law' with regard to paid health professionals, but a 'positive care law' with regard to informal care provided by friends and family.

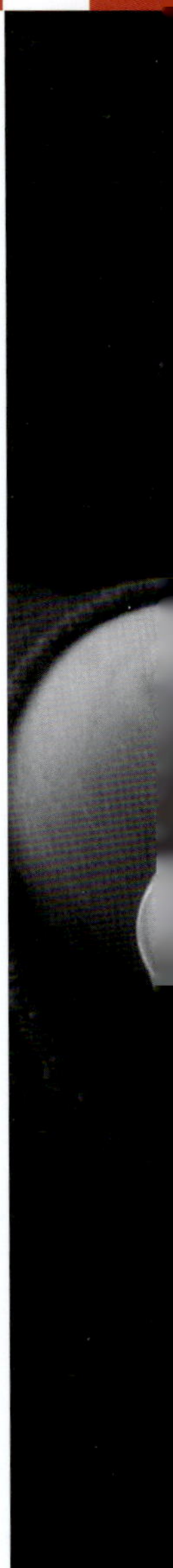

The i

Both maps in each figure represent the same places, shaded identically. The map on the left is a cartogram – each area is shown in proportion to the size of its population in 2001. The largest area is London, since it has the highest population of any of the places. The map on the right shows the actual boundaries of the areas.

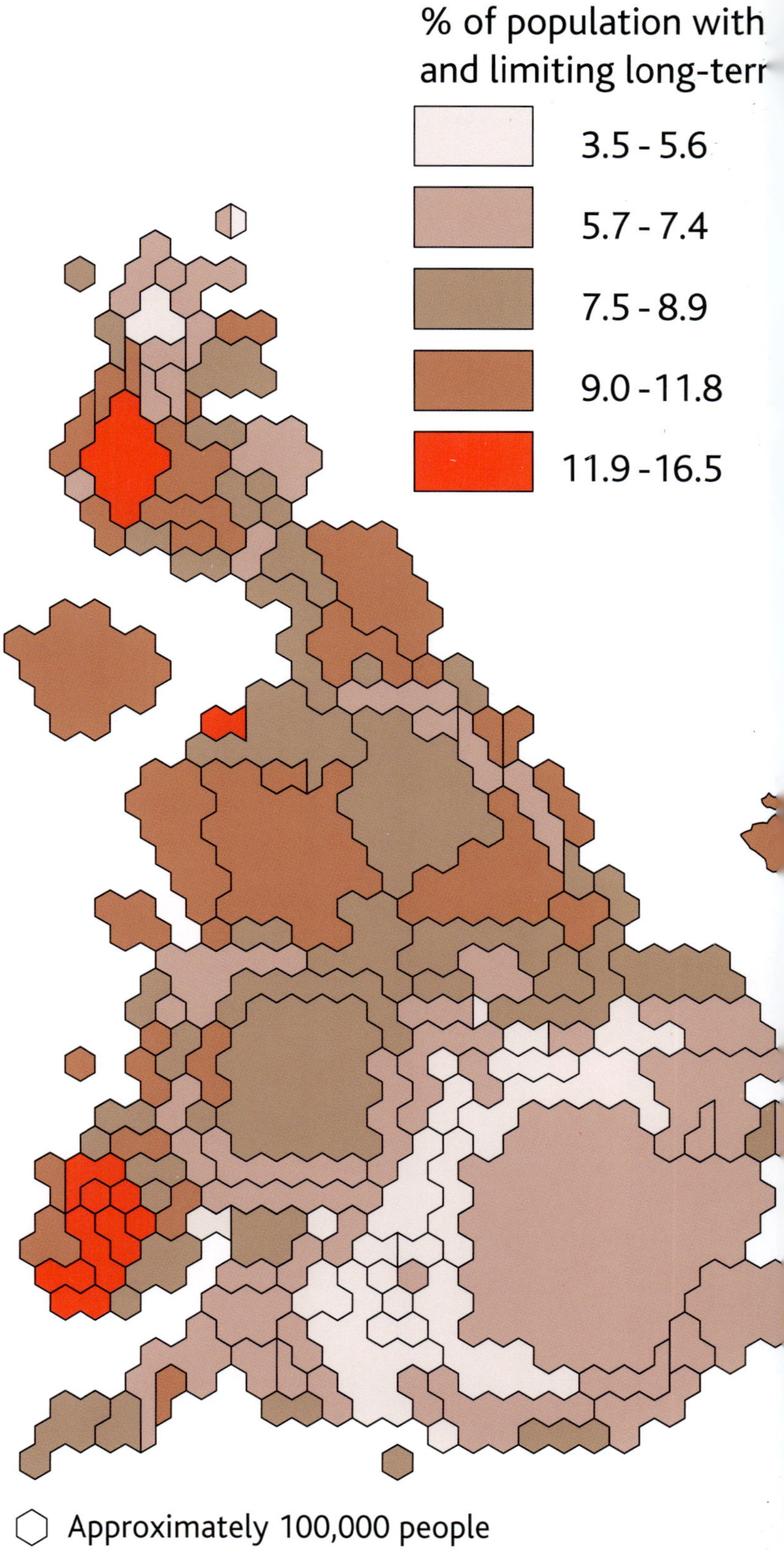

This poster accompanies a series of reports showing key patterns and inequalities in the UK revealed by the 2001 Census. The analyses focus on geographical inequalities, highlighting where services and opportunities appear not to be available or accessible to those people and places that need them most. Information on how to obtain the full reports that this poster is based on, along with the other topics covered by the project, are available at www.jrf.org.uk or www.sheffield.ac.uk/sasi

Poster and report
Bristol), Richard N
Text © University
Photographs © M
Design © The Poli
Project funder: Jo

r health
ness

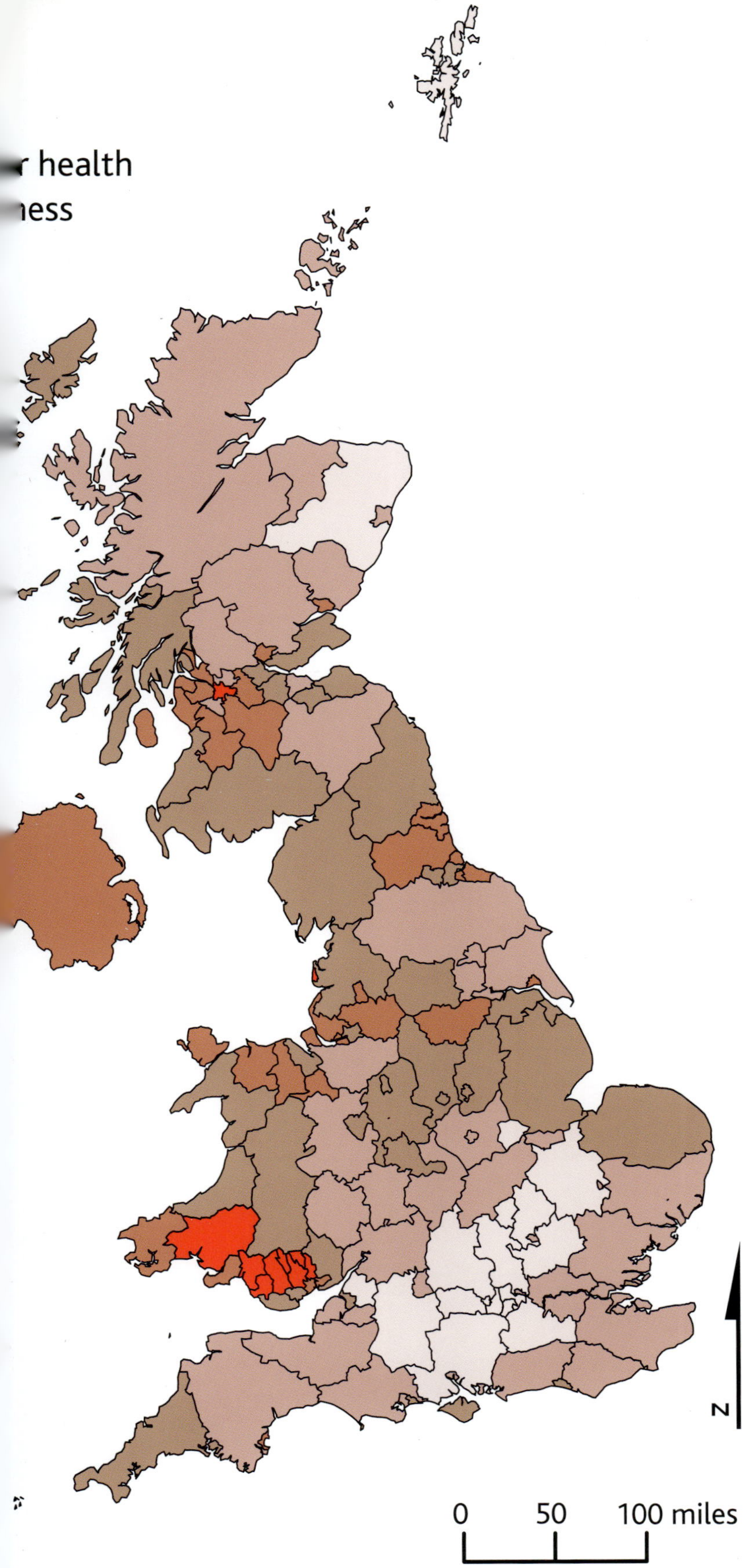

ıthors: Ben Wheeler (University of Sheffield), Mary Shaw (University of
chell (University of Edinburgh) and Danny Dorling (University of Sheffield)

JOSEPH ROWNTREE FOUNDATION
The POLICY PRESS

ıs data to understand poverty, inequality and place

ge above shows British Sign Language for 'access'

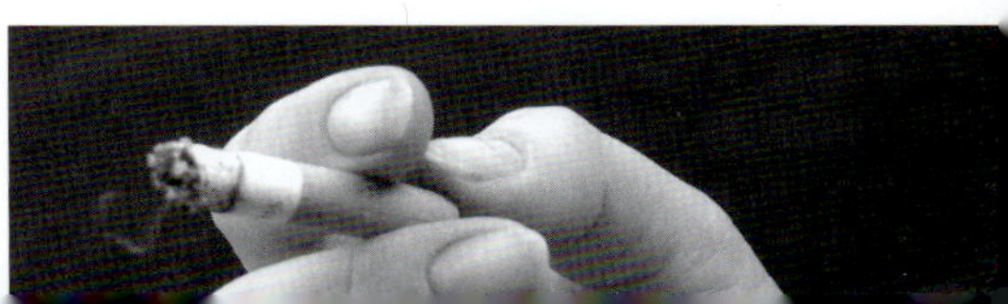

us data to understand poverty, inequality and place

NG

or 2
s

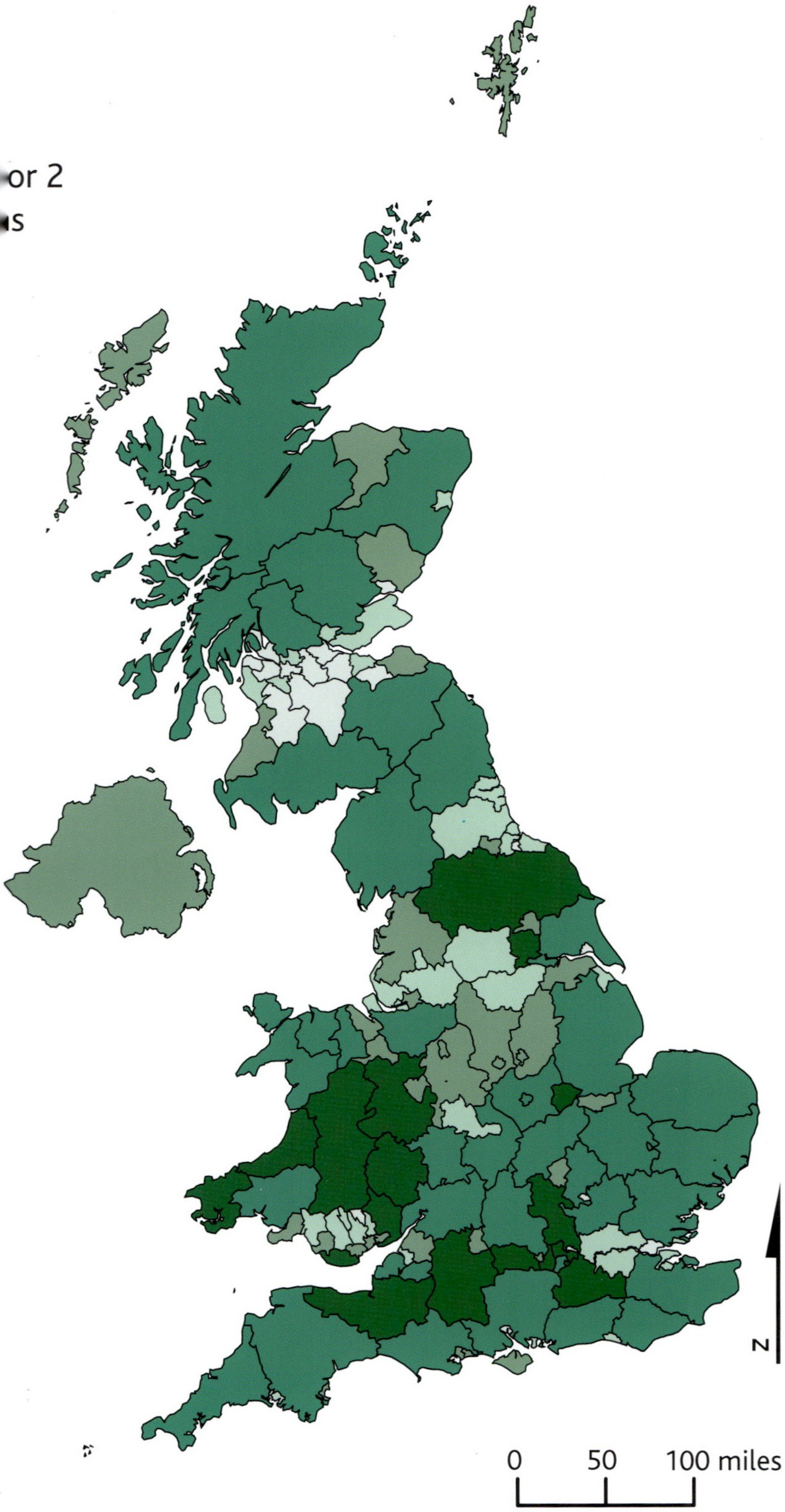

uthors: Ben Wheeler (University of Sheffield), Mary Shaw (University of
chell (University of Edinburgh) and Danny Dorling (University of Sheffield)

f Sheffield
y Shaw
Press
ph Rowntree Foundation

JOSEPH ROWNTREE FOUNDATION

The POLICY PRESS

tend to live in different areas.

Both maps in each figure represent the same places, shaded identically. The map on the left is a cartogram – each area is shown in proportion to the size of its population in 2001. The largest area is London, since it has the highest population of any of the places. The map on the right shows the actual boundaries of the areas.

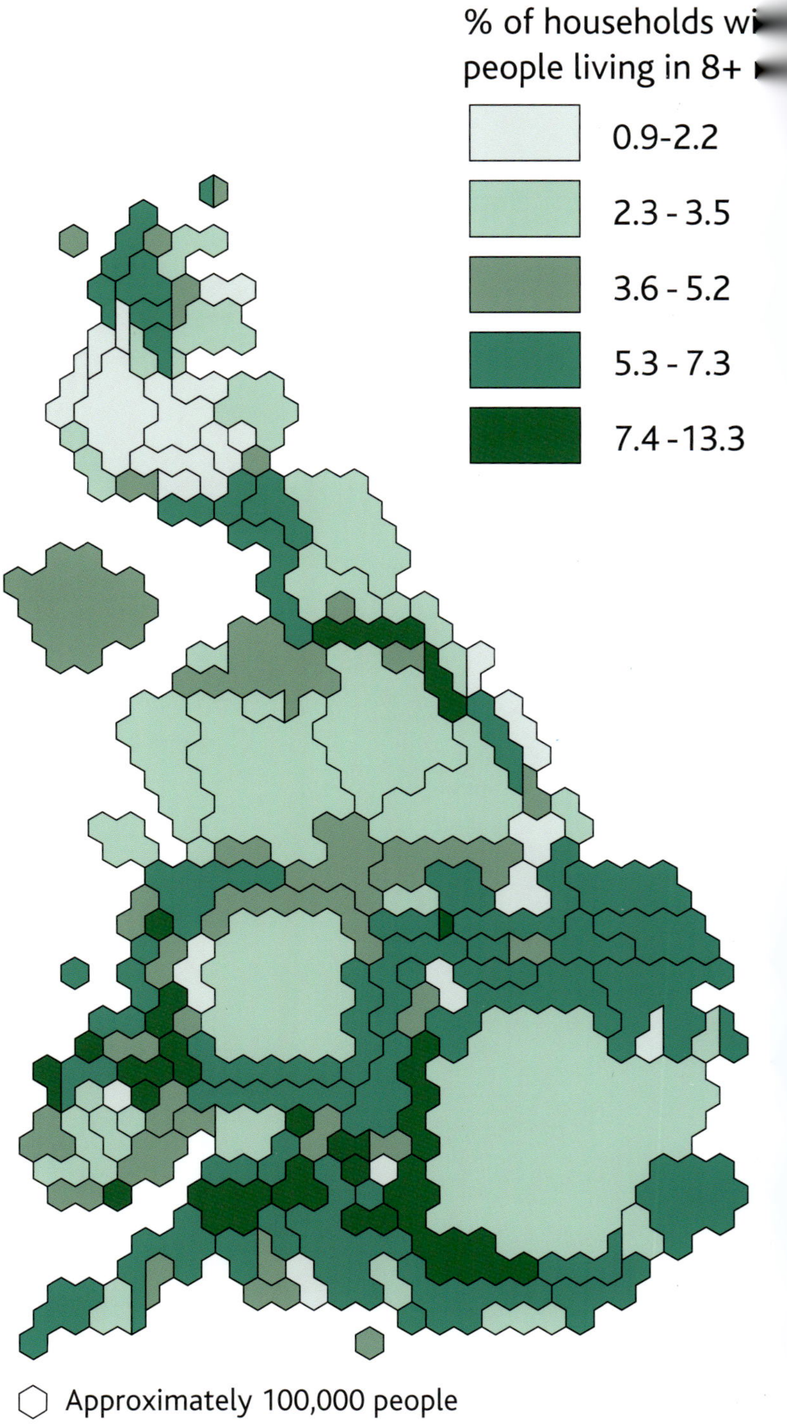

This poster accompanies a series of reports showing key patterns and inequalities in the UK revealed by the 2001 Census. The analyses focus on geographical inequalities, highlighting where services and opportunities appear not to be available or accessible to those people and places that need them most. Information on how to obtain the full reports that this poster is based on, along with the other topics covered by the project, are available at www.jrf.org.uk or www.sheffield.ac.uk/sasi

Poster and report
Bristol), Richard M

Project funder: Jo

LIFE IN BRITAIN Using millennial Cen

HOUSI

Of the 24.5 million households recorded in the 2001 Census, 466,000 (1.9%) had more people than rooms. About 1 million households – 4.3% – had one or two people living in eight or more rooms. Areas with a high rate of overcrowding tend to have a low number of 'underoccupied homes'.

This does not imply that people in households that have been classified as 'underoccupied' are doing something wrong. However, the analyses does show the geographical divide between people who live in overcrowded conditions and those who live in relatively spacious accommodation. These two groups

LIFE IN BRITAIN

Using millennial Census data to understand poverty, inequality and place

Technical report

Ben Wheeler, Mary Shaw, Richard Mitchell and Danny Dorling

JOSEPH ROWNTREE FOUNDATION

The POLICY PRESS

First published in Great Britain in September 2005 by

The Policy Press
Fourth Floor, Beacon House
Queen's Road
Bristol BS8 1QU
UK

Tel no +44 (0)117 331 4054
Fax no +44 (0)117 331 4093
E-mail tpp-info@bristol.ac.uk
www.policypress.org.uk

Published for the Joseph Rowntree Foundation by The Policy Press. The research and the material for the pack was developed as part of the Joseph Rowntree Foundation's programme of research and innovative development projects (www.jrf.org.uk).

ISBN 1 86134 773 1

British Library Cataloguing in Publication Data
A catalogue record for this report is available from the British Library.

Library of Congress Cataloging-in-Publication Data
A catalog record for this report has been requested.

Dr Ben Wheeler, Department of Geography, University of Sheffield. **Dr Mary Shaw**, Department of Social Medicine, University of Bristol and South West Public Health Observatory. **Dr Richard Mitchell**, Research Unit In Health, Behaviour and Change, University of Edinburgh Medical School. **Professor Danny Dorling**, Department of Geography, University of Sheffield.

Printed in Great Britain by TL Visuals, Bristol.

Contents

Acknowledgements

All photographs used in this technical report are © Mary Shaw, 2005.

Thanks to all who participated in the photographs, especially those who agreed to have their shoes photographed. Thanks also to Anne Harrop, David Dorling and a number of other reviewers for comments on earlier drafts.

Census data and boundaries are © Crown Copyright, and were obtained via ESRC/JISC agreements (see www.census.ac.uk) and directly from the national statistical agencies concerned.

Mary Shaw is funded by the South West Public Health Observatory (SWPHO). Richard Mitchell and the Research Unit in Health, Behaviour and Change are funded by the Chief Scientist Office of the Scottish Executive Health Department (SEHD) and NHS Health Scotland. The opinions expressed in this report are those of the authors and not of SWPHO, SEHD or the Health Education Board for Scotland (HEBS).

Summary

This project uses publicly available data from the 2001 Census to address aspects of inequalities in five key themes in the UK at the start of the 21st century: Health, Education, Housing, Employment and Poverty. These are, and have long been, important themes of interest and closely reflect the five 'Giant Evils' identified by William Beveridge (architect of the UK Welfare State): Disease, Ignorance, Squalor, Idleness and Want (Beveridge, 1942). This project provides an illustration, through 10 examples (two for each of the five key themes), of the overall picture of social inequalities in modern Britain. (See 'Areas' on page 4 of this report for our definition of geographical terms.)

The research takes a simple approach: it does not use complex analyses of small areas, it does not conduct international or longitudinal comparisons, nor contain systematic reviews of the literature for the wide subject areas covered. Instead, a selection of data from the Census are used, analysed with simple methods, and areas that are familiar and that have political and social meaning are used. This simple method is adequate to demonstrate that clear and obvious social inequalities in the UK remain to this day.

1

Introduction

This technical report provides background information and further detail on the analyses presented in the series of 10 reports and five posters, collectively entitled *Life in Britain*. The aim of this report is both to provide enough information to allow the work to be replicated and to demonstrate how all the reports are related. First, the use of the Census to record aspects of life in Britain is discussed. Then it is suggested that the Census can be used to reveal wide social inequalities for which more sophisticated analysis may be unnecessarily complex. Basic inequalities can be made clear to see through simple methods.

The Census is the decade's unique record of the extent to which poverty, work, overcrowding, good health, education and many other aspects of life have become more or less concentrated in particular places in the UK. No other source of information is as comprehensive. Similarly, the Census is the only means of determining whether policies aimed at reducing concentrations of poverty and inequalities in outcome and opportunity in particular places are working. The Census allows us to concentrate on long-term social changes and is a useful antidote to political emphasis on shorter-term evaluation. However, it is used here to simply consider a snapshot in time – to take a social photograph of life in Britain in April 2001. Each report also briefly mentions trends from the past up to 2001 and considers changes since 2001 in order to provide a little context.

Given the advantages of the Census it is surprising that in the past the Census tends to have been used to consider fairly narrow definitions of poverty and well being. People are more usually labelled as 'poor' in the Census if they are seen to lack certain attributes (such as employment or a car), and 'well off' if they have cars, are owner-occupiers or are employed. The most sophisticated work on poverty using the Census, such as the Breadline Britain study (Gordon and Pantazis, 1997), utilises the Census in conjunction with sample surveys to estimate the number of people living in poverty and to illustrate where the poor live. However, even this work only makes use of a fraction of what the whole Census can tell us about poverty, affluence, place and the processes that link them, and many other aspects of life in Britain.

Background

Previous work on the Census in Britain has tended to concentrate on aspects of poverty – who does not have what, where they are, and how such things are changing. To be poor is not to have, or not to have access to, certain things (possessions, resources and opportunities) that are increasingly seen as essential for a 'reasonable' standard of living. Money is the most obvious of these but the Census does not ask about income or wealth. What the Census does do well is to record where many of the possessions, resources and opportunities actually are which the poor are often claimed to lack. This project examined five themes of general resources and opportunities that the poor are often claimed to be lacking, each associated with one of the five great evils (see page v): employment opportunities, healthcare, housing provision, material needs and good education. Two reports were produced on each of these five themes. For each report, the Census was used to determine where these resources and opportunities are most highly concentrated.

There is plenty of research to show that good jobs, healthcare, better housing, material wealth and educational opportunities have been slowly and steadily moving geographically away from poor areas to concentrate in rich places. However, the concentration of research efforts on poor people and poor places has partly obscured our understanding of the processes that actually create poverty and maintain poor places. The Census counts everybody. It can be used to see a fuller picture. Without this fuller picture some of the processes by which poverty and affluence become concentrated in particular places are missed. The Census has already revealed that the relationship between the age structure of the population, and where people live within Britain, has been changing and that inequalities between richer and poorer people and places have grown (Dorling and Rees, 2003; Ballas, 2004; Boyle et al, 2004; Thomas and Dorling, 2004). The 2001 UK Census also updated our understanding of the population of the UK and contained several new questions. As more research on the Census takes place, it will change our understanding of society in this country. Even its basic count of the population revealed that a large group of mainly young men who were born in Britain and who were previously assumed to have been living here have actually left the country. The Key Statistics, released in February 2003, showed that Britain had polarised socially by area almost as much in the 1990s as it did in the 1980s (Dorling and Rees, 2003).

This project reveals the broad locations, circumstances and number of the most disadvantaged in society by contrasting the opportunities and resources to which they have access with those owned by, and available to, the more advantaged. The research uncovers the geographical relationship between poverty, affluence and area. It differs from work on 'deprivation indices' because it takes focused examples of the relationship between need and supply for very specific services or opportunities, rather than combining multiple indicators of circumstances that 'suggest' poverty. In simple terms, this work is about providing real examples of the different worlds in which the 'haves' and 'have nots' live in Britain.

Themes

The project has five main themes that are centred around the relationships between the need for, and the supply of, opportunity and resources. Where the supply of something is in proportion to – and meeting – need, the relationship between them is said to be 'positive'. However, when the availability of a resource or an opportunity is the opposite of the need for it (that is to say, where there is a great need for something yet it is hard to find or obtain, or where there is little need for it, but it is available in abundance), that relationship is said to be 'inverse'. A well-known example of an inverse relationship is called the inverse care law – first suggested by Tudor Hart in 1971 (Tudor Hart, 1971). He proposed that medical services are distributed inversely to population health needs, and that this law operates more completely where medical care is most exposed to market forces (see Shaw and Dorling, 2004). For each of the five themes, two reports consider different aspects of the relationship between supply and demand for resources and opportunities, and their geographies.

The five themes covered in the 10 reports and five posters this report supports are:

1) Health and care: the availability of health professionals and informal carers to ill people, updating Tudor Hart's study of the 1970s.
2) Education: young people's qualifications, the educational attainment of people in their parents' generation and the availability of teachers.
3) Housing: overcrowding, underoccupation, the prevalence of second residences and households that might be having difficulty getting on to the property ladder.
4) Employment: employment in well-rewarded high-status jobs, the distribution of skills, unemployment and people working long hours.
5) Poverty: the potential need for, and possible excess of, access to cars, the distribution of families with no working parent and young people providing informal care.

Methods

Simple quantitative methods are used for this project. Correlation coefficients are the most complex of the methods employed (and even they are only shown in this technical report, rather than in the 10 main reports). There is no need for complex models or analyses, given how strong and understandable many of the basic inequalities are. Graphics and maps are used throughout to illustrate findings. A crucial aspect of the project is the use of contemporary photography to bring life to the findings.

Sometimes those working with geographical areas are criticised for assuming that the findings for an area as a whole can be applied to all the individuals living there. This is called the ecological fallacy. However, working with the Census means that the information that almost everyone in each of the areas gave is being used. It also known from many other studies that the impact of the ecological fallacy is easy to over-estimate and that working in this way also avoids the (less well-known, but equally pernicious) atomistic fallacy. That is, where studies of individuals, rather than groups, leads to incorrect generalisations. The methods used here are appropriate for the purpose of the study.

The methods used in each report are broadly the same. The characteristics, opportunities and resources representing the 'supply and demand' of interest are selected. Appropriate Census data are extracted from the Census database and the distribution is explored using maps, graphs and charts. In determining which are the most appropriate data to use, the authors have often had to fall back on their experiences of working with the three Censuses before 2001. Thus their findings will be both influenced by, and may benefit from, their past work. The results are then commented on and illustrated with photographs and a discussion of contemporary trends.

Each report also contains an illustrative section on circumstances '100 years ago'. This section is intended to provided some historical context – where possible relevant information from the 1901 Census is included, otherwise other pertinent information from around that time is briefly mentioned. Although Censuses have been conducted since 1801 in the UK, these earliest surveys were only really population counts, and it is only since late Victorian times that poverty has featured prominently on the social and political agenda.

2

Technical details

Census data

The Census is the only means of assessing the socio-demographic make-up of (almost) the entire population of the UK. New systems to try and capture absolutely everyone and adjust the figures to estimate who was missed mean that the 2001 Census is the most complete and accurate social survey dataset available in Britain. However, it does not actually give very much detail on individuals or households because the Census takers promise that no one individual or household will be identifiable within the data they publish. That is why all of the analyses carried out for this project are 'ecological'. They compare groups of people, or areas, rather than individuals. The reports compare rates or percentages of the population with particular characteristics across areas of the country.

The Census database stores data via a system of data tables and table cells. The tables used to derive each variable selected for each report are given in Chapter 3. Chapter 3 also details the exact Census table cell references used to derive each variable. The tables can be obtained from the statistics agency for each country:

- England and Wales: National Statistics (www.statistics.gov.uk)
- Scotland: General Register Office for Scotland (www.gro-scotland.gov.uk)
- Northern Ireland: Northern Ireland Statistics and Research Agency (www.nisra.gov.uk).

As described above, the quantity of data analysed here and in previous work is vast, and yet it is only a small fraction of the Census dataset. Selection was made on the basis of keeping the analysis as simple as possible, using measures that are quite easy to understand and have direct relevance to the five key issues addressed, and given the authors' past experience of working with these data. The authors have no great concerns over the quality of the Census data that is far better than all other surveys (as they rely on it!) and recent Censuses (as they were not corrected properly for missing people).

Areas

Much has been made of the area-based nature of this research and here the authors explain what areas they use throughout this work. All reports in the series analyse data for counties, unitary authorities, former metropolitan authorities, council areas (in Scotland) and Northern Ireland as a whole. These areas were used in these analyses to provide a geographical framework of largely self-contained units with relevance and familiarity to non-specialist audiences. The areas were chosen for being familiar, with relevance to administrative units and to highlight national and regional rather than local (within city) divides. For convenience the terms Britain and the UK are used interchangeably throughout this report. Although the former term does not include Northern Ireland, the province is included wherever possible in the research.

As stated in the Summary, no complex small area analyses are carried out. Instead, the research is conducted at a spatial scale that has relevance to policy setting at local, regional and national (rather than micro/neighbourhood) levels. In many cases, the neighbourhood level would be too small, given that the authors discuss and analyse housing and job markets that operate across larger geographic areas. The availability of certain professionals (such as doctors) based on residential location is investigated, and the use of small-area data here would invalidate the analysis due to commuting patterns. The use of the former metropolitan authorities means that the large conurbations are considered in their entirety, rather than dividing them up along rather arbitrary political boundaries. In practice, given how clear many of the patterns are, the use of slightly different areas would have little impact on the results. The use of the formal administrative boundaries also means that the Census data used for the analyses can easily and precisely be identified, but the analyses could be replicated at any geographic scale.

Cartograms and maps

Cartograms as well as maps are used to show the spatial distribution of inequalities. A cartogram is an alternative way to represent a set of areas. Instead of representing the physical boundaries of areas, the cartograms show areas defined in proportion to some variable of interest. The counties and unitary authorities used in the analyses here are represented using a cartogram where the area is approximately proportional to the 2001 population. The cartogram is useful because it allows us to see the areas which are physically small, but which have large populations in them (such as cities). They also serve to de-emphasise rural areas that may be physically very large, but relatively small in population terms.

All of the maps presented in the reports and posters use an automated classification scheme based on Jenks' 'natural breaks' method (Jenks, 1977), available as standard in most geographic information system (GIS) software packages (ESRI, 2002). This method of classifying the data minimises variation within classes across the range of the data. While other classification schemes could have been applied here, the use of a single automated system across the series means that the maps have not been individually manipulated to produce any particular representation of the data. In short, if you were to download the data used for the standard geographies and were to then map them using the industry standard software package and the standard classification method employed, you would produce identical maps and cartograms to those shown throughout this work.

The cartogram 'shape files' are available from www.shef.ac.uk/sasi. Figure 1 provides a key to the cartograms used in all of the reports. Note that on the cartogram, the largest areas are the West Midlands, Greater Manchester, West and South Yorkshire former metropolitan counties, London, Glasgow and Northern Ireland. The smallest are the island communities of Orkney and Shetland. All of the areas very roughly equate to housing and labour markets, and all are familiar.

Figure 2 gives a similar key to the geographical map boundaries. Note how many areas are hardly visible on this conventional map; there was not even space to add small numeric labels within a number of the areas. Areas where the label has had to be displaced account for a total 2001 population of about three million, yet they are very difficult to see clearly on this map. The cartogram therefore aids interpretation of the geographical patterns described in the reports.

Figure 3 includes cartograms of a selection of variables from the reports. Each cartogram shows a pattern, and these can be summarised as north/south, urban/rural, core/periphery, or a combination of such. The South of England tends to be 'better off' than the North in terms of: population with limiting long-term illness and poor health; car ownership; unemployment; provision of informal care (including that provided by young carers, but with the acknowledgement that having to provide informal care has some positive as well as negative consequences); proportion of well-qualified people in jobs at the top of the socio-economic spectrum; well-qualified population (with the exception of most of Scotland, which also has a high proportion of older people with degrees); and medical practitioner availability. The North is only 'better off' than the South in terms of the availability of nurses, midwives and health visitors, and having fewer people working long hours (with the obvious caveat that a possible lack of full-time work opportunities may also have negative consequences).

Rural areas tend to have lower unemployment than urban areas, and also to have fewer families with dependent children where no parent is in employment. Rural areas also tend to have greater availability of teachers (per head of school-age population) and lower rates of overcrowded housing. However, they also have lower proportions of their well-qualified populations in jobs at the top of the socio-economic classification. The South East (of England) 'core' has greater availability of good jobs than the 'periphery'; more households with multiple car ownership; and fewer people with good qualifications in jobs at the bottom of the socio-economic classification. The 10 reports describe these patterns in greater detail, but Figure 3 gives a broad overview of the major patterns to geographical inequalities in the UK in 2001.

Figure 1: Key to cartograms

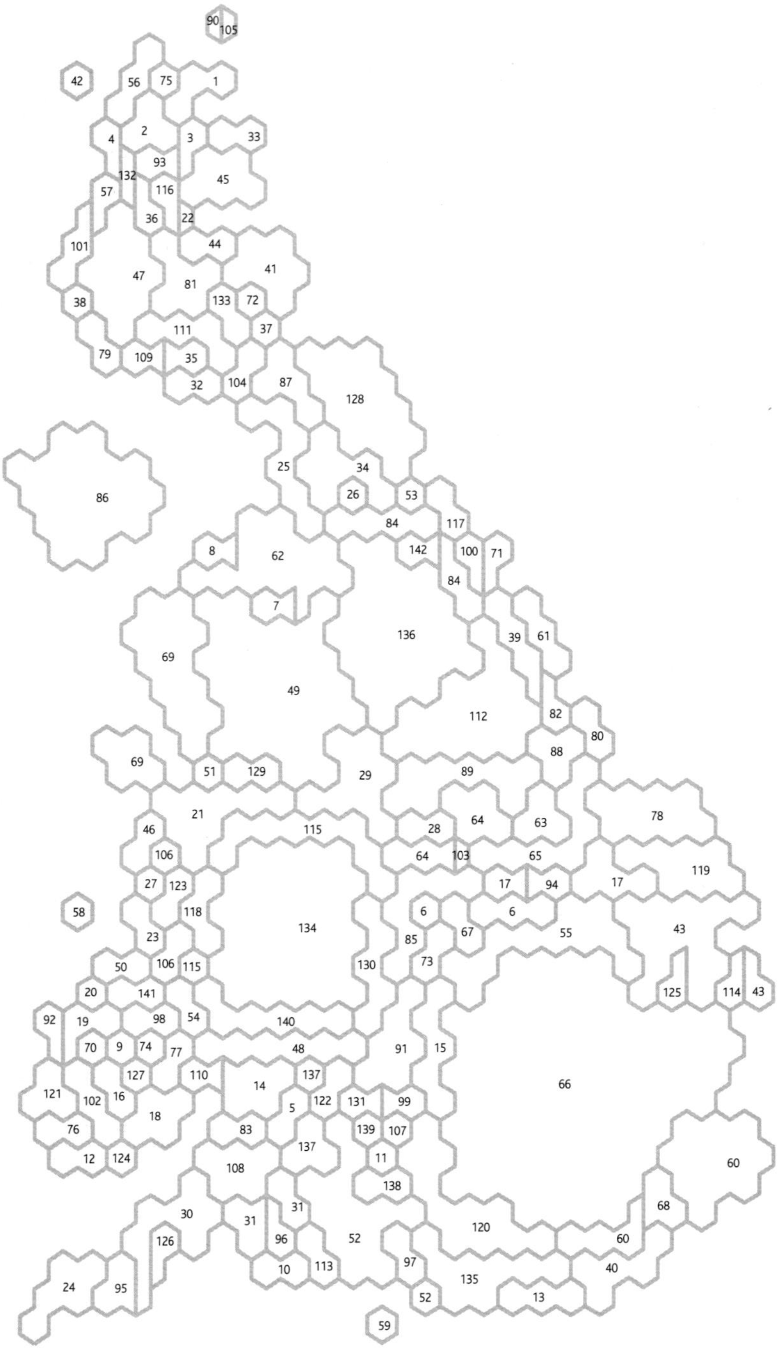

Area name	Label
Aberdeen City CA	1
Aberdeenshire CA	2
Angus CA	3
Argyll and Bute CA	4
Bath and North East Somerset UA	5
Bedfordshire County	6
Blackburn with Darwen UA	7
Blackpool UA	8
Blaenau Gwent	9
Bournemouth UA	10
Bracknell Forest UA	11
Bridgend	12
Brighton and Hove UA	13
Bristol; City of UA	14
Buckinghamshire County	15
Caerphilly	16
Cambridgeshire County	17
Cardiff	18
Carmarthenshire	19
Ceredigion	20
Cheshire County	21
Clackmannanshire CA	22
Conwy	23
Cornwall and the Isles of Scilly	24
Cumbria	25
Darlington UA	26
Denbighshire	27
Derby UA	28
Derbyshire County	29
Devon County	30
Dorset County	31
Dumfries and Galloway CA	32
Dundee City CA	33
Durham County	34
East Ayrshire CA	35
East Dunbartonshire CA	36
East Lothian CA	37
East Renfrewshire CA	38
East Riding of Yorkshire UA	39
East Sussex County	40
Edinburgh CA	41
Eilean Siar CA	42
Essex County	43
Falkirk CA	44
Fife CA	45
Flintshire	46
Glasgow City CA	47
Gloucestershire	48
Greater Manchester (Met County)	49
Gwynedd	50
Halton UA	51
Hampshire County	52
Hartlepool UA	53
Herefordshire; County of UA	54
Hertfordshire	55
Highland CA	56
Inverclyde CA	57
Isle of Anglesey	58
Isle of Wight UA	59
Kent County	60
Kingston upon Hull; City of UA	61
Lancashire County	62
Leicester UA	63
Leicestershire County	64
Lincolnshire	65
London	66
Luton UA	67
Medway UA	68
Merseyside (Met County)	69
Merthyr Tydfil	70
Middlesbrough UA	71
Midlothian CA	72
Milton Keynes UA	73
Monmouthshire	74
Moray CA	75
Neath Port Talbot	76
Newport	77
Norfolk	78
North Ayrshire CA	79
North East Lincolnshire UA	80
North Lanarkshire CA	81
North Lincolnshire UA	82
North Somerset UA	83
North Yorkshire County	84
Northamptonshire	85
Northern Ireland	86
Northumberland	87
Nottingham UA	88
Nottinghamshire County	89
Orkney Islands CA	90
Oxfordshire	91
Pembrokeshire	92
Perth and Kinross CA	93
Peterborough UA	94
Plymouth UA	95
Poole UA	96
Portsmouth UA	97
Powys	98
Reading UA	99
Redcar and Cleveland UA	100
Renfrewshire CA	101
Rhondda; Cynon; Taff	102
Rutland UA	103
Scottish Borders	104
Shetland Islands CA	105
Shropshire County	106
Slough UA	107
Somerset	108
South Ayrshire CA	109
South Gloucestershire UA	110
South Lanarkshire CA	111
South Yorkshire (Met County)	112
Southampton UA	113
Southend-on-Sea UA	114
Staffordshire County	115
Stirling CA	116
Stockton-on-Tees UA	117
Stoke-on-Trent UA	118
Suffolk	119
Surrey	120
Swansea	121
Swindon UA	122
Telford and Wrekin UA	123
The Vale of Glamorgan	124
Thurrock UA	125
Torbay UA	126
Torfaen	127
Tyne and Wear (Met County)	128
Warrington UA	129
Warwickshire	130
West Berkshire UA	131
West Dunbartonshire CA	132
West Lothian CA	133
West Midlands (Met County)	134
West Sussex	135
West Yorkshire (Met County)	136
Wiltshire County	137
Windsor and Maidenhead UA	138
Wokingham UA	139
Worcestershire County	140
Wrexham	141
York UA	142

Note:
UA: unitary authority
CA: council area

Figure 2 [For key to maps please refer to Figure 1]

Figure 3: Cartograms of a selection of the variables analysed in the reports (see note on page 9)

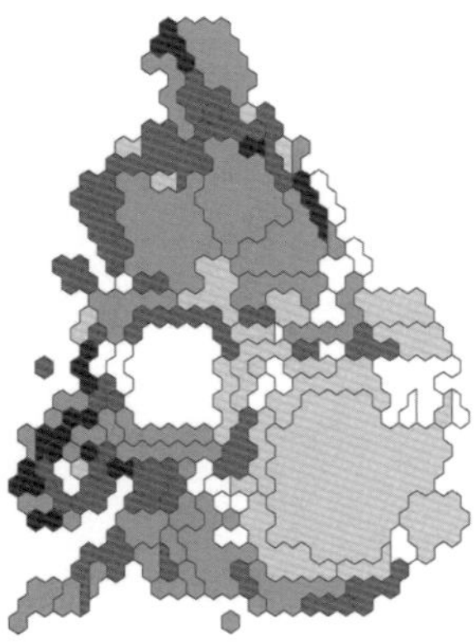

Working, qualified nurses, midwives and health visitors per head of population (north/south and urban/rural)

% of population with limiting long-term illness and poor health (north/south)

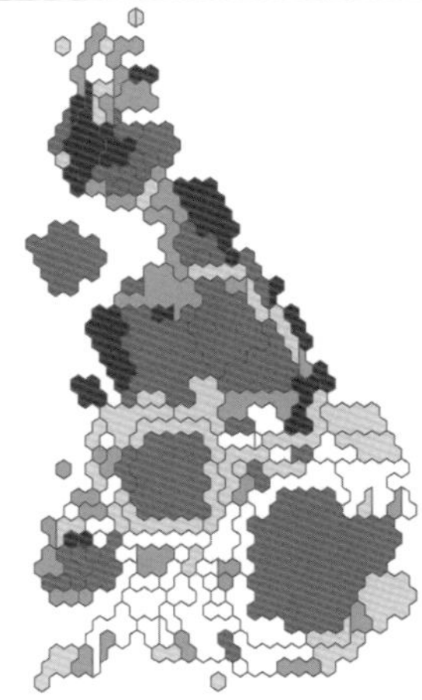

% of households that have dependent children and no car (north/south)

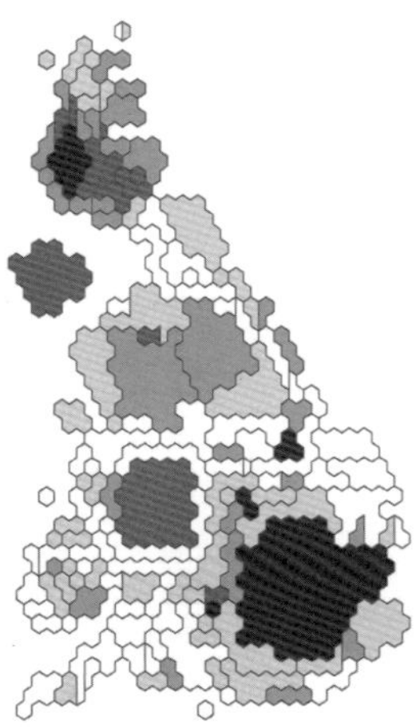

% of households with more people than rooms (urban/rural)

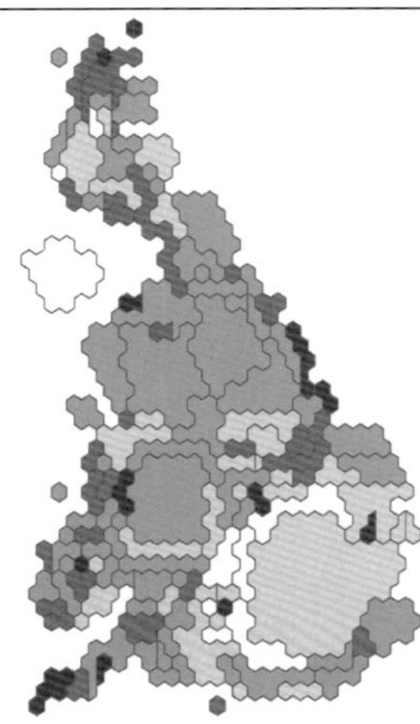

% of people with good qualifications doing jobs in the lowest levels of the socio-economic classification (core/periphery)

% of population providing 50+ hours of informal care a week (north/south)

% of population aged 30-54 that are unemployed (north/south and urban/rural)

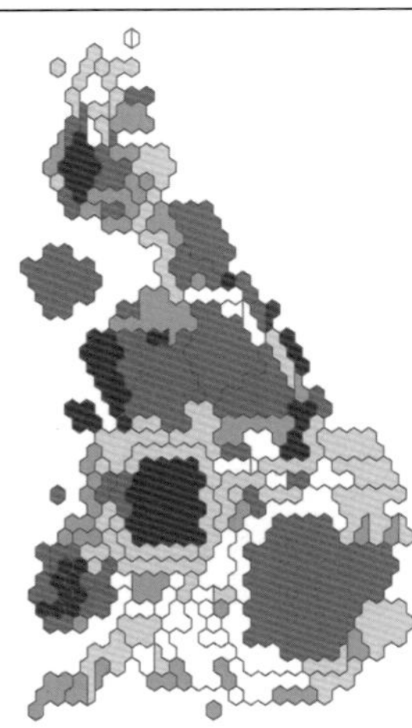

% of parents with dependent children in families where no parent works (urban/rural)

% of 5-17 year olds providing 20+ hours of informal care a week (north/south)

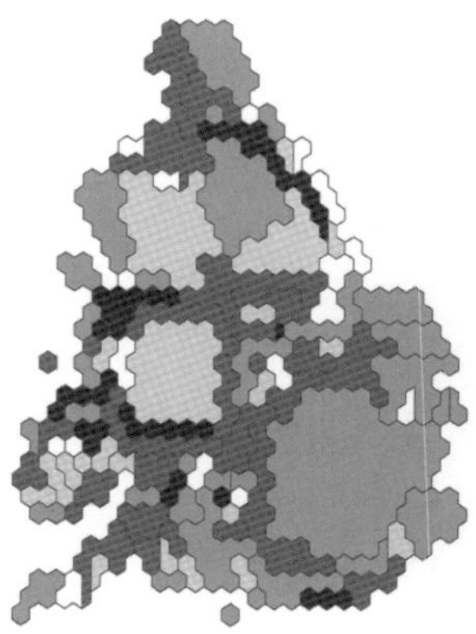

Working, qualified teaching professionals per 100 5-15 year olds in the population (urban/rural)

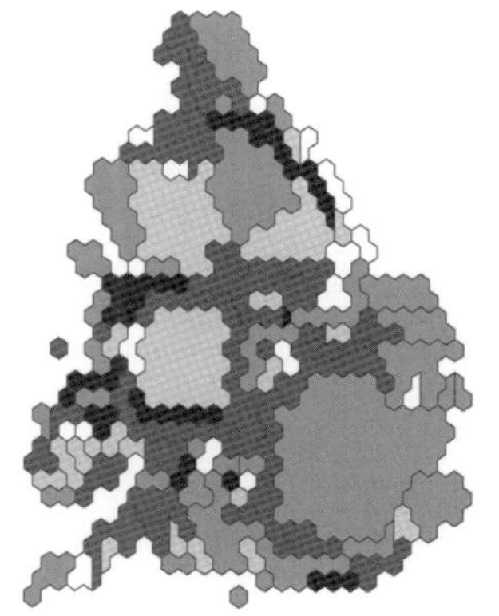

% of households with one or two people living in eight or more rooms (urban/rural)

% of people with good qualifications doing jobs in the highest levels of the socio-economic classification (urban/rural and north/south)

% of employed people aged 30-54 working 49+ hours a week (urban/rural and north/south)

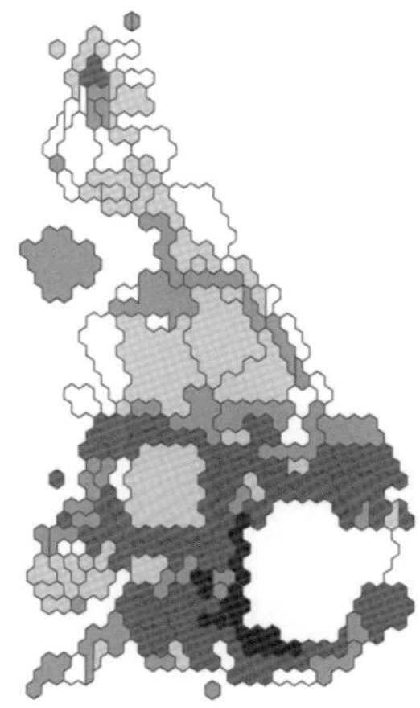

% of households that have three or more cars (north/south and core/periphery)

Other qualified health professionals (not doctors, nurses, dentists) per head of population (north/south)

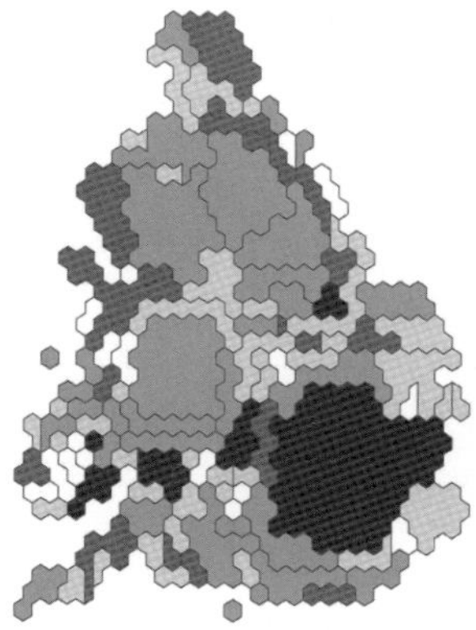

Working, qualified medical practitioners per head of population (north/south)

% of population working in occupations in the top levels of the socio-economic classification (core/periphery)

% of 40-54 year olds with degree-level qualifications (north/south excluding Scotland)

Note: In all maps, darker shades indicate higher percentages/rates per head of population. The dominant pattern as indicated in the text is noted for each cartogram.

Correlation coefficients

The correlation coefficient gives a statistical measure of how closely two variables are related. A good way to think about the relationship between variables is to see them on a graph (see Figure 4 for some examples). The correlation coefficient is a numerical way of describing how tightly the points on the graphs fit a straight line. The coefficient gives an indication of the strength of the relationship between the two variables, and a measure of statistical significance can be calculated to indicate the reliability of the coefficient. The coefficient can vary between +1 and –1. A correlation coefficient of +1 indicates a perfect, positive linear relationship between the two variables; –1 indicates a perfect, negative linear relationship and 0 indicates no linear relationship. The correlation coefficient does not tell us anything about the slope of the line – that is, to what degree one variable increases as the other increases/decreases.

Figure 4: Examples of the sign and magnitude of correlation between two variables, X and Y

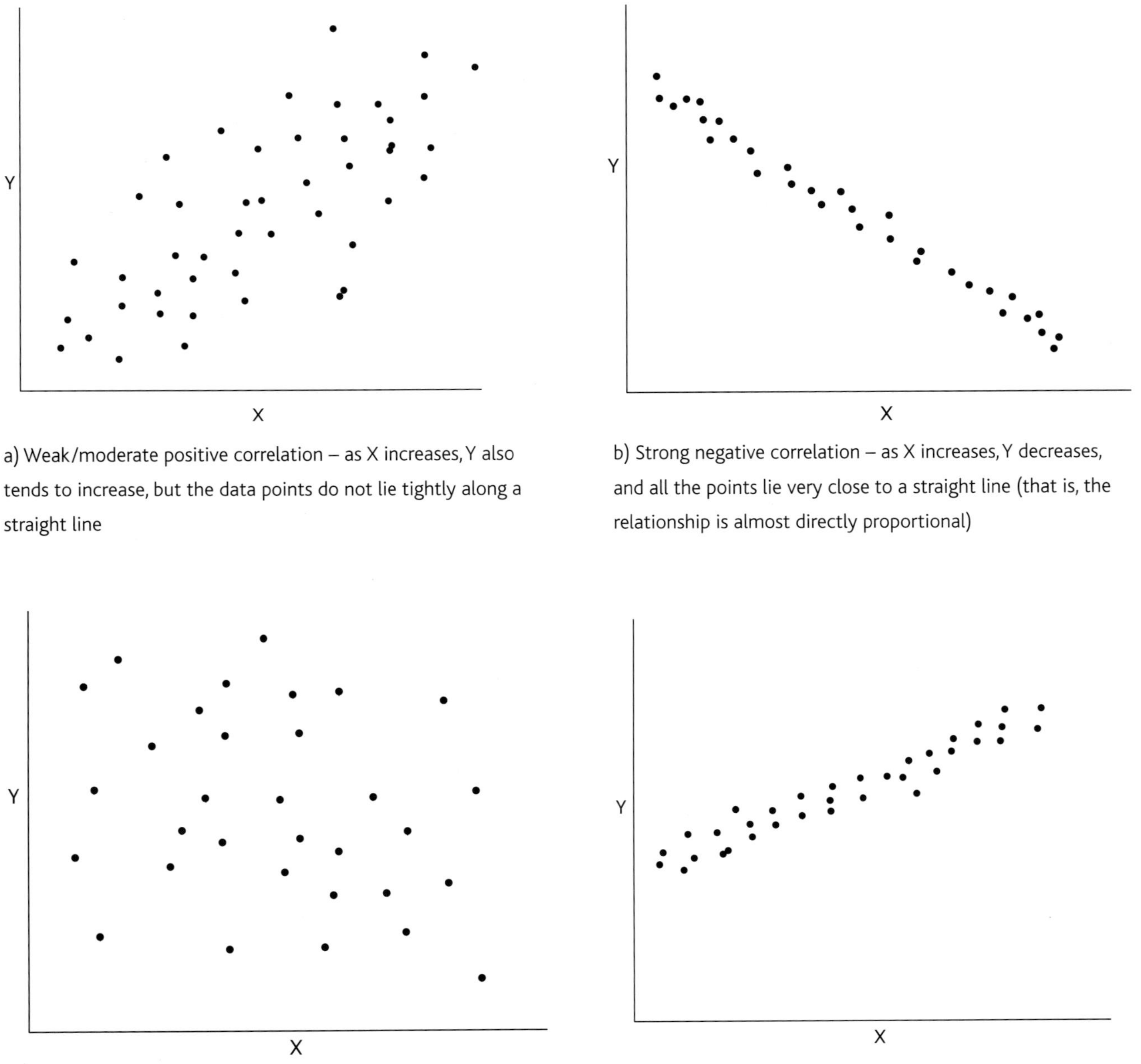

a) Weak/moderate positive correlation – as X increases, Y also tends to increase, but the data points do not lie tightly along a straight line

b) Strong negative correlation – as X increases, Y decreases, and all the points lie very close to a straight line (that is, the relationship is almost directly proportional)

c) No apparent correlation – there is no systematic change in Y with increasing X

d) Strong positive correlation – as X increases, Y increases

For each of the scatterplots included in the 10 reports, the correlation coefficient and its associated p-value have been calculated, and these are listed in Table 1. The p-value indicates the statistical significance of the coefficient, and typically p-values less than 0.05 indicate that the coefficient is statistically reliable (that is, unlikely to be due to chance variation alone). However, this is simply a rule of thumb, and does not mean that associations that just miss statistical significance are not important or real. In some cases data were not available for all 142 areas (due to differences in the Census in Scotland, Northern Ireland, England and Wales). The coefficients have been calculated on fewer areas in those cases.

The strongest relationship is found in the report *In sickness and in health*, between the percentage of the population with limiting long-term illness and poor health, and the percentage of the population providing informal care for 50+ hours a week. This unusually high correlation coefficient (0.96) suggests an almost perfect proportional association between the proportion of people requiring care, and the proportion providing it outside of the health services. Another very strong correlation is found for the association between the percentage of households with both dependent children and no car, and the percentage of households with three or more cars. In this case, the coefficient is –0.86, a strong negative correlation indicating a geographic divide between households that might be in need of a car, but do not have one, and households that might have an excess of cars.

The weaker correlations are those for associations between the availability of healthcare professionals and the proportion of people with limiting long-term illness and poor health. However, these correlations are still highly statistically significant, and also fit the inverse care law in that the care sectors with the greatest exposure to market forces (that is, the more 'private' sectors) are those with the greatest inverse relationships. This is illustrated by the increasing strength of inverse relationship from doctors to dentists to 'other practitioners' (including complementary/alternative medicine practitioners and so on).

Figures 5(a) to (e) illustrate associations between subsets of the variables using scatterplot matrices. These indicate the direction and the magnitude of the correlations between various pairs of variables analysed in the project.

Title pages of the 10 reports

Table 1: Correlation coefficients for all graphs in the reports

Report	Variable 1	Variable 2	Correlation coefficient	*p*-value	Number of observations (areas)
Doctors and nurses	% of population with limiting long-term illness and poor health	Qualified, practising health professionals per 10,000 population:			109 (England and Wales only)
		• medical practitioners	–0.22	0.022	
		• dental practitioners	–0.42	<0.001	
		• nurses, midwives and health visitors	0.31	0.0001	
		• other health professionals	–0.48	<0.001	
In sickness and in health	% of population with limiting long-term illness and poor health	% of population providing 50+ hours of informal care a week	0.96	<0.001	142
Teachers	% of 17 year old students with no (or unknown) qualifications	Working, qualified teaching professionals per 100 5-15 year olds	–0.51	<0.001	109 (England and Wales only)
Sons and daughters[a]	Scotland: % of 16-17 year olds with Group 1 qualifications	Scotland: % of 40-54 year olds with Group 3/4 qualifications	–0.32	0.076	32
	Rest of UK: % of 16-17 year olds with Level 2 qualifications	Rest of UK: % of 40-54 year olds with Level 4/5 qualifications	0.77	<0.001	110
Changing rooms[b]	% of households with more people than rooms	% of households with one or two people and eight or more rooms	–0.71	<0.001	142
A place in the sun[b]	% of household spaces that are unoccupied second residences or holiday accommodation	% of households with household reference person (HRP) aged 35-74 who is privately renting (or living rent-free)	0.70	<0.001	142
The office	% of population working in occupations in NS-SEC 1 or 2	% of people with Level 4/5 qualifications (Group 4 in Scotland) who are in an occupation in NS-SEC 5-7	–0.66	<0.001	142
		% of people with Level 4/5 qualifications (Group 4 in Scotland) who are in an occupation in NS-SEC 1-4	0.79	<0.001	
Open all hours	% of employed people aged 30-54 working 49+ hours a week	% of population aged 30-54 who are unemployed	–0.61	<0.001	142
Top gear	% of all households who have both dependent children and no car	% of all households who have three or more cars	–0.86	<0.001	142
Home front	% of parents with dependent children in households where no parent works	% of 5-17 year olds providing 20+ hours informal care a week	0.75	<0.001	142

Note: [a] Correlation coefficients are presented separately for Scotland and the rest of the UK for reasons described in the report.
[b] The associations in both housing analyses appear to be non-linear, and for this reason, the co-efficients and *p*-values are for Spearman's Rank correlation rather than Pearson's correlation as used in the other analyses.

Figure 5(a):Scatterplots for health variables

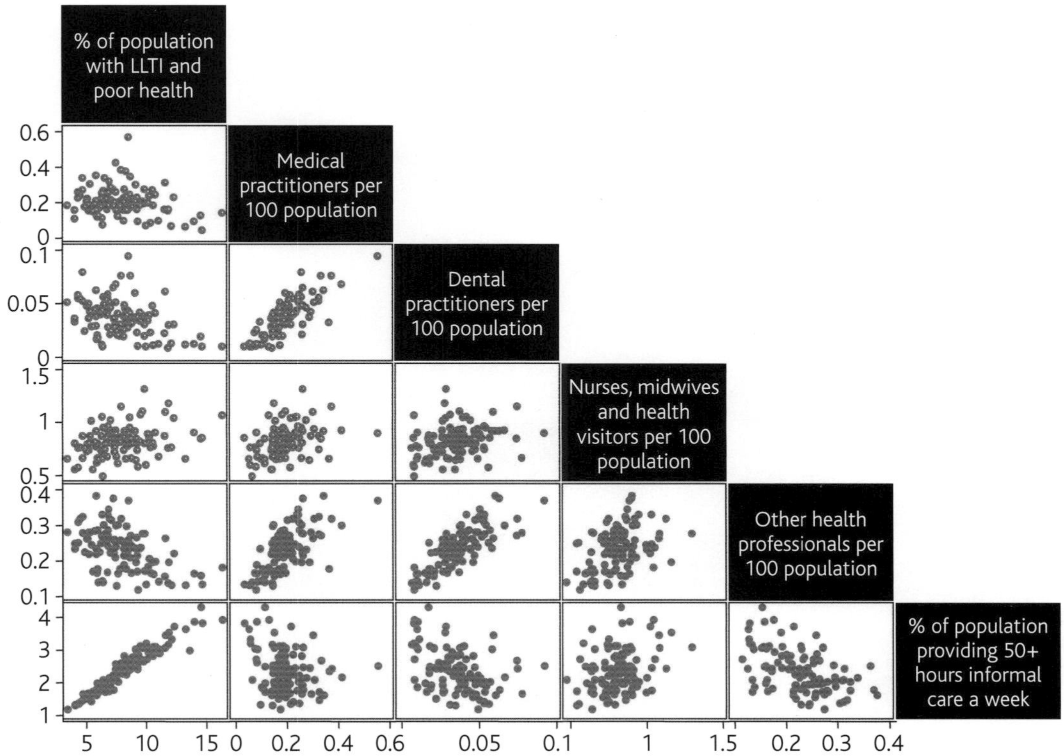

Note here that the strongest relationship is a near perfect positive correlation between the proportion of the population in need of care (percentage with limiting long-term illness [LLTI] and poor health) and the proportion of the population providing 50+ hours a week of informal care.

Figure 5(b): Scatterplots for education variables

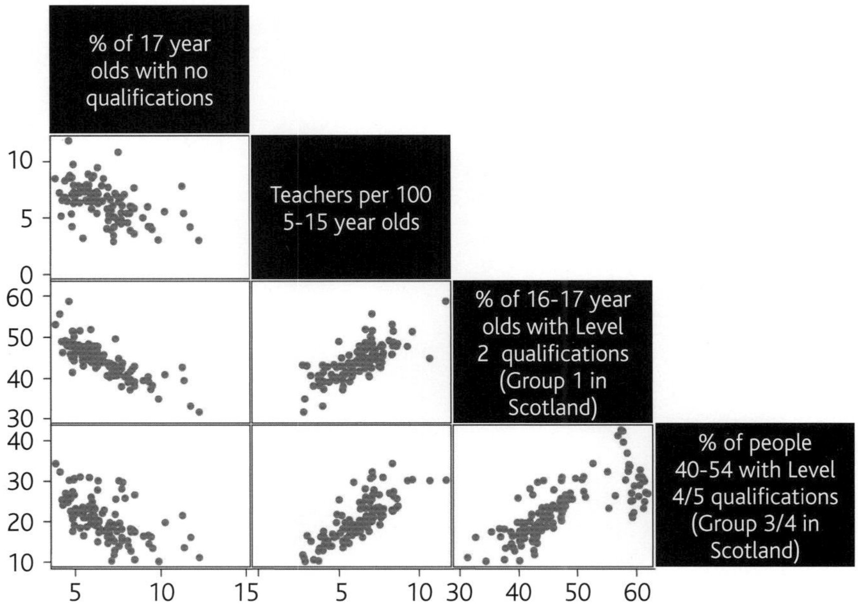

Note the strong positive relationship between areas with many teachers per child aged 5-15 and the educational achievements of children aged 16-17.

Figure 5(c): Scatterplots for housing variables

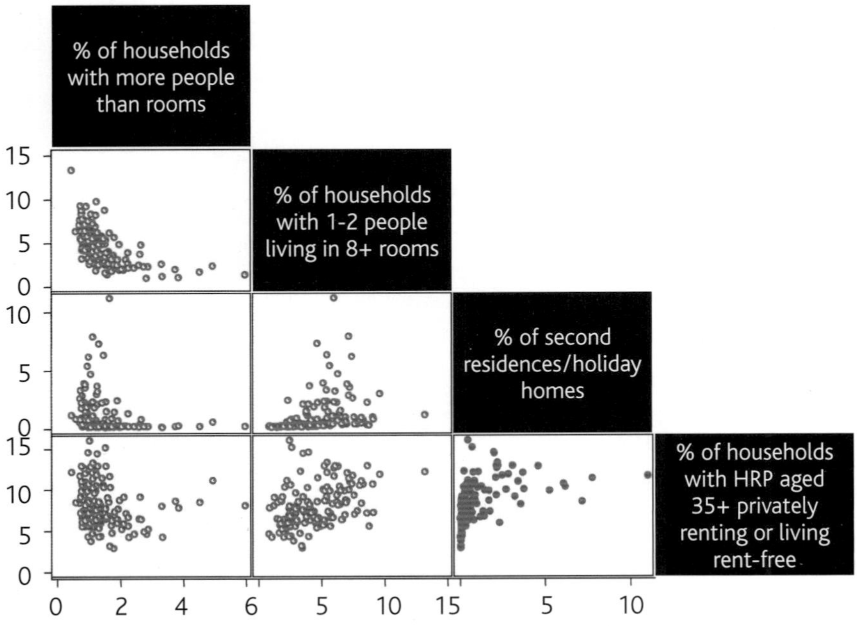

Note here the curvilinear ('boomerang' shaped) negative relationship between the proportion of households with more people than rooms and the proportion of properties that are second homes or holiday residences in an area (these are more common where there is less overcrowding).

Note: HRP = household reference person.

Figure 5(d): Scatterplots for employment variables

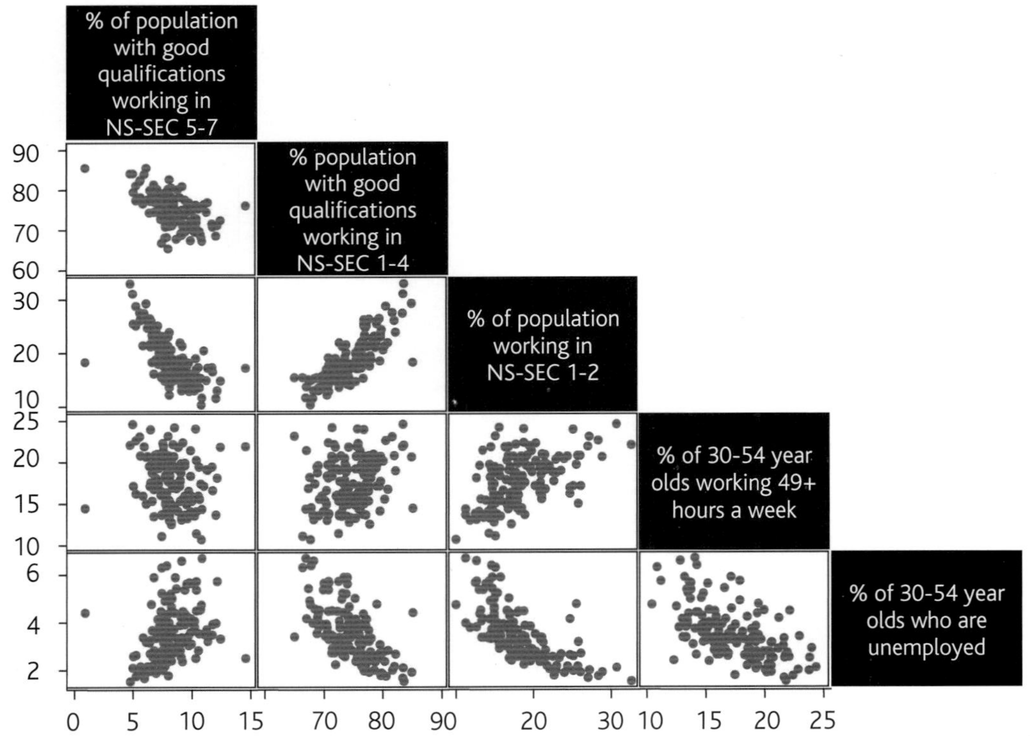

Note the strong inverse relationship between numbers of people working in high status jobs (NS-SEC 1-2) in an area and unemployment rates for those aged 30-54.

Note: NS-SEC = National Statistics Socio-economic Classification; variables relate to the population aged 16-74.

Figure 5(e): Scatterplots for poverty variables

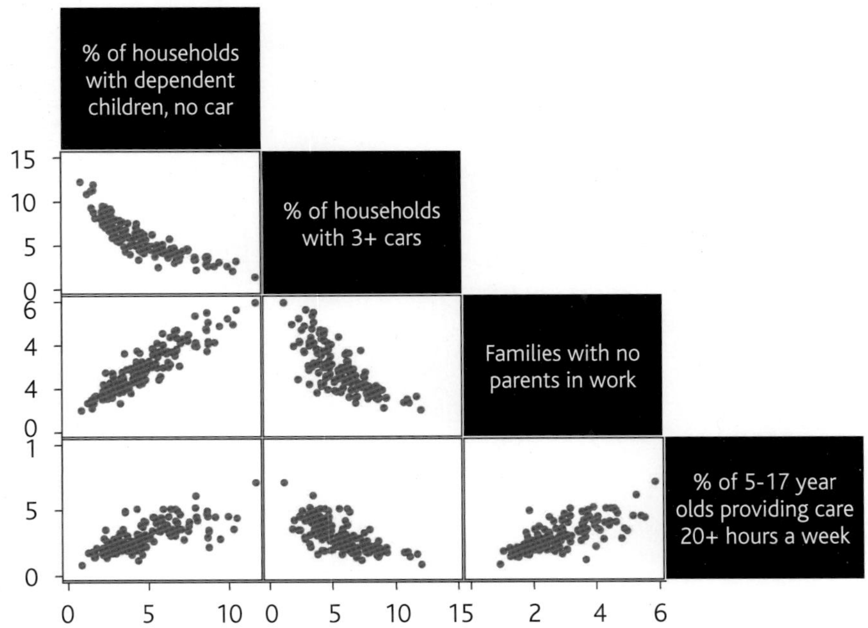

Note the strong positive relationship between areas where fewer households have cars and areas where many children have no parent in work.

Posters and photography

In addition to producing 10 reports with explanatory text, tables, maps and cartograms, five posters accompanying the reports have also been produced. The posters include photographs that comment on the reports and attempt to bring the data alive. A series of photographs were taken specifically for this purpose. Selected images are also used in each of the 10 reports.

Rationale and approach

Before going out to take photographs, some thought was given as to how to go about this element of the project. The following decisions were made, either before the project, or during the project as it took shape:

- The images should be visually cohesive, of a similar style, so that it is apparent that they are part of one series. One way of achieving this was by using one camera, the same lens, similar settings, and black and white rather than colour. A Canon G5 digital camera was used, allowing immediate re-shooting when necessary. In addition, a visual style that was very symmetrical, direct and with 'straight-on' perspective emerged.
- Images should invoke life in Britain without being stereotypical. This meant careful selection and presentation of subject matter.
- Images would be more engaging if the subject was not always immediately apparent, for instance if the viewer has to do some work to discern what it is that they are looking at.

Background research

A range of sources were explored, including looking at the work of photographers in the social documentary photography tradition (see, for example, Darwell, 1986; Baker, 2000; Danziger, 2001; Peralta, 2001; Salgado, 2003), as well as the use of photography in social science and the history of the poster.

For centuries posters have been produced for the purposes of information and advertising. Before radio and television, posters were the primary means of visual and mass communication – as most of the population were illiterate, the gripping images of posters were a way of reaching them (Le Coultre and Purvis, 2002). Posters have also traditionally been designed to have meaning and to motivate, to communicate and convince, for example, prompting political or commercial action. Posters usually include both images and text, and a good poster will both seize and retain attention (Le Coultre and Purvis, 2002). Features that contribute to their success are originality, clarity, directness and effective use of colour and typography.

Taking these characteristics into consideration, the posters have been designed to create an eye-catching, provocative introduction to the research project. The design is intended to be bold and straightforward, and common across all five posters to emphasise that they form a coherent series.

Photographing the five topics

Housing

This category was covered first and proved to be the most straightforward. It was decided to photograph a range of different types of housing: terraces, detached, old and newly built, with gardens and other surrounding features. For practical reasons they have only been photographed from the outside – it would have been much more revealing, but also much more difficult to arrange, to photograph inside people's homes.

Employment

For this category the authors wanted to represent a range of occupations. They stood in various public places and asked passersby if they would mind if their shoes were photographed. The authors explained about the project based on the Census, and carried contact information and ID for those who requested it. Only a handful of people refused; most were obliging and interested in the imaginative approach to the use of photography in the project. Each shot was framed in a similar way, but the location was varied and thus so too was the background. People were asked to state what they would describe as their occupation, and these descriptors have been used verbatim. When these individual images are placed together, as in the poster, the overall effect is enhanced.

Health

Here the method used for the employment category was built on by focusing on hands. The idea was that hands would be evocative of a range of activities related to health and well being. These shots were posed by various colleagues, friends and family. Both the shoes and hands shots have the advantage that the individuals are not identifiable.

Education

For this category the authors opted for collecting a variety of images to form a collage. This included outside shots from afar, as well as close-ups of educational objects (books, school bags, pencil cases, computers). They were careful to include subjects evocative of different levels of education, from primary to higher education.

Poverty

This was the most challenging category. To photograph recognisable images of poverty might easily appear stereotypical and hackneyed. The authors wanted to produce something less predictable, less immediately apparent. After some thought they decided to try to represent the side of poverty that is about deprivation – lack and absence – by photographing scenes of emptiness and bareness.

Ethical considerations

All photographers have to consider ethical issues. For this project the authors were careful not to include people as the subject of the photograph (other than as background passersby) unless they had been asked and their permission acquired. Where the people are recognisable, the consent form opposite was used (for the photographs of hands and feet this was not deemed necessary). Where practical and appropriate, the subjects were included in the decisions concerning the final choice of shots used in the posters.

The consent form used where people could be identified is shown next:

Life in Britain

Consent to use of photography

Background

We are taking photographs to use as illustrations for a series of reports and posters based on a research project funded by the Joseph Rowntree Foundation. The research uses information from the 2001 Census, supplemented by these photographs, to depict life in Britain today. The photos are intended to reflect various aspects of 'Life in Britain' and will be illustrative only – we will not require any personal information from you, with the exception of the information you give us on this form, and your full name will not be published with the photos. The reports and posters will be made publicly available, and may be published on the Internet.

Why do we need you to sign this form?

It is important that you understand why we are taking your picture, and what we may do with the photographs. We will also give you a copy of this form to keep so that you can retain the information and contact us at a later date if you need to. Please read the statement carefully before signing.

Consent statement

- I hereby confirm that I give consent for photographs to be taken of me for the purposes of the research project described above.
- I understand the photos have educational value. I consent to the photos being shown to appropriate professional staff and used in educational publications, journals, textbooks, posters and used in any other form or medium including all forms of electronic publication or distribution. As a result, I understand that the photos may be seen by the general public.
- All or part of the photos may be used in conjunction with other photographs, drawings, or other forms of illustration. Efforts will be made to conceal my identity but full confidentiality is not guaranteed.
- I may view the material by arrangement with the researchers. However, once published I realise that recovery of the photos may not be possible.
- I understand that no fee is payable to me in respect of the material either now or at any time in the future.
- I confirm that the purpose for which the material will be used has been explained to me in terms which I have understood.
- I have been given the option to refuse consent to be photographed.

To be completed by subject, or parent/guardian if subject is under 16:

I agree with the above consent statement
Name: ....
(BLOCK CAPITALS)
Date:..
Signature..(subject or parent/guardian)

Thank you very much for assisting us with this project.

Contact details
Dr Mary Shaw, Department of Social Medicine, University of Bristol.
Telephone: 0117 928 7353. E-mail: mary.shaw@bristol.ac.uk

Some of the key images used in the reports and posters are presented below:

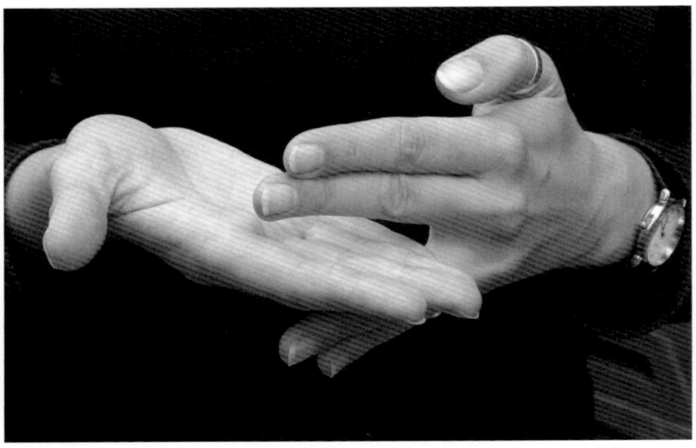

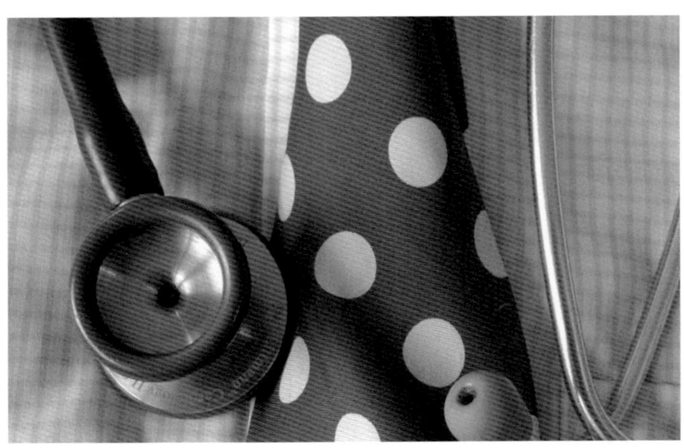

3

Report details

In this chapter, background details are provided for each report. Additional data and graphs for which there was insufficient space in the reports are also included.

Census tables and cell references

This section includes details of the Census tables and cell references from which each variable was derived. These cell references refer to the way that Census data tables output by the national statistical agencies are arranged, and can be used to find the exact data on which the analyses are based. In most cases, the table numbers and cell references for England and Wales, Scotland and Northern Ireland are the same. Where they are not, this is noted. In the case of Northern Ireland, specific cell references are unavailable, but even where table numbers are different, layouts are in most cases exactly the same as those for the other countries. All data used here have been extracted from the Census data series called 'Standard Tables', with the exception of some data on educational attainment from the series 'Theme Tables'.

Figure 6 gives an example of the layout of a Census output table. For example, the cell reference 'Standard Table 48: Cell 26' would refer to the total number of occupied flats, maisonettes and apartments in an area in 2001.

Health

1. Doctors and nurses

Redistribution

The following graph was excluded from the report due to lack of space, and gives an example of how numbers of medical practitioners in certain areas would need to change in order to bring about an even distribution of practitioners per head of population across all areas.

Figure 6: Example Census output table layout and cell references

			Unoccupied	
	TOTAL	Occupied	Second residence/ holiday accommodation	Vacant
ALL HOUSEHOLD SPACES	0001	0002	0003	0004
In an unshared dwelling	0005	0006	0007	0008
House or bungalow	0009	0010	0011	0012
Detached	0013	0014	0015	0016
Semi-detached	0017	0018	0019	0020
Terraced (including end terrace)	0021	0022	0023	0024
Flat, maisonette or apartment	0025	0026	0027	0028
In a purpose built block of flats or tenement	0029	0030	0031	0032
Part of a converted or shared house (includes bed-sits)	0033	0034	0035	0036
In a commercial building	0037	0038	0039	0040
Caravan or other mobile or temporary structure	0041	0042	0043	0044
In a shared dwelling	0045	0046	0047	0048
ALL DWELLINGS	0049	0050	0051	0052

Footnotes: In general a household's accommodation is defined as an unshared dwelling if all the rooms are behind a door that only household can use.

Source: Census 2001: England and Wales Standard Tables, Final layout

Census health measures and life expectancy

Self-reported illness is a good indicator of real levels of poor health as evidenced by the close relationship between the levels of limiting long-term illness in an area and local life expectancy. The graph opposite illustrates the strong relationship between limiting long-term illness and life expectancy, demonstrating that the illness measure from the Census is a good general indicator of real health status.

Figure 7: Vital Statistics: How to make the distribution of doctors better related to the distribution of the population

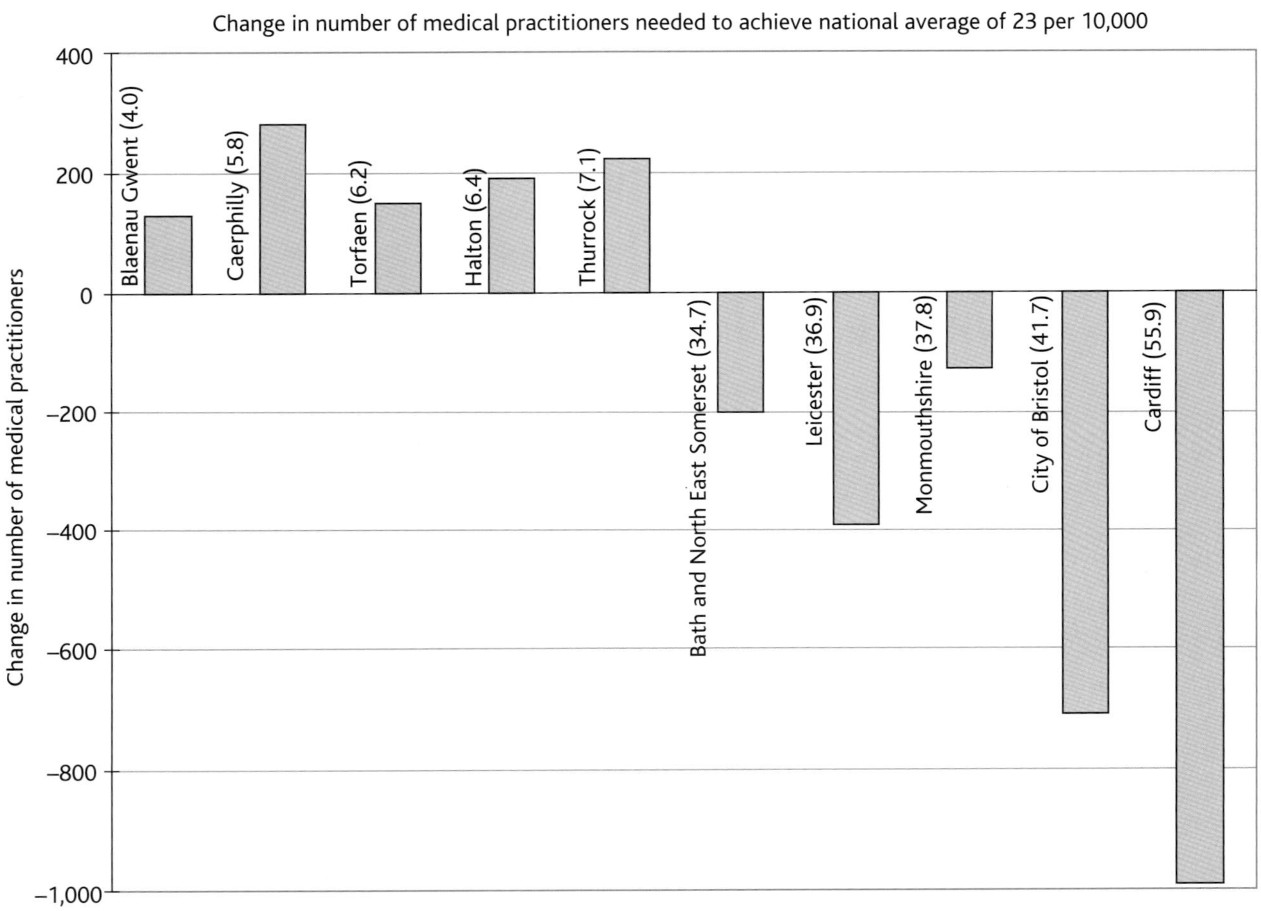

This chart shows the change in the number of medical practitioners that would be needed to achieve the national average rate of doctors per head of population for the five areas with the highest rates, and the five with the lowest (rates per 10,000 population are shown in brackets). For example, Halton would need to gain around 200 doctors to achieve the national average rate.

This redistribution would only serve to equalise the rate of doctors per head of population – it would not make the distribution of doctors more proportional to need, which would require even more extreme changes than indicated here. It also ignores the sometimes efficient concentration of doctors into specialist units in a few hospitals.

Figure 8: Graph illustrating the close association between the prevalence of limiting long-term illness (LLTI) (measured by the Census) and life expectancy (calculated using data from death certification) across local authorities in Britain

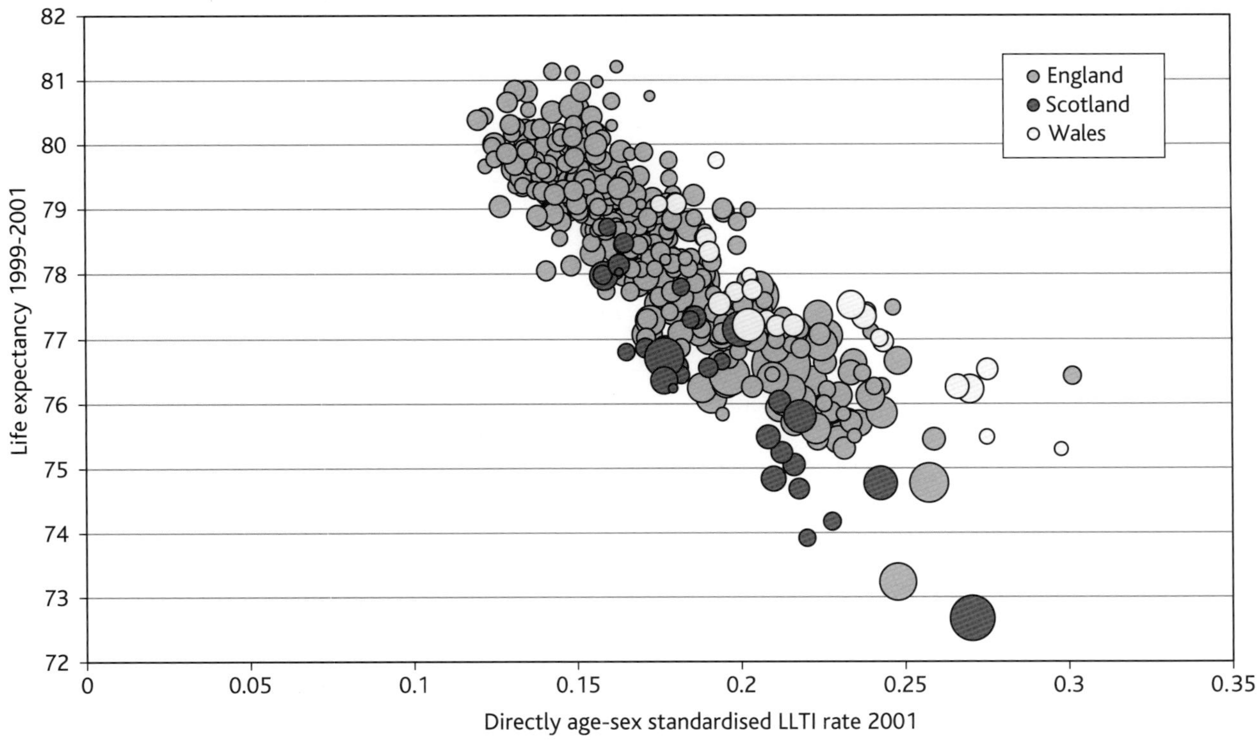

Note: Each circle represents a local authority, and its size is proportional to the local authority population.

Census tables and exact cell references used to derive main report variables

Variable	Census table and cell references	
	Numerator	Denominator
% of population with limiting long-term illness and poor health	st16: c11	st16: c1
Qualified, practising health professionals per 10,000 population		
Medical practitioners	st116: c25	st16: c1
Dental practitioners	st116: c33	st16: c1
Nurses, midwives and health visitors	st116: c37	st16: c1
Other health professional	st116: c45	st16: c1

Note: st = standard table; c = cell.

2. In sickness and in health

Figure 1 in the corresponding report shows the distribution of people providing differing amounts of informal care across economic activity categories. The figures clearly demonstrate that people who spend more time providing care are less likely to be economically active. The table below gives total figures and percentages that form the basis of that figure in the report.

Basis for Figure 1 (in report no 2):
The economic activity of informal carers aged 16-74, UK (2001)

UK	Providing 1-19 hours care per week	% of UK total	Providing 20-49 hours care a week	% of UK total	Providing 50+ hours care a week	% of UK total
Economically active	**2,586,704**	**69.8**	**323,822**	**53.1**	**347,193**	**32.1**
Employee – part time	615,764	16.6	87,288	14.3	104,371	9.6
Employee – full time	1,448,121	39.1	170,019	27.9	168,409	15.6
Self-employed – part time	112,242	3.0	12,133	2.0	14,789	1.4
Self-employed – full time	256,582	6.9	26,456	4.3	31,831	2.9
Unemployed	107,681	2.9	22,348	3.7	24,264	2.2
Full-time student	46,314	1.3	5,578	0.9	3,529	0.3
Economically inactive	**1,117,155**	**30.2**	**286,431**	**46.9**	**735,539**	**67.9**
Retired	569,910	15.4	100,507	16.5	275,215	25.4
Student	66,411	1.8	9,305	1.5	8,313	0.8
Looking after home/family	263,381	7.1	107,869	17.7	289,015	26.7
Permanently sick/disabled	144,557	3.9	46,714	7.7	124,884	11.5
Other	72,896	2.0	22,036	3.6	38,112	3.5
All persons aged 16-74	**3,703,859**	**100.0**	**610,253**	**100.0**	**1,082,732**	**100.0**

Source: Derived from Standard Table 26, UK Census 2001

Census tables and exact cell references used to derive main report variables

Variable	Census table and cell references: Numerator	Denominator
% of population with limiting long-term illness and poor health	st16: c11	st16: c1
% of population providing 50+ hours of informal care a week	st25: c25	st25: c1

Note: st = standard table; c = cell.

Education

3. Teachers

The table opposite demonstrates the distribution of 16- 24 year olds across economic activity categories by educational attainment. It shows that young people with higher qualifications are much more likely to be economically active and employed, and conversely, those without qualifications are more likely to be unemployed or economically inactive.

Percentage of 16-24 year olds in each economic activity category by educational attainment

	Economically active					Economically inactive					
	Total	Employee	Self-employed	Unemployed	Full-time student	Total	Retired	Student	Looking after home/ family	Perma-nently sick or disabled	Other
All 16-24 (%)	65.0	43.1	1.6	5.8	14.5	35.0	0.1	26.7	3.8	1.1	3.4
No qualifi-cations or level unknown (%)	45.2	25.2	1.7	10.1	8.2	54.8	0.3	35.2	8.3	3.5	7.6
Lower-level qualifications (%)	67.7	43.9	1.6	5.0	17.2	32.3	0.0	26.2	3.1	0.6	2.4
Higher-level qualifications (%)	78.8	65.6	2.0	3.8	7.5	21.2	0.1	16.6	1.1	0.2	3.1

Source: Derived from Standard Table 32, England and Wales Census, 2001

Census tables and exact cell references used to derive main report variables

	Census table and cell references	
Variable	Numerator	Denominator
% of 17 year old students with no (or unknown qualifications)	Theme table 2: c308	Theme table 2: c4
Working, qualified teaching professionals per 100, 5-15 year olds	st116: c15	st1: c11+c65+c119+c182

Note: st = standard table; c = cell.

4. Sons and daughters

In 'Since 2001' we refer to the attainment of 5 or more GCSEs at A*- C by 15 year olds, and also to the proportion of 15 year olds gaining no GCSEs or GNVQs since the Census. The tables overleaf, from the Department for Education and Skills (DfES), give figures for trends in these measures since 1988/89. The DfES constructs these statistics counting all pupils aged 15 at the start of the school year (30 August).

Percentage of pupils aged 15 achieving 5 or more GCSEs at grades A*-C, England (Table 5.5a)

School year	Boys	Girls	Total
1988/89	29.8	35.8	32.8
1989/90	30.8	38.4	34.5
1990/91	33.3	40.3	36.8
1991/92	34.1	42.7	38.3
1992/93	36.8	45.8	41.2
1993/94	39.1	47.8	43.3
1994/95	39.0	48.1	43.5
1995/96	39.9	49.4	44.5
1996/97	40.5	50.0	45.1
1997/98	41.3	51.5	46.3
1998/99	42.8	53.4	47.9
1999/00	44.0	54.6	49.2
2000/01	44.8	55.4	50.0
2001/02	46.4	57.0	51.6
2002/03	47.9	58.2	52.9
2003/04	48.4	58.4	53.3

Source: DfES GCSE Statistics (www.dfes.gov.uk/trends/)

Percentage of 15 year old pupils achieving no GCSE/GNVQ passes, England (Table 5.5d)

School year	Boys	Girls
1988/89	8.8	6.2
1989/90	8.7	5.8
1990/91	8.0	5.5
1991/92	9.7	7.0
1992/93	8.2	5.8
1993/94	8.7	6.6
1994/95	9.3	6.8
1995/96	8.9	6.6
1996/97	8.8	6.5
1997/98	7.7	5.4
1998/99	7.0	5.0
1999/00	6.5	4.6
2000/01	6.5	4.4
2001/02	6.4	4.3
2002/03	6.3	4.1
2003/04	6.5	4.2

Census tables and exact cell references used to derive main report variables

	Census table and cell references	
Variable	Numerator	Denominator
% 16-17 year olds with Level 2 (Group 1 in Scotland) qualifications		
England and Wales	st105: c11	st105: c8
Scotland	st204: c8	st204: c7
Northern Ireland	st320	st320
% 40-54 year olds with Level 4/5 (Group 3/4 in Scotland) qualifications		
England and Wales	st105: c55+c62+c69	st105: c50+c57+c64
Scotland	st204: c46+c47+c52+c53+c58+c59	st204: c43+c49+c55
Northern Ireland	st320	st320

Note: st = standard table; c = cell.

Housing

5. Changing rooms

Alternative overcrowding/underoccupancy measure

In 'Findings' we describe the use of an alternative measure of occupancy that can be used to look at the number of people, rather than households, living in overcrowded or underoccupied circumstances.
The Census calculates an 'occupancy rating' for each household based on a number of factors. The occupancy rating provides a measure of underoccupancy and overcrowding. A value of –1 implies that there is one room too few and that there is overcrowding in the household; a rating of +1 indicates that there is a surplus of one room relative to the basic needs of the household; and a rating of 0 indicates a household that is neither overcrowded nor underoccupied. The occupancy rating assumes that every household, including one-person households, requires a minimum of two common rooms (excluding bathrooms).

The Census Standard Table 54 gives counts of population by age and occupancy rating of the household in which individuals live.

Basis for Figure 1 (in report no 5)

Population by occupancy rating	Aged 0-17	Aged 18+	% aged 0-17	% aged 18+
+2 or more (underoccupied)	4,857,535	21,708,010	36.6	48.8
+1	3,311,356	11,161,915	25.0	25.1
0	3,350,603	8,016,745	25.3	18.0
–1 or less (overcrowded)	1,739,006	3,597,284	13.1	8.1
Total	**13,258,500**	**44,483,954**	**100.0**	**100.0**

Source: Derived from Standard Table 54, UK Census 2001

Census tables and exact cell references used to derive main report variables

	Census table and cell references	
Variable	Numerator	Denominator
% of households with more people than rooms		
England, Wales and Scotland	st52: c25+c33	st52: c1
Northern Ireland	st356	st356
% of households with one or two people and eight or more rooms		
England, Wales and Scotland	st51: c18+c27	st51: c1
Northern Ireland	st355	st355

Note: st = standard table; c = cell.

6. A place in the sun

Census tables and exact cell references used to derive main report variables

Variable	Census table and cell references	
	Numerator	Denominator
% of household spaces that are unoccupied second residences or holiday accommodation		
England, Wales and Scotland	st48: c3	st48: c1
Northern Ireland	st363	st363
% of households with HRP aged 35-74 that are privately renting (or living rent-free)		
England, Wales and Scotland	st13: c181+c241+c301+c361	st13: c133+c193+c253+cc313
Northern Ireland	st327	st327

Note: st = standard table; c = cell; HRP = household reference person.

Employment

7. The office

Full details of the National Statistics Socio-economic Classification (NS-SEC)

The report includes a truncated version of the table opposite, describing NS-SEC classes 1 to 7. Here the table is reproduced in full to include class 8 ('never worked' and 'long-term unemployed') and the 'unclassified' class. The National Statistics Socio-economic Classification (NS-SEC) is the replacement proposed for the Registrar General's 'social class' classification. It places people into a socio-economic category based on their occupation and certain characteristics of the work that they do (whether they are an employer, self-employed or an employee; whether or not they are responsible for supervising others; and the number of employees at the place of work). Of the classifications for people in work, the highest group is NS-SEC 1, 'Higher managerial and professional occupations', and the lowest is NS-SEC 7, 'Routine occupations'. The NS-SEC classes are listed with the population in 2001, example occupations and relative risk of death for those in work.

	National Statistics Socio-economic Classification	Population 2001[a]	Examples of occupations[b]	Relative risk of death[c]
1	Higher managerial and professional occupations	3,182,614	Doctors, directors of large organisations, clergy	70
2	Lower managerial and professional occupations	6,990,083	Journalists, nurses, school teachers	94
3	Intermediate occupations	3,532,894	Travel agents, police officers (sergeant and below)	99
4	Small employers and own account workers	2,626,067	Farmers, taxi drivers, hotel managers	86
5	Lower supervisory and technical occupations	2,687,927	Train drivers, electricians, bakers	102
6	Semi-routine occupations	4,393,965	Scaffolders, traffic wardens, dental nurses	113
7	Routine occupations	3,410,122	Building labourers, waiters, cleaners	126
8	Never worked and long-term unemployed	1,404,188		
	Never worked	*1,021,800*		
	Long-term unemployed	*382,388*		
	Not classified	9,379,577		
	Full-time students	*2,648,991*		
	Not classified for other reasons	*6,730,586*		
	Total (aged 16-74)	**37,607,437**		

Notes:

[a] People aged 16-74 only.

[b] Drever et al (2004).

[c] The relative risk of death was the chance of men classified by their occupation in 1981 dying in the period 1986-90. The national average was 100, so a relative risk of 126 indicates 26% greater risk than the average. Thus, after allowing for differences in age distribution men in NS-SEC class 7 were 1.8 times more likely to die in a given period as compared to men in class 1 (126/70=1.8). The NS-SEC classification includes more people in these top and bottom categories and thus this ratio is slightly smaller than that found for men classified at the extremes of the Registrar General's classification over the same period (130/66=1.97) (Fitzpatrick et al, 1997). Note that no data were provided for group 8.

Census tables and exact cell references used to derive main report variables

	Census table and cell references	
Variable	Numerator	Denominator
% of population working in occupations in NS-SEC 1 or 2		
England and Wales	st114: c7+c8+c9+c10+c11+c12+c25+c26+c27+c28+c29+c30	st16: c1
Scotland	st215: c7+c25	st16: c1
Northern Ireland	st321	st16
% of people with Level 4/5 qualifications (Group 4 in Scotland) who are in an occupation in NS-SEC 5-7	st114: c47+c53+c59	st114 c5
England and Wales	st215: c47+c53+c59	st215: c5
Scotland	st321	st321
Northern Ireland		
% of people with Level 4/5 qualifications (Group 4 in Scotland) who are in an occupation in NS-SEC 1-4	st114: c11+c29+c35+c41	st114 c5
England and Wales	st215: c11+c29+c35+c41	st215 c5
Scotland	st321	st321
Northern Ireland		

Note: st = standard table; c = cell.

8. Open all hours

Figure 1 in the report shows the distribution of weekly working hours for people aged 30-54. This graph is based on the following figures from Standard Table 29.

Basis for Figure 1 (in report no 8)
Data for all people aged 30-54 in employment in the week before the Census, UK (2001) (Total: 16,351,098)

Part time (30 hours or less per week)				
Total	1-2 hours	3-5 hours	6-15 hours	16-30 hours
3,797,566	21,578	112,439	879,499	2,784,050
Full time (31 hours or more per week)				
Total	31-37 hours	38-48 hours	49-59 hours	60 or more hours
12,553,532	3,038,566	6,563,594	1,796,568	1,154,804

Source: Derived from Standard table 29, UK Census 2001

In 'Findings', we describe that 79% of people employed part time (30 hours or less per week) are women, compared with 35% of those working full time. The following table gives population counts and percentages from Standard Table 29 that are the source of these figures.

Distribution of full-time and part-time employment among men and women

	Total population aged 16-74 in employment in the week before Census		Working part time (30 hours or less per week)		Working full time (31or more hours per week)	
Males	14,361,337	(54.0%)	1,373,526	(21.0%)	12,987,811	(64.8%)
Females	12,214,342	(46.0%)	5,162,171	(79.0%)	7,052,171	(35.2%)
Total	26,575,679	(100%)	6,535,697	(100%)	20,039,982	(100%)

Source: Standard Table 29, UK Census 2001

Census tables and exact cell references used to derive main report variables

Variable	Census table and cell references	
	Numerator	Denominator
% of employed people aged 30-54 working 49+ hours a week	st29: c87+c88+c98+c99+c109 +c110+c120+c121+c131+c132	st29: c78+c89+c100+c111+c122
% of people aged 30-54 who are unemployed	st28: c121+c137+c153+c169+c185	st28: c113+c129+c145+c161+c177

Note: st = standard table; c = cell.

Poverty

9. Top gear

Figure 1 in the report demonstrates that the percentage of households who might need a car is very similar to the percentage of households who may have more cars than are really needed. The basis of this graph, from Standard Table 62, is the table of figures below, and the total number of households from the same table (24.5 million).

Basis of Figure 1 (in report no 9)

UK households with dependent children and no car (numbers)	UK households with three or more cars (numbers)
1,243,571	1,394,786
% of all UK households with dependent children and no car	*% of all UK households with three or more cars*
5.1	5.7

Source: Standard Table 62, UK Census 2001

In 'Findings', we state that "... nearly two thirds of households that have three or more cars contain just two or fewer employed people". Figures on the number of employed people and vehicle access in each household are only available for England, Wales and Northern Ireland (figures are from Standard Table 118, which is not available for Scotland). This table reveals that of 1,311,276 households with three or more cars, 554,703 (42%) have three or more employed people.

Census tables and exact cell references used to derive main report variables

Variable	Census table and cell references	
	Numerator	Denominator
% of all households who have both dependent children and no car	st62: c50+c68+c86	st62: c1
% of households who have three or more cars	st62: c5+c6	st62: c1

Note: st = standard table; c = cell.

10. Home front

Census tables and exact cell references used to derive main report variables

Variable	Census table and cell references	
	Numerator	Denominator
% of people who are parents with dependent children in households where no parent works	st31: c100	st16: c1
% 5-17 year olds providing 20+ hours informal care a week	st25: c44+c45+c64+c65+c84+c85+ c104+c105+c124+c125+c144 +c145	st25: c41+c61+c81+c101+c121+ c141

Note: st = standard table; c = cell.

4

Conclusions

While the analyses, data, and aggregations used here are fit for the purpose for which they are intended, a number of other possibilities for more in-depth analyses exist. In some cases, small area analysis may be appropriate and provide further insight into patterns of inequalities at higher resolution. In the use of relatively large areas, very localised social patterns are ignored. For example, in the case of the analysis of the availability of teachers and the qualifications of young people locally, variation between schools within each area is ignored; however, such analysis would be impossible with Census data, which are not released for aggregations of teachers and children by school.

Further investigation of issues covered here may also be possible using data from previous censuses to look at changes over time. This would be complex and beyond the scope of this project, given changes in Census questions, definitions and areas over time. However, this situation may improve, with the advent of 'future-proof' Census geography from 2001, and with the availability of time-series datasets through projects such as 'Linking Censuses through Time' (http://census.ac.uk/cdu/software/lct).

The 10 reports and this technical report consider only a tiny fraction of information revealed from one Census of population. Comparisons are not made with other Censuses, other social data, longitudinal data, nor with other countries or for small areas. Nevertheless, the amount of information presented here is vast and many illustrations and examples are given of the overall patterns of social inequalities in the UK at the beginning of the 21st century.

References

Baker, S. (2000) *Streets and spaces: Urban photography*, Salford: Lowry Press.

Ballas, D. (2004) 'Simulating trends in poverty and income inequality on the basis of 1991 and 2001 census data: a tale of two cities', *Area*, vol 36, no 2, pp 146-63.

Beveridge, W. (1942) *Social insurance and allied services*, Cmd 6404, London: HMSO.

Boyle, P., Exeter, D. and Flowerdew, R. (2004) 'The role of population change in widening the mortality gap in Scotland', *Area*, vol 36, no 2, pp 164-73.

Danziger, N. (2001) *The British*, Hammersmith: HarperCollins Publishers.

Darwell, J. (1986) *Working lives*, Stockport: Stockport Museums and Gallery Service.

Dorling, D. and Rees, P. (2003) 'A nation still dividing: the British Census and social polarisation 1971-2001', *Environment and Planning A*, vol 35, pp 1287-313.

Drever, F., Doran, T. and Whitehead, M. (2004) 'Exploring the relation between class, gender, and self rated general health using the new socioeconomic classification. A study using data from the 2001 census', *Journal of Epidemiology and Community Health*, vol 58, pp 590-6.

ESRI (Environmental Systems Research Institute) (2002) *ArcMap 8.3*, Redlands, CA: ESRI.

Fitzpatrick, R., Bartley, M., Dodgeon, B., Fifth, D. and Lynch, K. (1997) 'Social variations in health: relationship of mortality to the interim revised social classification', in D. Rose and K. O'Reilly (eds) *Constructing classes: Towards a new social classification for the UK*, Swindon: ESRC/ONS, Chapter 7.

Gordon, D. and C. Pantazis (eds) (1997) *Breadline Britain in the 1990s*, Aldershot: Ashgate.

Jenks, G.F. (1977) *Optimal data classification for choropleth maps*, Department of Geography Occasional Paper No 2, Lawrence, KS: University of Kansas.

Le Coultre, M. and Purvis, A. (eds) (2002) *A century of posters*, Lund Humphries: Aldershot.

Peralta, M. (2001) *Nearly invisible: Photographs by Moyra Peralta, writings by John Berger and Alan Bennett*, London: Lansdowne Press.

Salgado, S. (2003) *The end of Polio: A global effort to end a disease*, New York, NY: PixelPress.

Shaw, M. and Dorling, D. (2004) 'Who cares in England and Wales? The positive care law: cross-sectional study', *British Journal of General Practice*, vol 54, no 509, pp 899-903.

Thomas, B. and Dorling, D. (2004) 'Endpiece: mapping changes and the 2001 census for the UK', *Area*, vol 36, no 2, pp xxiii-xxxviii.

Tudor Hart, J. (1971) 'The inverse care law', *Lancet*, vol1, pp 406-12.

Wheeler, B., Shaw, M., Mitchell, R. and Dorling, D. (2005a) *Life in Britain: Doctors and nurses*, Report 1, Bristol: The Policy Press.

Wheeler, B., Shaw, M., Mitchell, R. and Dorling, D. (2005b) *Life in Britain: In sickness and in health*, Report 2, Bristol: The Policy Press.

Wheeler, B., Shaw, M., Mitchell, R. and Dorling, D. (2005c) *Life in Britain: Teachers*, Report 3, Bristol: The Policy Press.

Wheeler, B., Shaw, M., Mitchell, R. and Dorling, D. (2005d) *Life in Britain: Sons and daughters*, Report 4, Bristol: The Policy Press.

Wheeler, B., Shaw, M., Mitchell, R. and Dorling, D. (2005e) *Life in Britain: Changing rooms*, Report 5, Bristol: The Policy Press.

Wheeler, B., Shaw, M., Mitchell, R. and Dorling, D. (2005f) *Life in Britain: A place in the sun*, Report 6, Bristol: The Policy Press.

Wheeler, B., Shaw, M., Mitchell, R. and Dorling, D. (2005g) *Life in Britain: The office*, Report 7, Bristol: The Policy Press.

Wheeler, B., Shaw, M., Mitchell, R. and Dorling, D. (2005h) *Life in Britain: Open all hours*, Report 8, Bristol: The Policy Press.

Wheeler, B., Shaw, M., Mitchell, R. and Dorling, D. (2005i) *Life in Britain: Top gear*, Report 9, Bristol: The Policy Press.

Wheeler, B., Shaw, M., Mitchell, R. & Dorling, D. (2005j) *Life in Britain: Home front*, Report 10, Bristol: The Policy Press.

s data to understand poverty, inequality and place

TION

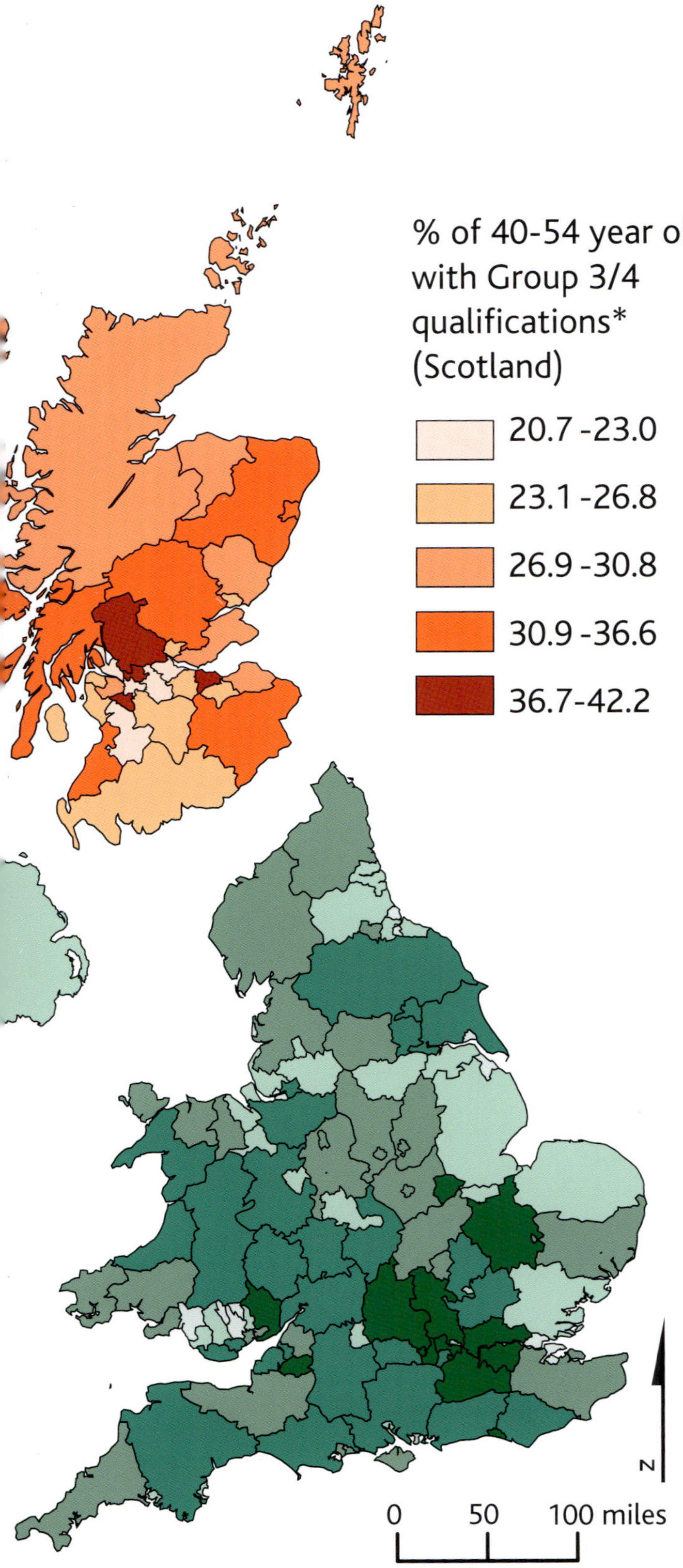

* Census qualification Level 4/5 and Group 3/4 include first and higher degress, HNCs, HNDs, NVQ Level 4-5 and certain professional qualifications

thors: Ben Wheeler (University of Sheffield), Mary Shaw (University of
hell (University of Edinburgh) and Danny Dorling (University of Sheffield)
Sheffield
Shaw
Press
h Rowntree Foundation

JOSEPH ROWNTREE FOUNDATION

The POLICY PRESS

LIFE IN BRITAIN Using millennial Cen

EDUCA

In England, Wales and Northern Ireland, 16-17 year olds are more likely to have obtained good GCSEs and equivalent qualifications if they live in an area where a high proportion of their parents' generation (people generally aged 40-54) are well qualified.

Because children's achievement is so strongly related to that of their parents' generation, geographical inequalities in educational attainment across the country are maintained over time. However, this is not the case in Scotland, where there is much less geographical variability in the proportion of young people who have qualifications.

Both maps in each figure represent the same places, shaded identically. The map on the left is a cartogram – each area is shown in proportion to the size of its population in 2001. The largest area is London, since it has the highest population of any of the places. The map on the right shows the actual boundaries of the areas.

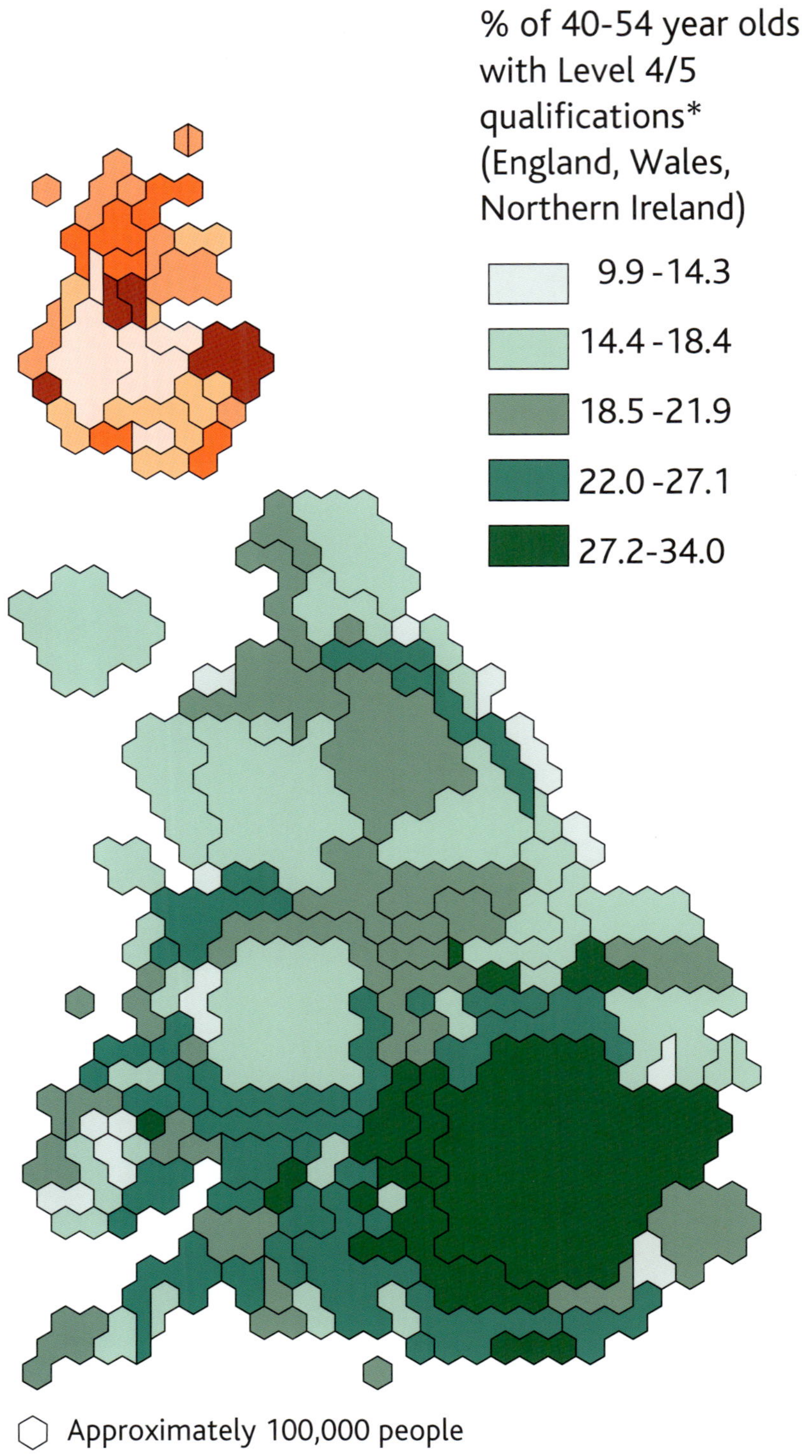

This poster accompanies a series of reports showing key patterns and inequalities in the UK revealed by the 2001 Census. The analyses focus on geographical inequalities, highlighting where services and opportunities appear not to be available or accessible to those people and places that need them most. Information on how to obtain the full reports that this poster is based on, along with the other topics covered by the project, are available at www.jrf.org.uk or www.sheffield.ac.uk/sasi

Poster and repo
Bristol), Richard
Text © Universit
Photographs © I
Design © The Po
Project funder: J

LIFE IN BRITAIN

Using millennial Cen

EMPLO

Well-paid, high status jobs are not evenly distributed across the country. Most jobs falling into the top levels of the National Statistics Socio-economic Classification (NS-SEC) are found in London and the South East of England.

In areas where there are relatively few of these jobs available, people with good qualifications are more likely to have a job in the lower levels of the socio-economic classification. Therefore, it seems that the place in which someone lives can sometimes be a more important influence on their prospects of a well-

rewarded job than their qualifications.

Both maps in each figure represent the same places, shaded identically. The map on the left is a cartogram – each area is shown in proportion to the size of its population in 2001. The largest area is London, since it has the highest population of any of the places. The map on the right shows the actual boundaries of the areas.

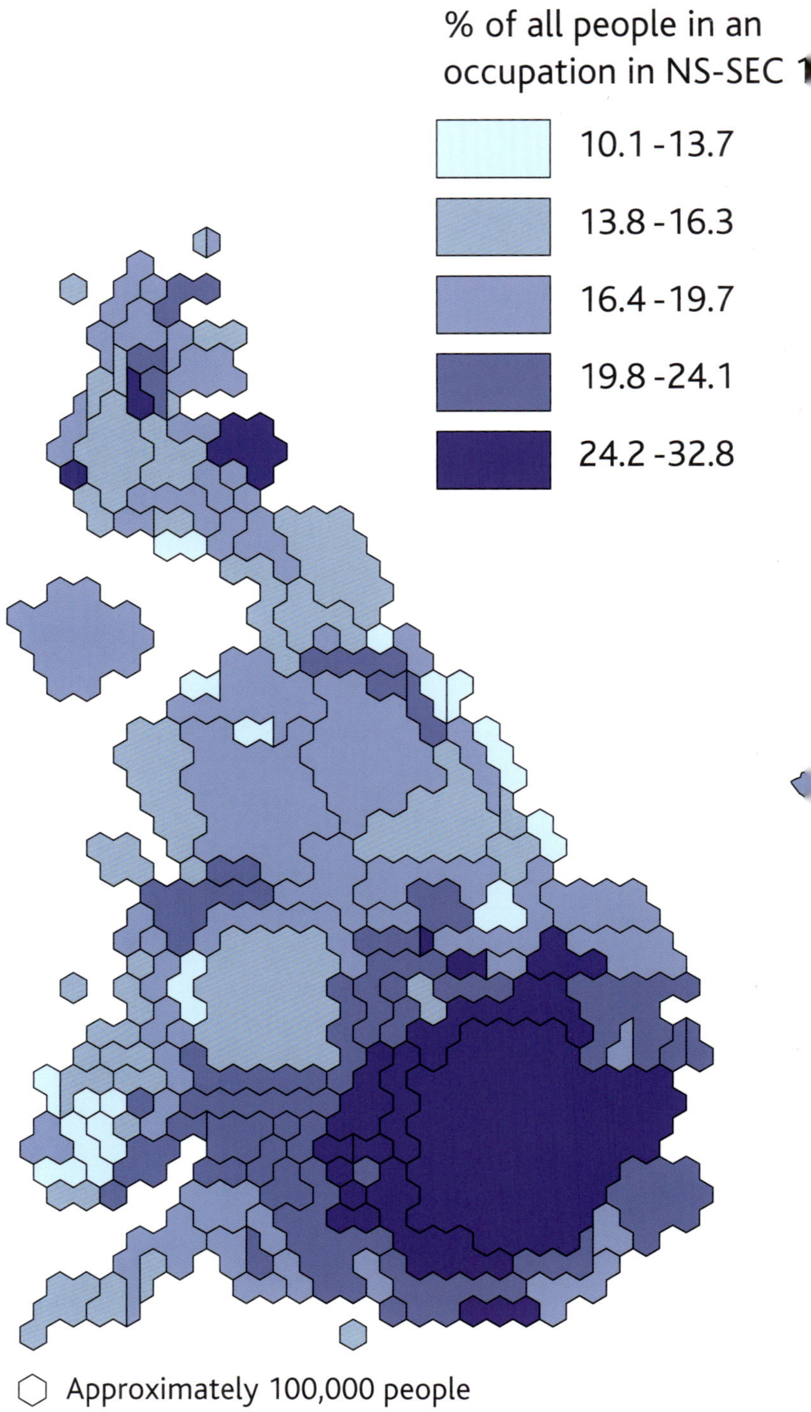

This poster accompanies a series of reports showing key patterns and inequalities in the UK revealed by the 2001 Census. The analyses focus on geographical inequalities, highlighting where services and opportunities appear not to be available or accessible to those people and places that need them most. Information on how to obtain the full reports that this poster is based on, along with the other topics covered by the project, are available at www.jrf.org.uk or www.sheffield.ac.uk/sasi

Poster and repo
Bristol), Richard
Text © Universi
Photographs ©
Design © The Po
Project funder: J

POVERT

The 2001 Census revealed that 175,000 young people (aged 5-17) in the UK provided care on an informal basis for relatives and friends. Of these, 30,000 were providing care for 20+ hours per week, a substantial undertaking given that almost all of these children were also in full-time education.

There were around 1.3 million families with dependent children where no parent was in employment. Areas with the highest percentages of young people providing care also tend to have high proportions of families where no parent is in paid work.

s data to understand poverty, inequality and place

TY

Both maps in each figure represent the same places, shaded identically. The map on the left is a cartogram – each area is shown in proportion to the size of its population in 2001. The largest area is London, since it has the highest population of any of the places. The map on the right shows the actual boundaries of the areas.

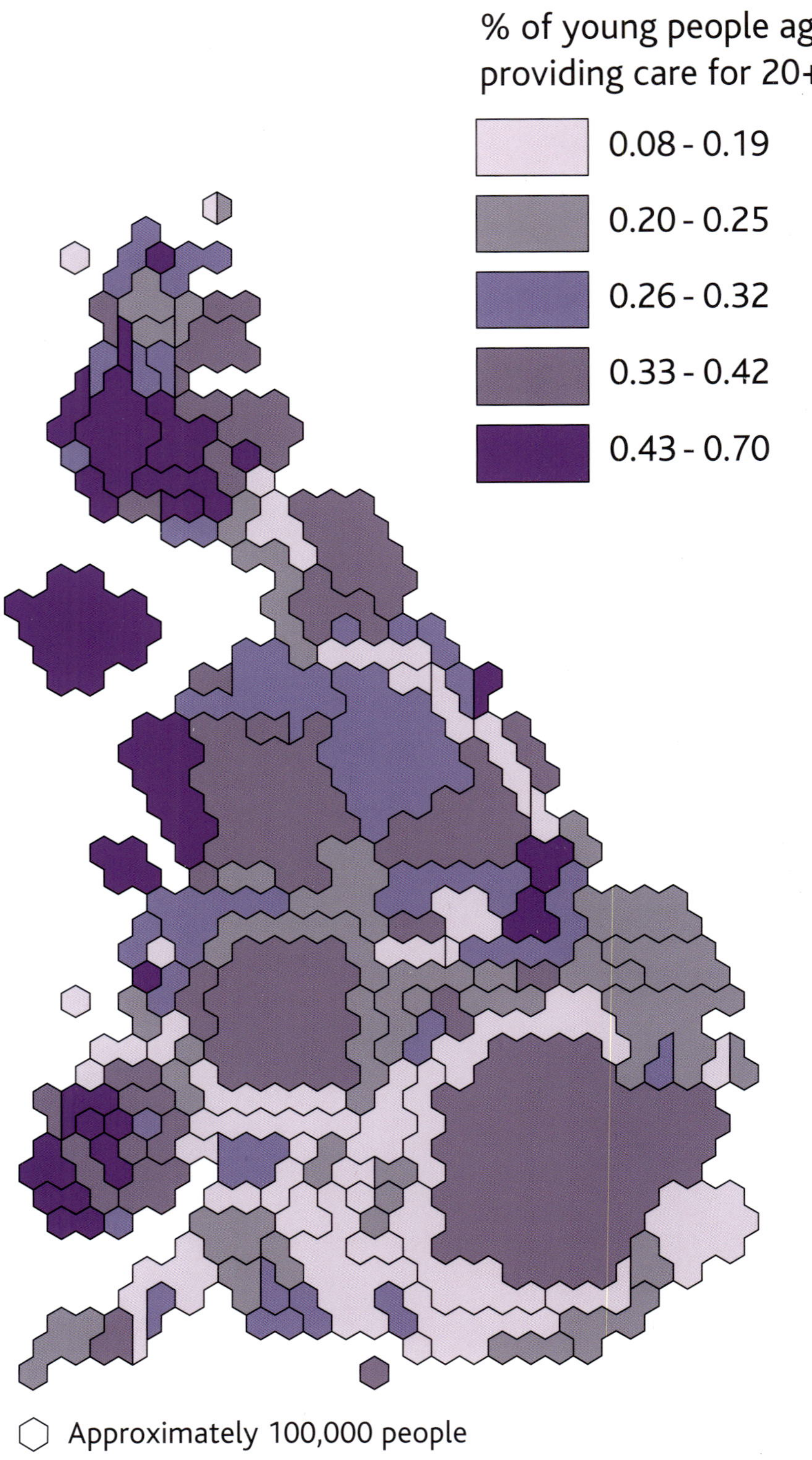

This poster accompanies a series of reports showing key patterns and inequalities in the UK revealed by the 2001 Census. The analyses focus on geographical inequalities, highlighting where services and opportunities appear not to be available or accessible to those people and places that need them most. Information on how to obtain the full reports that this poster is based on, along with the other topics covered by the project, are available at www.jrf.org.uk or www.sheffield.ac.uk/sasi

Poster and repo
Bristol), Richard

Project funder:

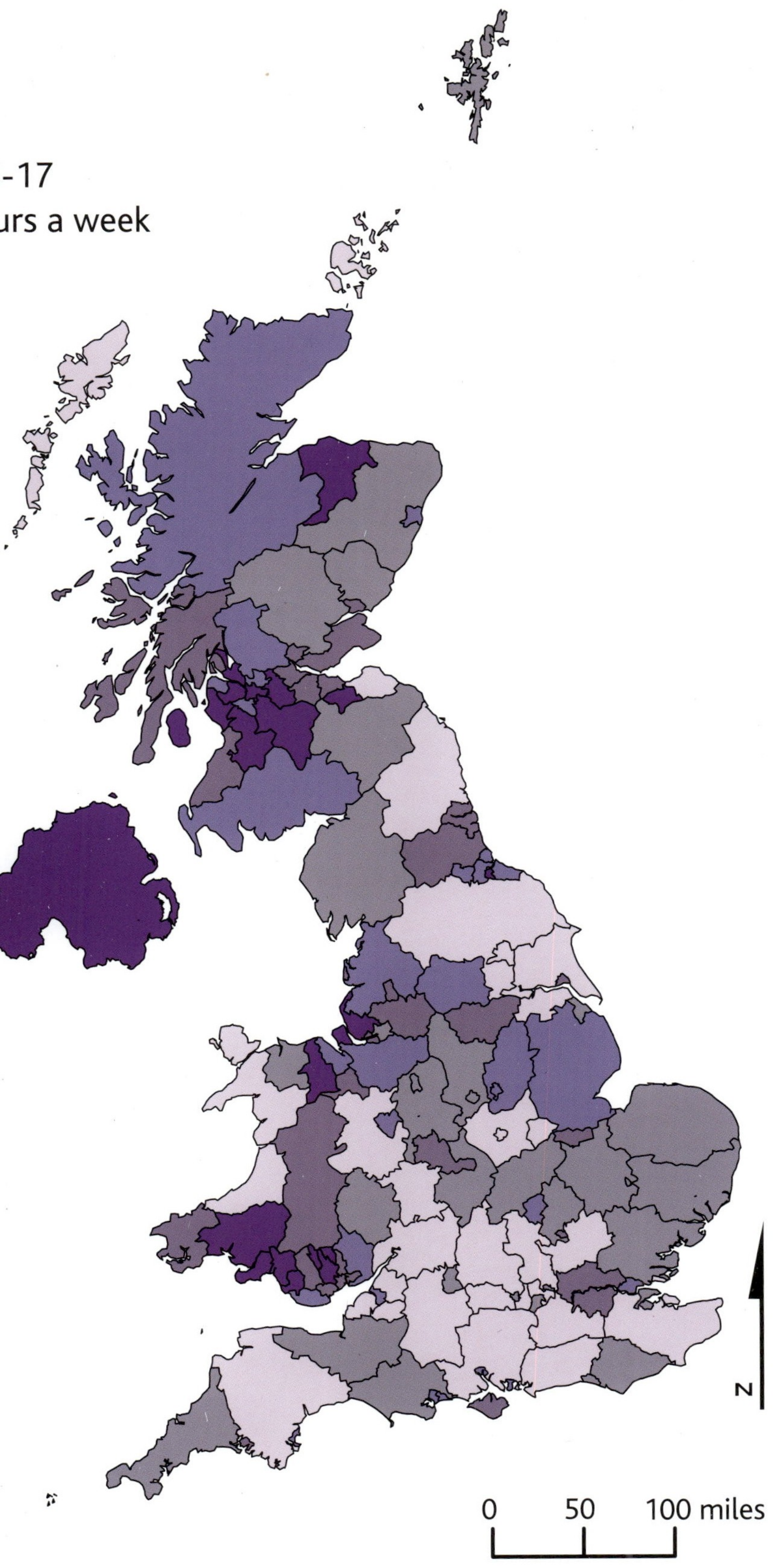

hors: Ben Wheeler (University of Sheffield), Mary Shaw (University of
hell (University of Edinburgh) and Danny Dorling (University of Sheffield)

JOSEPH ROWNTREE FOUNDATION

The POLICY PRESS